Issues in Ethics and Applied Ethics Series

Volume-III

Socio-Political Ethics

Issues in Ethics and Applied Ethics Series

Vol. 1 Ethics in Business, Applied and Environment
Vol. 2 Ethics in Feminism
Vol. 3 Socio-political Ethics

Forthcoming volumes

Vol. 4 Biomedical Ethics (Part I)
Biomedical Ethics (Part II)
Vol. 5 Metaethics (Part I)
Normative Ethics and Virtue Ethics (Part II)
Vol. 6 Practical Economics, Corporate and Educational Ethics
Vol. 7 Cārvāka/Lokāyata, Morality and Secularism (Part I)
Philosophy and Ethics of the Jainas (Part II)
Philosophy and Ethics of the Buddhas (Part III)

About the Editors

Shiva Nath Prasad, after completing his studies, served Bihar Government in several capacities. After retirement he became a full timer in the pursuit of philosophy. He edited a bilingual journal "Abhrant" later edited two journals separately one in English namely *Journal of Bihar Philosophical Research* and *Darshan Digdarshan* in Hindi. He authored one book *Cārvāka/Lokāyata Analytical and Hermeneutics Study,* a very unique book, which is a "singular attempt to reconstruct this almost a vanished system of India." He also published an Anthology namely Phenomenology: Methodological Introduction with Prof. V.T. Sebastian of Punjab University. His Multi-Volume Anthology on Ethics and Applied Ethics (22 volumes) are being published by Concept Publishing Company Pvt. Ltd. and some are being processed. Recently, he published this book "Reflections of Cārvāka/ Lokāyata, the *Gita* and Rajneesh," a book of immense value.

Avinash Kumar Srivastava, born, December 1955 (Nalanda District Bihar) completed Master's degree (Philosophy) from Patna University, Ph.D. on the topic "A Comparative Study of the Samadhi (Yoga) in Early Buddhism and *Bhagavad Gītā*" from Magadha University, Bodh Gaya. Presently he is Associate Professor and Head, P.G. Deptt. of Philosophy, Magadha University, P.G. Centre Darshnik Traimasik (Patna), Nalanda College Biharsharif. He is a prolific writer. He has authored two books *(Living Buddhism and Bharatiya Darshan Ki Mool Samasyayen)* and edited three Anthologies. His about forty research chapters have been published in India and abroad. He is a widely known scholar of India. He was Joint Secretary and Secretary of Akhil Bharatiya Darshan Parishad and General Secretary, Bihar Darshan Parishad, Vice President of Indian Society for Buddhist Studies. And member of editorial board of 'Bauddha Prajna Sindhu, and Ocean of Buddhist Wisdom (Delhi), *Journal of Bihar Philosophical Research, Darshan Digdarshan* (Patna).

Issues in Ethics and Applied Ethics Series

Volume-III

Socio-Political Ethics

Edited by
Shiva Nath Prasad
Avinash Kumar Srivastava

CONCEPT PUBLISHING COMPANY PVT. LTD.
NEW DELHI-110059

ISBN-13: 978-81-8069-976-4 (Series)
ISBN-13: 978-81-8069-979-5 (Volume-III)

First Published 2017

Published and Printed by

Concept Publishing Company Pvt. Ltd.
A/15-16, Commercial Block, Mohan Garden
New Delhi-110059 (India)
T : 25351460, 25351794, *F* : 091-11-25357109
E: publishing@conceptpub.com, W: www.conceptpub.com
Editorial Office: H-13, Bali Nagar, New Delhi-110 015, India.

Cataloging in Publication Data—*Courtesy:* D.K. Agencies (P) Ltd. <docinfo@dkagencies.com>

Socio-political ethics / edited by Shiva Nath Prasad, Avinash Kumar Srivastava.
pages cm. -- (Issues in ethics and applied ethics series ; volume - III)
Contributed articles.
Includes bibliographical references and index.
ISBN 9788180699764 (series)
ISBN 9788180699795 (volume-III)

1. Social ethics--India. 2. Political ethics--India. I. Prasad, Shiva Nath, editor. II. Śrīvāstava, Avināśa, 1955- editor. III. Series: Issues in ethics and applied ethics series ; volume - III.

BJ123.S63S63 2015 DDC 170.954 23

Foreword

The Book entitled "Ethics and Applied Ethics, Vol. III" edited by Shri Shiva Nath Prasad and Avinash Kumar Srivastava comprises Twenty chapters. It is a pleasant job to read and understand such collections. The work is a collection of different articles of eminent scholars of philosophy.

The first chapter deals with "Paradox of Fundamentalism" by D. North of Standford University. This chapter appeared in *Radical Humanism*, Vol. 72, Nov. 12. The word 'fundamentalism' requires to be used with care. The term "fundamentalism" dehumanises people and justifies killing of them. In Western United States, a fundamentalist was a Christian Bible thumper. Fundamentalist were regarded as backward and dogmatic. The term is now widely understood to include adherents of Jewish, Christian, Hindu, Buddhist, Jainism, Sikh and Islamic culture. The word fundamentalism sounds dangerous. Fundamentalists are conservative. By conservative, it is meant that fundamentalists seek to conserve their own brand and their religious heritage.

The second chapter entitled "Nehru's Contribution to Secularism and Scientific Attitude. A Critical Study by Prof. Y.V. Satyanarayana stipulates that secularism is the product of the West. The doctrinal basis for secularism was found in the declaration of Christ. "Render unto Caesar the things that are Caesar's and to God the things that are Gods". The struggle between the church and the state in the medieval period was a crucial factor in the emergence of secularism in the West. The secular spirit is the gift of scientific temper. Secularism separates politics from the church. Here Dr. Satyanarayana has very aptly made it clear that "*scientific*" does not mean only positive sciences. It means the *spirit of free enquiry*. According to Chambers Dictionary, "Secularism is the belief that the state, morals and education etc., should be independent of religion". Dr. Satyanarayana upholds that secularism is a philosophy of life which can be applied to all aspects of human life. Secularism as understood in the West is alien to India. The spirit of religious tolerance is the distinctive feature of secularism in Indian context. The need for secularism and the relevance of secular state have been emphasized by Mahatma Gandhi and Pandit Nehru. In pluralistic society like India, the practice of secularism must be an essential aspect of Indian democracy. Nehru was an ardent lover of democracy, socialism and secularism. Nehru's rational approach was quite evident in his attitude to life, society and nation.

The third chapter deals with "Indian Culture and Technological Society : A Philosophical Perspective." Here Dr. R.C. Sinha adheres that technology in itself is value free, but assumes value when linked with cultural activities. Secondly, technology is not logically incompatible with Indian culture because Indian culture is integral in nature. It integrates technological society with cultural values. Thirdly, it also gives ontological basis to secular values of technological society. By Indian culture, he means a set of values dear to Indians. Dr. Sinha upholds that in technological society, man leads a mechanical life. Man is under bondage of technology. Indian culture can harmonize between spiritual and secular values and other worldly and this worldly life.

The fourth chapter entitled "Morality and Political Obligation" by Y.V. Satyanarayana, has raised the problem of political obligation. Why does the citizens have an obligation to obey the laws of the state ? Dr. Satyanarayana has placed the views of Socrates and M.K. Gandhi regarding citizen's obligation to obey the laws of the state. According to Gandhi and Martin Luther Jr., the system of laws must meet moral criteria as well. They refused to consider an unjust law as a law. It is not enough to sanction a law by the state, but that law must have adequate justification. Therefore, to have an obligation to obey the law, the law must be morally justified. Martin Luther King Jr. opines that unjust law is a code that is out of harmony with the moral law. John Locke regarded that citizen's obligation to the state holds good only the state does secure justice. Thus, political obligation is not absolute and the citizens are not obliged to obey anything that the state will decree. Thoreau's classic treatise on "civil disobedience" adopts this approach and justifies disobedience. John Rawls in his essay on "Civil Disobedience" admits that one does have a right to disobey if one is subjected to deliberate injustice which violates the liberties of equal citizenship. Civil disobedience is a form of non violent protest against unjust laws of the state. It is an instrument of struggle against evil and injustice. Gandhi observes, that civil disobedience is civil breach of immoral statutory enactments. Gandhi stipulates that a *Satyagrahi* breaks the law in order to register his moral protest.

The fifth chapter deals with "Non-Violence, Sovereignty and Security—Gandhian Thought in the Modern Context" by L.G. Chincholkar. He has tried to consider and evaluate Gandhian thought in the context of sovereignty and security of the state. The modern world is deeply ridden with almost universal terrorism and clash of social, economic, religious and political interests appears to question the very principle of non-violence as a stabilizing force in the human society. If the concept of state implies that it must protect its sovereignty and ensure security of its people and if relevant measures of the state for the purpose imply and sanction reference to violence, would it be inconsistent with the responsibilities of the state ? Is violence under such circumstances antithetic to Gandhian concept of non violence ? If so, how could the state discharge its responsibilities without endangering its basic liabilities? How would Mahatma Gandhi help to solve such problems? These are some of the issues Dr. Chincholkar has considered and given realistic evaluation in the context of Gandhian concept of non-violence and the concept of sovereignty and security of the state.

The sixth chapter entitled "Relevance of Gandhian Measures in Tackling Terrorism" by Dr. L.G. Chincholkar is quite apt in the contemporary world situation. The whole world is haunted with the threat of terrorism. The event of *Beslan* tragedy in Russia where in hundred of school children along with their parents and others were mercilessly scorched to death by the Chechen terrorism has once again forced the global attention on the problem of terrorism in the world. The problem came to be widely acknowledged after the Islamic terrorist attack on 11.09.2001 on the World Trade Centre in U.S.A. India has been facing Pakistan sponsored terrorism for the last more than 50 years not only in Jammu & Kashmir but also in various parts of the nation. .

Now, the question is as to how Gandhian methodology of *Satyagraha* is relevant ? Gandhian methodology to combat terrorism or any type of violence may not be practical. Roma Rolland has very aptly observed, "Some of the suggestions of Gandhi for the use of *ahimsa* in the world of diplomacy appear unrealistic and unconvincing to me" (Roma Rolland, *Mahatma Gandhi*, p. 8) Gandhian methodology of 'Non-violence' as Political Methodology may not be very effective in face of terrorism. Dr. Chincholkar admits that non-violence has no instrumental value. Gandhian means lies in its emphasis and trust to effectuate Catharsis of the hearts of the terrorists. Terrorism is self destructive. The heart of terrorist requires to be touched and changed.

The seventh chapter is concerned with a very burning problem of *social justice* from a Vedic Perspective by Dr. Shashi Prabha Kumar. She has done an excellent wonderful treatment to the modern problem from ancient perspective. Justice is the first virtue of social institutions. The principle of social justice provides a solid foundation for social structure. It tries to establish that basically all human beings are equal. The demand of the concept of social justice is that there should be no discrimination amongst human beings on the basis of religion, caste, colour and creed. Social justice is based on social equalities. It does not mean that there will be no disparities at all. The persons of higher capabilities should not be equated with the persons of lower capabilities. Social justice demands social security. It means that social structure should be such in which every member gets a fair share according to his capabilities. Dr. Shashi Prabha Kumar very rightly observes, "Vedas inculcate the ethics of collective living through mutual love and promote social harmony by upholding social virtues like fidelity and friendship". She further observes, "we can *study three aspects of social justice in the Vedic perspective namely, gender equality, class equality and economic equality, since these are three main parameters of the social justice.*" She has illustrated her point very aptly when she says that "the equality between man and woman is the cornerstone of social justice and the Vedas distinguish themselves from all other Indian literature by the high regard in which they hold woman". She has very ably shown that gender equality, class equality and economic equality are found in Vedas. She observes, "The Vedic seers, who were great social philosophers gave a very serious thought to the basic principles which contributed to the evolution of an unshakable structure of social justice." In the end, she admits that there is no expression like "social justice" used in the Vedic literature yet we find an ideal concept of a just society. There seems to be no place for inequalities in ancient Indian society. Dr. Shashi Prabha Kumar deserves all appreciation for analyzing the modern concept of social justice in the framework of ancient Vedas.

The eighth chapter entitled "Secularism : An Imperative for Indian Society" by Prof. S.A. Shaida requires fresh thinking since it is one of the controversial themes. Dr. Shaida has rightly pointed out that some people equate secularism with Atheism. There is a pressing need to understand the meaning of secularism and work out its relevance to Indian society. He says, "Majority of our people share the views that for peace, progress and development secularism is the only available way of life which most appropriately suits the Indian character". Further, he says that in a country like India, with its beautiful mosaic of multi-culturalism, multi-religious and mutli-linguistic people, the secular character of the country is inevitable. It is true that society can't function without secular principles. But secularism does not mean Atheism. It is respect to all religions. It is a wrong notion that only Godless people fall in the lap of secularism. India has its own notion of secularism different from Western conception. It is respect for "other religions". Secularism is not disbelief in religion or God. In current sense, utmost we can say that secularism can be understood as separation of religion from politics. The original spirit of secularism was the separation of church from state. Dr. Shaida has rightly contended that if we want to maintain the democratic set-up with the ideals of universal justice and equality enshrined as guiding principles, a country like India has no other choice except to develop secular values and attitudes in social and political action.

In the ninth chapter, we have a very scholarly treatment of the burning social and political problem of 'secularism' by Prof. Dharmendra Goel. His chapter is entitled "Secularim and Contemporary India". He attempts to clear the misconceptions prevailing regarding the concept of secularism. Dr. Goel has also formulated his own reflections on secularism. He has made a clarification about multi-religious Indian society and secularism. Dr. Goel had contended that ordinarily secularism means "*Sarva Dharma Samabhava*". In India, we have respect for all religions. It is true that days of theocratic states are gone. But this view of "*Sarva Dharma Samabhava*" as secularism stipulates is not tenable. Dr. Goel says that, "It is my considered view that we ought to go beyond this inert and ineffective doctrine of "*Sarva Dharma Samabhava*' because it fails to wage a very important struggle against obscurantism and blunts the edge of rational criticism against traditionalism. Dr. Goel wants to substitute science and humanism in place if secularism as *Sarva Dharma Samabhava.*

In the tenth chapter, we find a very interesting and enlightening chapter on "Terrorism : A Conceptual Analysis" by Shri Shiva Nath Prasad. Sri Prasad gives the etymological meaning of terrorism. The term "terrorism" came from the French word 'terrorism'. It is also based on the Latin verb "*terrere*" which literally means, "to cause any one to tremble". The exact definition of the word "terrorism" is elusive. Terrorism is unlawful use of force to coerce or intimidate to achieve Political or Religious or Ideological objectives. According to the word "terrorism" as unlawful use of force covers the method of all terrorist acts. Terrorism is a violent act instead of peaceful act. The violence is the end result. Terrorism is pre-meditated act of violence. The intention is to spread chaos. It targets to destroy individual of government property. But one person's terrorist was another person's freedom fighter. So, this requires to be clarified. There is a difference between freedom fighter and terrorist. A freedom fighter is guided by the love for country, while terrorist has no such aims. Terrorists kill innocent people to create a sense of horror. Terrorism is neither legally nor morally approved act. There is a criminal intent in terrorist acts. There is a difference between revolution and terrorism. Revolution aims at change of social structure and it is backed by ideology. Terrorism has got no ideology. It lacks definite goal. Terrorism leads to anarchy but Revolution changes, all of a sudden, the existing social structure. Mr. Prasad has raised a significant question : Is terrorism a philosophy ? Terrorism is negative frame of thought. It is an act of desperation. Mr. Prasad admits that anarchism cannot be said to be a sound philosophy. He mentions C.E.M. Joad and says that anarchism is useless concept.

In the eleventh chapter, Mr. Prasad has streamlined the views of Acharya Rajneesh on Terrorism. Rajneesh is against fundamentalism. He suggests that terrorists require therapy of meditative silence. Communism is no remedy to terrorism, because it is Psychological. It is another tyranny of the proletariat. It is just another trap. Rajneesh says that violence is not engrained in man. Violence is animal's nature. It is the nature of the beasts. Animals kill, man murders. Animals have only present, and no history. Man has a past and a future. He has a history. He owes obligation to past and responsibility to future. Man can take a decision to be non violent. Man has freedom to choose. Sri Rajneesh makes a distinction between *real Jehad* and *unreal one*. *Real Jehad is purity, creativity and compassion*. It is *moral Jehad*, to kill the *evil in man*. Real Jehad is *reply to Jehad of tyranny*, *Jihad* of terrorism. For my convenience, I spell real *Jehad* as *Jehad*, and unreal *Jehad* as '*Jihad*'.

The twelfth chapter of the book is the Gandhian Concept of "welfare" by Bijayananda Kar. Dr. Kar asserts that Gandhi's concern for human welfare need not be underestimated. He advocates for human dignity. Dr. Kar has pinpointed that ideal of *Sarvodaya* stands for the welfare of all and not of some. He transcends the popular view of democracy. Gandhi upholds the spirit of democracy and does not subscribe to the letters of democracy. Gandhian vision of welfare to all is not utopian. I should not be taken as impractical. Gandhi concedes that the objective of *Sarvodaya* is difficult to achieve. This is an ideal. But, simply because, an ideal as such cannot be made actual, there is no justifiable ground as to why it cannot be pursued. Gandhian concept of human welfare seems to have been grounded on a sort of moral secularism.

The thirteenth chapter deals with the problem of "Religious Integration" by Prof. Bijaynanda Kar. In contemporary age, a great emphasis is laid upon the issue concerning the integration of all religions (*Sarva Dharma Samanvaya*) particularly in the Indian context. Gandhi advocated the idea of religious integration. Secularism according to Gandhi is proper political ideal. This move is a definite step for social harmony. Akbar had attempted to evolve a religion called *Din-e-Illahi*. The attempt was not very successful. Kabir has made a sincere effort to unite Hindu and Muslim community. In the twentieth century, Ramakrishna Paramahansa advocated Hindu-Muslim unity. Dr. Bijaynanda Kar admits that inter-religious unity and integration has not achieved considerable amount of success in Indian context. Right after the post-independence there has been great emphasis laid by the politicians, social workers, reformers and general intellectuals on the issue of religious integration. Both Hindus and Muslims talk about lofty values and welfare of humanity at large. Divergences are noticed among different faiths. Prof. Kar adheres that the issue of religious integration no more remains as mere theoretical ideal but can easily be concretised in the actual situation. Prof. Kar honestly admits that issue of religious integration has not attained success in the actual front. Mutual distrusts persist among different religious communities.

Dr. Kar has very ably suggested that theological framework has to be replaced by an ethical framework that can avoid religious fundamentalism considered to be the root cause of clashes. Dr. Kar suggests to boost up the sense of moral order which is a harmonious blending of the individual and social requirements in a balanced manner. The ethical framework will avoid any religious rigidity. "Religious Integration" is possible in the ethical framework.

The fourteenth chapter entitled "Trusteeship Theory : A Means of Social Justice in Indian Context" by Dr. Vinod Kumari attempts to the social reality of India. Attempts are made to lessen the gap between different social groups in society. The inner nature of the society is the value structure. The trusteeship theory has been gradually formulated by Gandhi. Dr. Vinod Kumari says categorically that trusteeship is an alternative to Marxian theory of class struggle and violent revolution. Gandhi was speaking for subalterns, but he was not averse to elite class. The elite class has responsibility towards subalterns. Gandhi does not approve class conflicts. He is against class hatred. He does not see the necessity of class struggle. He wanted harmony between elitist and subalterns. He wants that subaltern should be co-sharer of power structure of elitists.

The fifteenth chapter dwells on "Gandhi and Secularism" by Dr. Manisha Barua. Secularism is popular in contemporary India. It is a fashion to accuse someone as non- secular. As a matter of fact, Gandhi believed in true secularism and not Pseudo Secularism. He is not anti-religion but truly a religious person. Secularism is defined as a moral code of conduct based on the well-being of mankind. A secular state has no particular religion of its own. This word secularism is alien to ancient India. The Indian mind is deeply rooted in spirituality. Our forefathers did not coin the word like secular to maintain the unity of the masses. Hindus used the word *dharma.* The goal of *dharma* is to create spiritual fellowship. *Dharma* supports the entire society. *Dharma* is concerned with particular religion. India is called 'Bharat'. People who live in this land are all 'Bharati' irrespective of caste, creed or religion. *Dharma* transcends religions. It transcends Hinduism, Christianity, Islam and all other religions. *Dharma* cannot be equated with any particular religion. Thus, Gandhi's concept of secularism did not reject spirituality and religion. It gave a new dimension to 'secularism' which preached equality, humanity and universal love and tolerance. It did not mean anti-religion. It meant equality of all religions.

In the sixteenth chapter Prof. Dipak Basu attempts to give "the Meaning of 'Secularism'." In the opening sentence. Prof. Dipak Basu says that in India everyone is confused about the definition of secularism. They equate secularism with religious tolerance. Secularism is defined in the Webster's Dictionary as, "A system of doctrine and practice that rejects any form of religious faith and worship". If we accept secularism as rejection of religious faith, then Sri Aurobindo, Vivekananda, even Ramakrishna Paramahansa though highly tolerant and respectful of other religions, were not secular. Similarly, Mahatma Gandhi, Rabindranath Tagore, Maulana Azad and Khan Abdul Ghaffar Khan were not secularists. In India, secularism is ordinarily, translated as *Pantha Nirapeksha*. India is not secular if we accept the literal meaning of term. As a matter of fact, India is not religious neutral or *Dharma Nirapeksha*. Actually, it is *Panth Nirapeksha*. The author has tried to interpret the meaning of secularism with reference to several countries.

The seventeenth chapter, "Was the Buddha : A Misogynist ? expreses typical of monastic sentiment not to have any sympathy with women. Women is attractive, but dangerous. When Ānanda asks, "Master, how shall we behave with women?" The Buddha says, "You should shun their gaze and if you happen to see her, you should not speak to her and if you should speak to her, you must watch over yourself". But Buddha accept Ambapāli's invitation and refused the alternative invitation of the Licchavi Princes. In the above chapter, the author has tried to bring out the Buddha's overall view of women. Buddha in the heart of his heart did not approve of the idea of women entering the order. But he yielded to the request of Ānanda on behalf of women for long time, women were looked down upon, were regarded as no better than chattels and were subjugated by men. A time came when daughters were regarded as unwelcome. Dowry may have been one of the reasons. By the time of the Buddha, women came to have a very low place. But later on Buddha saw clearly that women did deserve a higher status than they had been given. Buddha took a liberal view against the views prevalent during the period. Did Buddha consider women inferior to men as far as religious aspirations and ascetic practices are concerned ? He asserts that women are not incapable of ascetic practices. He has no prejudice against women. He says that doors of Nirvāṇa is not closed for women. They are not unfit to attain Nirvāṇa. Can we call him a misogynist ? The author depicts that Buddha is full of sympathy for women. In view of the author it is not reasonable to call him as misogynist.

In the eighteenth chapter of the book, Dr. Avinash Kumar Srivastava in his chapter entitled "Religious Pluralism and National Integration" asserts that National Integration may be understood as cohesive attitude among different groups and individual at the national as well as local level. It implies a feeling of common fraternity and oneness among the nationals of a country. In fact, this common cause of Integration is Nation itself. Dr. Srivastava has pinpointed three elements in national integration :

1. It is an attitude of mind that regards loyalty to the nation being above group and sectional attitudes.
2. It is an attitude of keeping the interest of groups or sections subordinate to the wider interest of the nation.
3. It is an urge to think of the interest of every citizen of the country irrespective of caste, creed and religion.

Now, it can be said that by "national integration", we mean a harmonization of loyalties.

Religious pluralism consists of a multiplicity of equivalent. It is opposed to monism. There is a plurality of religions such as Hinduism, Buddhism, Jainism, Islam, Christianity, Zoroastrianism and Sikhism, etc. Every religion has got sub-sects. Thus entire human race has been divided into several religious camps. If we look back and take into account the history of mankind, we will find that religion had been one of the potent factors responsible for disintegration. Religions put up a great obstacle in the way of solidarity in nation because it functions in isolation. But religion has positive functions too. It plays the role to unite human beings.

Religious tolerance should be developed. Jain religion believing in *Anekantavada* does not ask anyone to give up his religion. Hinduism is tolerant. It believes in unity of all religions. If we understand religion as store house of positive values then its role is integrating. We have to respect 'others' in order to maintain cohesiveness. We have to maintain the dignity of differences and cherish the ideal of National Integration amongst religious pluralism.

In the nineteenth chapter, Mahi Pal Singh in, his chapter "Civil Liberties and the Armed Forces (Special Powers) Act", points out that the commitment to protect civil liberties and human rights has received a serious jolt. This is due to mad pursuit of self-centred motives. Sri Mahi Pal Singh suggests that if the people of the country are to be saved from the onslaught of inhuman laws and not to be pushed, against the wall of them into taking to arms, which is not the solution of the problem, an awareness campaign about human rights education should also be started among the people so that the state can be pressurized to tackle such political issue politically through talks with all concerned groups instead of resorting to the use of armed forces which are best kept confined to their barracks except in times of external aggression.

In the twentieth chapter Mahi Pal Singh in his chapter entitled "Questions Arising from the Mumbai Terrorist Attack" suggests that in order to meet the challenges of terrorism, we have to set our house in order. We have to plug the holes through which they sneak into the country. We have to address the problems of those who give shelter to them. Sri Mahi Pal Singh suggests that diplomatic efforts can achieve what armed forces cannot. There are peace loving people everywhere. Such people will not like *Jihadi* terrorism.

R.C. Sinha
Senior Fellow
Indian Council of Philosophical Research
New Delhi

Preface

The present book has raised some of the most pertinent, persistent, burning social and political issues of the day, beginning with a paper written by an American Scholar, entitled "Paradox of Fundamentalism" and ends with the paper on the topic "Questions arising from Mumbai Terrorism Attack of 26/11", coming from the pen of a great social activist. 'Fundamentalism' is inseparably wedded to 'terrorism', through religion as the fountain spring and 'terrorism' as an "epithet" as end result of political discourse, involving mass massacre requiring social and humanistic solution, bringing justice, social justice by demolishing all sorts of violence to usher in a world with a peaceful living based on equality, liberty, fraternity, goodwill, social welfare, religious, social integration, led by properly deliberated and humanely grounded sentiments and ideals, as also driven and guided by social, political accountability, moral, political obligation, creating a healthy world of secularist, egalitarian scientific society, dissociating state interference on the religious presumptions that result in terrorist attacks on innocent populations, for which Gandhian principles of non-violence, sarvodaya, trusteeship are the proven remedies for all times. The word 'Jihad' is used very frequently, but Osho Rajneesh in the present time, even 'Allah' used the word to end all egoity, anger, hatred, jealousy, arrogance as 'Allah' seemed really to mean, a Jihad which can be termed Jihad-e-Aazam, rather go for the madness of violence. In fact, Jihad in terms of 'terrorist attack' on the innocents is a maniac emanations of a sick mind. It is really a disease born out of insane mind which is a quality of animals; never implying sanity.

Shiva Nath Prasad

Avinash Kumar Srivastava

Acknowledgements

Our inspiration to attempt an anthology of this genre has come form Dr. S. Radhakrishnan who has edited great volume of '*Eastern Religion and Western Thought*' and from Dr. Rajendra Prasad of IIT Kanpur", whose personal anthology entitled '*Karma Causation and Retributive Morality*', published by Concept Publishing Company Pvt. Ltd., New Delhi. These are their amazing works and their genius that opened the portals of socio-cultural, ethical and philosophical ideas. We would like to express our deep sense of gratitude to them and all other authors who have provided inspiration to us.

We are thankful to all the authors who have contributed their learned chapters in this volume and for expressing their confidence in us as well as for their continuous support.

We are thankful to our family members whose unstinting support and advice has been a major source of sterngth and a vital contribution to the completion to this anthology.

Lastly, we express our indebtedness to the entire team of Concept Publishing Company, Pvt. Ltd., New Delhi in general and Sri A.K. Mittal in particular for their support and cooperation in this *Jnana Yajna*.

Bhavatu Sabba Mangalam

Avinash Kumar Srivastava

Contents

List of Contributors

1. **Basu, Dipak :** Professor of International Economics, Nagasaki University, Japan. He is reputed for his critical writings studed with facts. Contact Email Id. Bose66@hotmail.com
2. **Barua, Manisha :** Professor of Philosophy, Guwahati University, Guwahati, Assam. She has contributed a number of scholarly chapters in various Philosophical Journals in India and abroad.
3. **Choudhary, Angraj :** Retired Professor of English, Navanalanda Mahavihar, Nalanda, Bihar. He is an expert of Early Buddhism and received President Award for his enormous works on Pali Buddhism. Presently, he is at V.R.J. Dhammagiri, P.O. Igatpuri Dist., Maharashtra. Mobile No. 9370609940
4. **Chincholkar, L.G. :** Professor of Philosophy, Nagpur University. He is an outstanding scholar with great specialisation in ethics. He has authored several books of outstanding merit. His hundreds of chapters are published in Hindi, English and Marathi. His mailing address is — Back Road, Congress Nagar, Nagpur, Maharashtra.
5. **Goel, Dharmendra :** He is a retired Professor of Philosophy, Punjab University, Chandigarh. He has his specialisations in Eastern Philosophy, Philosophy of Science, and Philosophy of Language, Phenomenology, and Existentialism, Social and Political Philosophy. He is widely known for his critical thinking and difficult comprehensive scholarly writings.
7. **Kar, Bijayanand :** Retired Professor of Philosophy, Utkal University, Bhubaneswar, Odisha, has to his credit hundreds of research chapters published in different Philosophical Journals in India and abroad. He has also authored several books from reputed Publishing Houses including Indian

Council of Philosophical Research, Ajanta International, Indian Institute of Advance Studies, Shimla and the Concept Publishing Company Pvt. Ltd., New Delhi. He was a Visiting Professor in Australia's University. His address is AM 26 V. S. S. Nagar, Bhubaneswar, Orissa.

8. **Kumari, Shashi Prabha :** She is a retired Professor of Sanskrit from J.N.U. She is a rare scholar of Sanskrit and Philosophy. She has authored a number of research chapters and books in Hindi, Sanskrit and English published from India and abroad. She has received prize for her book on Vaisheshika Philosophy.
9. **Kumari, Vinod :** She is a Professor and Head in the Department of Philosophy, Meerut University. She is widely known for her brilliant writings. She has authored several books and contributed a number of research chapters in different Journals of Philosophy. She has participated in many conferences, seminars and workshops all-over India.
10. **North, D.,** Email.danorth@stanford.edu
11. **Prasad, Shiva Nath :** Shiva Nath Prasad, M. A. in Philosophy from Patna University. After retirement from Government of Bihar, wherein he served in different capacities, started the publication of a bilingual Journal of Philosophy, *Abhranta*, as an editor. Later on the persistent requests of scholars of Philosophy, he started two unilingual journals entitled '*Darshan Digdarshan*' in Hindi and the Journal of Bihar Philosophical Research in English. Presently, he is the editor of Philosophical Quest, a bilingual Journal of Philosophy. He has authored a book entitled "Charvaka Lokayata an Analytical and Hermeneutic Study", published by Janki Prakashan, Patna. Besides, he has edited an anthology 'Phenomenology : An Introduction' with V.T. Sebestian, Punjab University, Chandigarh. Presently, he is working on an ambitious multi-volume series, "Issues in Ethics and Applied Ethics". His mailing address is, Road No. 20, Plot No. 39, S.K. Nagar, Patna-800001, Mobile No. 09905292070, Email Id is: shivanathprasad51@yahoo.com
12. **Satyanarayana, Y. V. :** He is a retired Professor of Philosophy

of Andhra University, and Professor Emeritus Vishakhapatnam A.P. He has completed three Major Research Projects on Applied Ethics that was later on published in book form by a reputed publisher, M.S. Pearson Education. His book on Bio-Medical is also under publication.

13. **Shaida, S.A. :** He is a retired Professor of Philosophy, I.I.T., Kanpur. His field of specialisation is Existentialism, Phenomenalism, Ethics, Applied Ethics and Religious Ethics with special reference to Islam. He is widely known for his scholarship in India and abroad.

14. **Singh, Mahi Pal,** Editor– "The Radical Humanist", G-3/617, Shalimar Garden, Extension 1, Rose Park, Sahibabad, Gaziabad-201005, (U.P.)

15. **Sinha, Ramesh Chandra :** He is a retired Professor of Philosophy, Patna University. Presently, he is a Senior Research Fellow of Indian Council of Philosophical Research. He is a Visiting Professor in different Universities in England and America. He is a widely known scholar in the Philosophical world because of his academic tours. He has presided over many academic sessions in national and international seminars, symposium and conferences in India and abroad. He has contributed hundreds of scholarly chapters in national and international Journals of Philosophy. He is considered to be an introducer of the concept of *'Subaltern Morality'* in Bihar. However, his field of specialization is Post-Modernism, Socio-political Philosophy and Buddhism. His interests are multi-dimensional and divers to cover every philosophical topic that is posed before him to deliberate. Because of his humility and social activity he is loved and respected by all. Presently, he is the Chief Editor of *Darshnik Traimasik*, a *Journal of Akhil Bhartiya Darshan Parishad.*

16. **Srivastava, Avinash Kumar :** He is Professor and Head Centre, Nalanda College, Biharsharif. He completed his M.A. from Patna University and Ph.D. from Magadha University, Bodh Gaya, on the topic of "A Comparative Study of the

Concept of Samadhi (Yoga) in Early Buddhism and *Bhagavad Gita*". He was awarded Minor Research Project of U.G.C. on the topic of "Adaptable Nature of Buddhism". He has authored two books, "*Bhartiya Darshan ki Mool Samasyaen*" and "Living Buddhism". Besides, he has edited three anthologies : 'Ethics at the core of Globalization', 'Buddha Darshan: Adhunik Sandarbh' and 'Tulnatmak Dharma Darshan'. Dr. Srivastava is a prolific writer and widely known scholar. His about fifty research chapters have been published in India and abroad. He was Joint-Secretary and Secretary of Akhil Bhartiya Darshan Parishad, General Secretary of Bihar Darshan Parishad and Vice President of Indian Society for Buddhist Studies. Besides, he was member of the editorial board of "Darshnik Traimasik", 'Ocean of Buddhist Wisdom' and 'Bauddha Prajna Sindhu' (Delhi). He is also the member of the editorial board of, '*Darshan Digdarshan*' '*The Journal of Bihar Philosophical Research*' and *The Philosophical Quest*. His mailing address is: Amber Chauraha, beside Mahadeva Temple, Biharsharif, *Nalanda*-803102. His Email : avinash.srivastava@gmail.com

Introduction

The present volume is the third book, amongst the present Multi-volume series under the broad head of " Issues in Ethics and Applied Ethics".

The materials of this book were humbly placed before Prof. R.C. Sinha (Retd. Head, Deptt. of Philosophy, Patna University and at present Senior Research Fellow I.C.P.R.) for favour of writing its foreword. It may be mentioned, that Prof. Sinha is one such scholar, who does not feel proper to write a perfunctory report/preface of a book by way of customary, conservative, formal and stereotyped way, since such formalized and customary reports are merely throwing out the responsibility in a haphazard way, rather than giving a mind to the subject and doing some mental exercise. Such types of foreword reports do not hit the bull's eye, rather hits at the periphery and do not qualify for a foreword, in the true sense of the term. Having received the request, Prof. Sinha very wilfully and pleasantly, taken the cudgel to write the foreword, after carefully, absorbingly, minutely reading all the chapters, time and again, reach at the core of theme taken up by individual authors and after keen deliberation, start writing a critical commentary-cum-foreword. The way in which the same has been brought out is very fine. The editors do not have words to express their debt of gratitude to him in this regard. More importantly, he has reduced the job of editors to a zero point. Hence, any attempt at further writing about the chapters would be mere repetition worth nothing, as well as "sheer drudgery".

In the present volume, there is first chapter by D. North, entitled "Paradox of Fundamentalism" which appeared in *Radical Humanism......* The same was so much impressing that requests were made to him to allow recycling the same in the series and he has been kind enough to allow for it and the same is placed in the beginning of this book. The contents of the materials of this chapter have added allegiance with two chapters at serial 6, entitled "Relevance of Gandhian Measures in Tackling Terrorism" by Prof. L.G. Chincholkar (Retd. Nagpur University) a prolific scholar, who has contributed hundreds of research chapters in all the philosophical Journals of India, authored several books, attended great number of seminars, symposia, conferences and addressed lots of philosophical gatherings. Also at Sl. 10 and 11, there are two chapters on Terrorism which throws limelight on the ticklish matter and has posed threat of global dimension, without any immediate solution, near in sight. India is the worst sufferer of this threat for decades; the big powers only gave lip service without joining hands to eradicate it in right earnest. Terrorism is a disease, a social and political evil, a malaise rooted in the name of religion, done to destabilize the government/state in the garb of or in the cloak that "what is one man's terrorist is another man's freedom fighter", but freedom for whom, for what, why, are unknown freedom to kill the innocent goers, passers by, a crime against humanity at large. What a game/what a tyranny? What a principle? At an enormous price! It is not known how long this menace of terrorism will continue. Would we have to wait for a prophet or Messiah to come forth and do the right thing for the humanity that dehumanizes, that robs the life given to human kind, by way of the gifts of the God, the Almighty? Why has man snatched the power of God, disobeyed God's law, one may imagine that the result of Adam and Eve's, disobedience in the garden of Adam, brought in the world 'sin' for endless times to come, and the perpetrators of terror are causing mass genocide. Has God lost all his powers, or have the terrorists made God crippled to take any action and is avoiding to give proper justice for ill or evil, murder and slaughter, in such vast scale, beyond imaginable proportion.

It may be noted, that the present book contains three chapters on terrorism in this one volume, though some more chapters on religious fundamentalists, *Jihad*, etc. have been left out for the next volume. One may be curious to know, why so many chapters in one volume on one subject alone. The answer is quite simple and realistic, especially in the context of India. India is facing the menace of terrorism time and again, but is not able to control and contain it and due to their there inability to check it, the terrorist have taken our country as a soft state and the terrorist activities have gained considerable deterrence. This fact can be discussed with reference to some events of India, which have encouraged the terrorist's ambitious designs of more and more fresh attacks, in several novel ways. It is known to all Indians, that on 13th December, 2001, five terrorists armed with most lethal and sophisticated arms attacked the Parliament of India, which is a temple of democracy. The armed terrorists continuously fired indiscriminately for a long time, killing several security personnel, gardeners, etc. Though legal case took long time, but on 22 August, 2005, Afzal Guru's appeal was dismissed by the Supreme Court of India, taking his death sentence as appropriate. Curative petition was also dismissed by the Supreme Court (four Bench) on January 12, 2007, then mercy petition was filed and the same is pending with President, but the file which is so much sensitive and which could have taken a day or two to dispose of, is still kept pending, without any rhyme or reason, being an act of terrorist, which disgraced a nation, brought shame to all Indians. Does it not mean, that the Indians who were disgraced, has not got the uprightness to punish the guilty of dastardly, ghastly and most heinous criminal act. Where the Indians are faltering is not taken into account? Does it not sound something foul in the state of Denmark? What may possibly have aroused national sentiment seems to be at bay. Can we rise to the occasion and be straight forward and do as per the provisions of the law? One another example, Kasab's terrorist acts rocked the entire nation. The mercy stage may come and remain pending for years and decades as in the above cited case, and we are spending crores of rupees in his maintenance and security. The founding fathers of the Constitution have provided in Article 72 for the President of India to allow mercy petition or reject at the advice of the Prime Minister, but they (the founding fathers) were not aware that a minor latch was that they did not fix a definite time limit to hasten the disposal of such cases, hence such dastardly act, goes unpunished and a waivering approach is adopted on flimsy pretexts. This is not a small matter for any country/any democratic state. The time demands a fixed limit for disposal of such cases by the President. What is the reason of all this waivering? It is one and only APPEASEMENT POLICY. It is simply **Vote** policy, **Vote** diplomacy; it is due to greed of power and chair.

While India was groaning in the guttural tones, with the scourge of Fundamentalism, terrorism, what was the reaction of the other great countries of the world, say, England, America? Only lip service, and crocodile tears. But as against our cold approach, we may compare the hard and harsh approach of the U.S. which faced terrorist attack on the World Trade Centre, masterminded by Osama Bin Laden which cost about 5000 lives. The U.S. response was amazing as compared to our weak and humble one. What America did? Within weeks, U.S. came up with Patriot Act which gave sufficiently wider power to the agencies to deal with terror. The result-oriented approach is worth everyone to see, with eyes azar. Osama was traced, caught and killed from the very country on which U.S. spends huge funds. Is not terrorist killing a great violation of the Human Rights? Does it not cost enormous innocent lives? If the U.S. could make laws to contain terrorism, why is it that India did withdraw anti-terror laws like POTA and TADA? For whom and for what? No other simplistic answer can be given except vote politics, political appeasement, for coming into power and earn dividends, without any let or hindrance. Is it not a kind of political corruption, a safe haven for power, prestige, crime, corruption at the cost of the voters who can do nothing against them, else they meet their doom in the hands of goons/goondas? Taken into the immensity and magnitude of the problem, the readers would feel satisfied that such acts or laws of U.S. were justified to save their land (U.S.) and countrymen. Perhaps U.S. stand seems to be appropriate, so one would feel satisfied and justified in the sense that several chapters placed here in this book are meant to show different angles of vision from which a problem may be seen and a proper remedy found out for our country. Politician of

India may try to take it in right earnest and save our land from perils any further.

As we have seen above, we easily, come to another set of chapters on "Secularism", which follows our electoral prospect's politics or secular and non-secular parties. The group of the so called secular parties raise their accusing finger against the non-secular parties. In the race of secular, non-secular, the entire political leaders cry and argue almost fiercely. The word 'secular' has so much been flung, that it is most essential to discuss what is it that is called "secular". The great divide between the two opposed forces, attempt has been made here to place more than one chapter in this present volume, so that enough awareness is created between what is what and what is not what.

We have at serial 8, one chapter by Prof. S.A. Shaida, a very fine chapter coming from the pen of a great scholar of India. At serial 9, is another chapter coming from a most incisive intellect by Prof. Dharmendra Goel. The next chapter on this topic occurs at serial 15, by Dr. Manisha Barua and at serial 16, a chapter by Prof. Deepak Basu of Tokyo University, Japan. They have discussed about it very minutely and thoroughly with deep intellection and *Prof. R.C. Sinha has already written the gist of their chapters after thoroughly going through the texts and has given much matured opinion.* The important fact is that, as Russell has said once, there are words which are definable, there are words which are not definable and according to him, secularism is a word which is not definable. That the question that Russell has said is not very much worth-noting. It is not the question of giving a definition. The question is, that nobody wants to understand it, for their own gains and losses in political achievement, in political appeasement, political aggrandizement. The politicians feel, it is better to pretend innocence and gain dividends, till the mind of the general mass get matured, to separate the husk from the grain. This process takes time and till that time, bake their bread and grease with butter, that is the best way to befool others, the time till others are befooled is the best time for harvesting self-interest.

In this context apart from whatever the materials given therein, it would be very advantageous to suggest that a very recently published book, edited by the one of the greatest stalwart in Philosophy of India, Prof. B. Kar (Orissa) and whose contribution to philosophy in India has been monumental, since to his great credit there are more than a dozen books and nearly 150 research chapters published and are still flowing in abundance like the natural stream. The book is entitled *Secularism and National Integration*. This title is itself very significant, since 'secularism' is a political subject and has by far more been debacling persons and acting in the direction of dividing men, disintegrating rather than uniting or integrating, as such to the most reader/scholar, 'secularism' is abhorent of 'integration', far more national disintegration'. When one political party comes in power, it enacts laws like POTA and TADA, when another party comes into power, it annuls all those, not because undoing was good in the interest of the country's unity integrity and sovereignty, but such government created an air on the political grounds, just to show down the former government, that such acts are secular. What was put to loss in the fight between two groups, the divide was on the plea of secular and the division harmed the whole country, due to soft pedalling of the one party towards the very terrorists activities, destroying not only innocent human lives but the country as a whole, shaming and disgracing the entire people. Such is the part played by the political persons for voter's appeasement. So, it seems a conundrum, how secularism could be related to 'National Integration', when secularism acts divisively and when once a division is committed, it needs a reintegration process. Scholars will find enough materials in the book of Prof. B. Kar, at least, what are the key powers processes, points, pleas that relate humanity, etc. for National Integration and the role of Orissa to this end, specially. A chapter 'Secularism' by Prof. Kar is included which is so much compact, crystal clear, like which, it is difficult to find in any book. This can be said with most impartiality.

The very word 'National' or even the call for 'National Integration' would sound distasteful to the ear drums of man, in general, who has now developed leaning towards globalization, global village, globalization as a reminder of the Greek Genius Diogenes. Rabindra Nath Tagore wrote the book *Nationalism*, the Western scholars, even the Indians, found it not appealing, amidst the craze for globalization. But globalization is more a craze than a wish fulfilment and a positive actualization or achievement. Many Western scholars disdain the concept of 'Nationalism', thus it is a pertinent question, if we should relish the ideas of Integration, whether National, Religious or International. The chapters presented on these topics are meaningful in the context of Secularism, Fundamentalism, Terrorism which have damaged the entire social fabric of India. None other than the 'National Integration' can be the proper reply to the problems of secularism, fundamentalism, terrorism and cry for social justice against the backdash of this political tyranny. Only a well concerted effort can remove these social evils as mentioned above in the pattern of the U.S. term policy of Patriot Acts as against the waivering or weak attitude of latches, indecisiveness approach of India, in the eradication of the tyranny of terrorism, fundamentalism, etc.

In the present context of India, integration in its several senses can be a Time Honoured Demand, or a First Priority demand just now, may not be so later, or till the sky is cleared of controversies, cleavages, led by deep thirsts of territory of our neighbouring countries, or the political Power Blocks which always drowns the dim voices of the weak, which robs the economy of the underdeveloped or undeveloped countries with loud, resounding voices of globalization, without letting the poor countries know how much is globalization the right remedy for the economic maladies facing the poor countries, as also how globalization pays the powerful rather the poor, depressed. In this state of affair, the presentation of Prof. Kar's book is quite incidental and timely. His approach is quite appreciable.

Let me quote a few of the words of Prof. Kar in respect of "Secularism" and see how the appropriate answer to 'secularism rather Pseudo Secularism, can be met by adopting an approach towards integrations of several kinds. Prof. Kar says, (1) secularism, and sacerdotalism are two opposed views (p.128), but it has to be noted if sacerdotalism has done harm, while secularism has desisted from doing harm? Since both of them are opposed. What one has done, the other should have undone, such a phenomenon is not found in practical practice, both have equally harmed. (2) Prof. Kar says, "secularism has been viewed as a logical neighbour of humanism. It implies concern for humanity" (p. 29), further, has secularism really contributed to humanism in the true sense of the term. Obviously not, to my mind. (3) While not taking into consideration any linkage between spirituality and morality, "secularism is committed to the free flow of dispassionate rational enquiry", it is a fact that secularism came into existence from the backdoor of rationalism but have the adherents of secularism done anything for humanity? Secularism is a principle of "this worldliness", but is it in practice? not so, it is merely in the achievement of individual self-seekingness, selfishness and the like, the mission is not met in true sense. Prof. Kar says that secularism is 'equidistance from religions' of which its another version is *sarva dharma samabhava*. It has also missed this version, even trying to meet the demands of common man, one cannot find a concept as such, secularism + religion. This is impossible, what we find in actuality is a mere show, a pretension, flattery, hypocrisy. The reply to secularism's mode of thinkers is given by Prof. Kar himself "under the plea accepting equal treatment to all religions, our political leaders have either while in power or aspiring to get power – come forward eagerly to make themselves associated with festivals and functions organized by different religions communities in order to gain cheap popularity there, appeasement is made solely with a selfish motive and evil design to capture vote bank and to be in power, sacrificing socio-political justice. This means that under the garb of religious tolerance, religions groupism/ communalism is politicized and is. . . . . . for political gain and that, in turn, ... the prospect of social justice as also equilibrium of the state" (p. 35). If such is the fate of the word secularism, better discard it once for all.

It is to these realistic problems, facing our country, we find reply in the different sets of chapters collected in this volume ranging from terrorism, integration (religions and national) including welfare, social justice, Gandhian methods of trusteeship, sovereignty and security of the nation, civil rights etc. If the present volume may be taken in that light, this volume may prove fruitful, in true sense of the term. The poet Byron said, "if you can't wage a war really, a military war, the words can also be not less fruitful armoury against tyranny, scycophants which does not require physical strength, but really a moral power, which can change even the metal iron into a watery shape." Byron says "let us wage war with words", this may be termed in hindi "BOLI KI GOLI", that is, fiery words.

The reason why this editorial note has to refer to Prof. B. Kar's book is that, it hits two birds in one throw, one stone. Further, here in this book, there are two chapters on Integration; one chapter entitled 'Religious Integration' by Prof. Kar himself and another chapter by Avinash Kumar Srivastava entitled Religious Pluralism and National Integration. These two chapters provide general guidelines, besides the roots/causes that lead to National Disintegration, they are unique in their own right, throwing much light to a man in the dark and groping.

Another topic which is in common coverage in the present day, is social justice, which is more social than not. Even those who claim themselves to be its torch-bearers, are no better than proving the popular adage of "much boast little roast or another, empty vessel sounds much", why? Because, doing a thing is one thing, while saying is another, when saying and doing are not in consonance, then hypocrisy buds forth and hypocrisy results into flattery and flattery is inmmoral, if not a sin. Further, the word 'social justice' is a word, which linguistically is redundant and repetitious, for the reason, the word 'justice' is a political concept and political framework can work only within a social context. The word is alluded to Greeks, but perhaps 'social' was not attached to justice then. There was an occasion when it was asked from one Prof. of Linguistics, how should the concept be analyzed, he kept silent and said jokingly, it is not known, why the tail of 'social' has been attached with justice and who added it and for what purpose. Really speaking, justice beyond the ken of society is unmeaning, justice is always social. The chapter 'social justice' included in this volume by Prof. Shashi Prabha Kumar, who is one of the greatest Sanskrit scholar of India and also philosophy, beats all bounds of excellency of approach and is most praiseworthy.

Chapters at serial 5, at serial 12 and 14 are related to Gandhian thought, are fine pieces coming as they do from great scholars of repute and add value to the book.

There are two chapters of Prof. Y.U Satyanarayana of Andhra University which are master pieces in their own way, coming as they do from a mastermind, known for his transparency, clarity and precisive writing. The chapter on Gandhi by Prof. L.G. Chincholkar is befitting in our present turmoiltwisted world today, facing political crisis owing to political highhandedness bordering on the verge of corruption, instability and self seeking at the cost of the other. The chapter on Civil Liberty by the President of Civil Liberties, Sri Mahipal Singh is a very timely presentation, packed with facts, without wasting a word, he is a prolific writer in every sense of the term. He is a social activists too, a lover of Human Rights and a good soul, besides.

Shiva Nath Prasad

Avinash Kumar Srivastava

1

The Paradox of Fundamentalism in a Democratic State

D. North

1. Observations and Definitions

When I say the word "fundamentalism", I call to mind a set of personal and subjective experiences which may be very different from yours. The definition and underlying assumptions of the word are shaped by geography, time, socio-economic circumstances, and the like. Thus, we must recognize the meaning of the word "fundamentalism" as approximate. We nonetheless continue to use the word as a shortcut to discourse. But given that the word itself is subject to various meanings, confusion and misunderstanding are likely. Accordingly, the word must be used with care.

It must likewise be acknowledged that use of the term "fundamentalism" may itself be counter-productive. As the term is used to describe various and complex groups of people who may otherwise have little in common, it tends to paint with too broad a brush. Use of the term may also encourage over-simplification and deflect deeper and more precise inquiry.

* This was published in *The Radical Humanist* and here it is published by permission–*Editor*.

Moreover, the term can be, and often is, used to dehumanise people and to justify killing them. Nonetheless, with these cautions in mind, and recognizing that some word or another has to be used, we settle with the term "fundamentalism".

The concept of who and what is a "fundamentalist" has tended to evolve over time. To me, growing up in the western United States, a fundamentalist was a Christian Bible-thumper. That is, a Protestant Christian who claimed the literal truth and inerrancy of the Christian Bible. They were the people who claimed that the world was literally created by God in six days. By close study of the scriptures, they had established that the world was 5,000 years old and that its end was imminent. Scientific evidence such as carbon-dating and the like was viewed by them as irrelevant to the higher authority of scripture.

Such people were mostly objects of scorn among my family and friends. They were isolated cultists and were not perceived to pose any danger to us personally or to society in general. More often than not, they were regarded as backward fuddy-duddies who would, in time, die, taking their unevolved ideas with them.

Today, however, as the world seems to grow smaller and smaller, with social interactions taking on global relevance, the terms "fundamentalist" and "fundamentalism" have taken on more complex meanings. The term is now widely understood to include adherents of Jewish, Christian, Hindu, Buddhist, Sikh and Islamic cultures. Recent experience of the Bush administration's misadventures in Iraq has revealed to European and American observers warring strains of Islamic fundamentalism previously unknown to westerners. Likewise, the years of the "troubles" in Ireland highlighted the competing strains of fundamentalism within Christianity.

More than that, however, the term "fundamentalism" now sounds dangerous, where before it just sounded dismissive. Today, to call someone a "fundamentalist" is an accusation and a challenge. For the past eight years of the Bush administration, the words "fundamentalism" and "terrorism" have been used synonymously and interchangeably.

What, then, is the real nature of fundamentalism? What precisely do we mean by the word? Is there in fact a widely accepted definition of the term? Are there common elements operating among the various strains of fundamentalism? Can valid generalizations be made about fundamentalism? More important, are all fundamentalisms equally threatening to democratic functioning? And what should be the response to fundamentalism?

The challenge to anyone wishing to explore the issue of fundamentalism in relationship to the democratic experience is to try to determine if it can reasonably be said that there are identifiable characteristics which recur among the diverse groups we call "fundamentalist."

In exploring this topic, I have looked for guidance to the comprehensive five-volume series of the *Fundamentalism Project*, edited by Marty and Appleby and published by the University of Chicago Press, Chicago, IL, over the years 1991-1995. Likewise, I have been influenced by personal conversations with the late Professor Gabriel Almond of Stanford University, who was one of the editors of the *Fundamentalism Project*.

Additionally, I have been guided by the collection of essays collected under the title, *Fundamentalisms*, edited by Christopher H. Partridge, and published in 2001 by Paternoster Press, Carlisle, Cumbria, UK.

The term "fundamentalist" was first used by Baptists in the northern United States. A series of pamphlets called *The Fundamentals* was published between 1909 and 1915 as a reaction to the perceived assault of Darwinism and liberal Protestant theology. Use of the term among contemporary Christian groups in the US has at times both been embraced and rejected. Antagonistic sects have likewise used the term as a disparagement against others.

Use of the term is now generally accepted to include diverse religions which embrace various conservative agendas and orthodoxies.

After the collapse of the Soviet Union, observers began to

speculate about where the next threat would come from. What ideology might replace Reagan's "evil empire" as the challenge to Western democracy? A common prediction among scholars was that fundamentalism would take the place of Marxist ideology as a threat to democracy. (The implications associated with the assumption that there would necessarily be another threat is, itself, interesting to ponder.)

According to John Garvey, there are three traits common to fundamentalists: they are "conservative, popular and practical." [see Prof. John Garvey, *Fundamentalisms and the State*, Vol. 3 of the Fundamentalism Project, p. 15.

By "conservative" it is meant that fundamentalists seek to conserve their own brand — and their own interpretation of — their religious heritage. That is, they resist anything perceived to be a revision of that which they claim to be based on ancient texts and practices.

By "popular" it is meant that fundamentalists adhere to a simplistic gloss or interpretation of their ancient texts in order to produce easily understood and easily disseminated messages to their supporters. It can be argued that this leads to over-simplification and actual misinterpretation of the scriptural texts. For example, Islamic fundamentalists urge strict adherence to Shari'a, while skipping over the complex and elaborate history of Islamic jurisprudence. (See, for example, the penetrating and persuasive discussion by R.A. Jahagirdar, "*Talaq: Talaq: Talaq*" in Vol. 72, No. 5 of the *Radical Humanist*.)

By "practical" it is meant that fundamentalists are not big on theory. Rather, they offer practical, everyday codes of behaviour which both give reassurance to their followers and provide unifying identity to the group. Exacting and specific directives are given, for example, in matters of dress, dietary restrictions, social interactions, and the like.

Fundamentalists likewise believe that God, or his agents, actively participate in the affairs of the world. Thus all over the globe we hear the concept that AIDS is God's punishment to sodomists and drug abusers. No mention is made of AIDS transmission to innocent, unwitting victims such as recipients of blood transfusions or continent and faithful wives who contract the disease from their husbands.

Another, perhaps paradoxical, characteristic of fundamentalists is that they actively engage and confront the world despite the backward-looking trajectory of their message. They also tend to encourage the perception of the wider community that they are "different", by actively seeking to set themselves apart by distinctive dress, customs, diet and the like. In this way, by seeking to establish subservience to the divine while challenging and rejecting modern ideas and customs, fundamentalists are caught up in the push-pull of ideas. The problems posed by this dilemma often require a strong, authoritarian and charismatic leader and a subservient, unquestioning set of followers.

As secularists, we accept the division of society into distinct public/private spheres. We accept that one of the functions of the state is regulation of actions and relationships in the public arena according to secular rules. Moreover, those rules are subject to transformation as necessary. No claim to eternal or divine truth is made for the laws of the secular state. A basic tenet of secularism is that in their private lives, people are free to act as they wish in religious or other matters.

An example is the Constitution of India, which provides that all persons are equally entitled to freedom of conscience and the right freely to profess, practice and propagate religion. Similarly, the First Amendment to the Constitution of US provides that "Congress shall make no law respecting an establishment of religion, or prohibiting the free exercise thereof".

Fundamentalists, however, reject the distinction of public/private spheres. They actively seek to unite the public sphere with their own brand of religious world view. Thus, to the extent that fundamentalists overtly reject the idea of a secular state, they reject a fundamental element of the modern democratic state. Other issues arise, of course, among fundamentalists not living in democratic states when their religious views conflict with those of the dominant state religion.

2. Practical Considerations: What is to be done?

Many paradoxes are presented when contemplating a strategy of practical action in response to fundamentalism. In the first place, to the extent that religious fundamentalists seek to promote their cause by persuasive means through media, preaching, etc., the secular state not only must tolerate them but must also protect them. Fundamentalist Christian anti-abortionists who wish to demonstrate, for example, in front of medical clinics where abortions are performed, must be given protection to express their views, however antithetical they may seem to others.

The opposite, of course, is more often the case. That is, more often than not it is the fundamentalists who spur their followers on to the call of violence against those they perceive as agents of secularism. Fundamentalists are empowered to take to violence because, viewing themselves to be singled out for special favour with God. they often lack fear of death, or actually believe that their violent acts will be rewarded in another life. Additionally, they often perceive that the media notoriety engendered by retaliatory actions against them is helpful to their cause and raises sympathy, donations and converts. Nonetheless, within the laws of the secular state, such people must be afforded protection and the freedom to follow their beliefs.

The reaction to this paradox-protection of the state and its citizens *vs*. protection of the individual's right to pursue religious beliefs—requires a very delicate balancing act on the part of the democratic state. Make no mistake: overreaction—repression, indiscriminate retaliation, etc.—does nothing but strengthen the hand of the fundamentalist. As repressive and retaliative action is pursued, people become radicalized and align themselves to the fundamentalist cause which they previously may have rejected. Likewise, the state must act honourably and truthfully in its dealings with fundamentalists.

In formulating the response of the democratic state to the challenges of fundamentalism, it is imperative to understand that fundamentalism is a nuanced concept. Although, as described above, fundamentalists share elements common to their causes, they are not necessarily monolithic in their thinking and strategies; even within each group there are shades of meaning and degrees of commitment. The same response, repeated over and over, to differing groups or to the same group, whose philosophy and strategies may be shifting, is likely to be doomed or even counter-productive. The example of the Bush administration is Exhibit 'A' in the case of what not to do. The Bush administration has not the slightest understanding of the underlying philosophy or motivating views of the fundamentalists against whom they have declared war. In fact, they have given no indication of wanting to understand.

Moreover, the argument can be made, and I make it, that elements of the Christian fundamentalist movement have hijacked US foreign policy through the agency of the Bush administration, which has led to war and nasty entanglements all over the world and has resulted in countless more deaths than any bomb-throwers could ever have hoped. US Christian fundamentalist thinking is thus indirectly terrorist in nature and poses a threat to the democracy and to the international standing of the US.

The greatest threat to democracy posed by fundamentalism is panic and ill-considered overreacting policies by the government. 9/11 was an economic threat to the US and it caused horror and panic. However, the real assault to democracy came not from the fundamentalist terrorists themselves, but from the overreactions and repressive actions of the Bush administration in instituting torture, in opening prison at Guantanamo, etc.

But no legitimate government can stand idly by and watch its citizens murdered and its treasury depleted by the acts of violent terrorists. It is, I suppose, predictable and even understandable that governments will resort to actions which turn out to be counter-productive, but which actually eat away at the very roots of democracy.

Given the horrific potentials of fundamentalist violence, imposition of the death penalty is frequently offered as a solution. The death penalty is argued to serve two purposes. First, it is argued that it serves as a deterrent. Second, it is argued that the death penalty offers a sense of justice to the outraged populace and satisfies the atavistic urge for retribution.

But since many fundamentalists actually seek a martyr's death, believing that death for the cause leads to reward in a next life, the death penalty is likely to have the opposite effect of deterrence and may actually spur the fundamentalist on to violent acts in the quest for martyrdom.

Are there, then, pre-emptive actions—other than the blunt instrument of force and war—available to counter fundamentalism before it erupts into violent acts? In this connection, it is good to remember that fundamentalism breeds in the dark neglected corners of society. Moreover, fundamentalism does not spring up from nothingness; it arises out of the circumstances and events of its social and cultural environment.

In her book, *Memo to the President*, former U.S. Secretary of State Madeleine Albright addresses the issue by detailing three relevant points :

1. *Be precise:* just because radically fundamental Islamists undertake specific attacks does not make all Islam our enemy. It does not even make all radical fundamental Islamists our enemy. It is imperative that we target only those who are actually responsible for violent acts. To do otherwise radicalizes more moderate adherents and provides a central, unifying impulse to fundamentalists who might otherwise be at odds within their own movement. By focusing on this precision, various factions of the fundamentalist movement may be isolated and kept from aligning themselves into larger, more dangerous entities or they may actually be motivated to take positions at odds with other factions, thereby weakening the movement.

2. *Exploit their weaknesses:* Most fundamentalist movements have no economic or intellectual programme to offer the rank and file. This weakness may be exploited by offering people economic and intellectual hope.
3. Engage right-minded members of the religion. In the case of Islamic fundamentalism, for example, terror and violence are inherently un-Islamic. Give a forum for this message to be disseminated by moderate adherents of the Islamic world.

This discussion highlights another paradox, one that is peculiar to the secularist. By our very nature, secularists are not usually driven by passion into action. The secularist more likely runs the risk of being paralyzed by the tendency to over-analyze and to add unnecessary complexity and layers of theory to issues.

As W.B. Yeats wrote in his poem, "The Second Coming":

> The best lack all conviction, while the worst
> Are full of passionate intensity.

How passionate are we, then, as secularists, about secularism and democracy? What contagious passion do we bring to our cause? Do we have a vehicle—a method, a symbol—to make secular democracy as exciting and enticing to the common man and woman as the fundamentalist does for his ideology? Does our passion for secularism and democracy stand up to the passion for fundamentalism? This may be the challenge for the secularist today.

2

Nehru's Contribution to Secularism and Scientific Attitude : A Critical Study

Y.V. Satyanarayana

Secularism, as we understand it is a product of the West. The doctrinal basis for secularism was found in the declaration of Christ: "Render unto Caesar the things that are Caesar's, and to God the things that are God's". The struggle between the Church and the state in the medieval period was a crucial factor in the emergence of secularism in the West. The secular spirit was the gift of scientific revolution which separated politics from the church. Secularism and scientific attitude are closely associated with one another. Here the word "scientific" does not merely mean positive sciences. It also means the spirit of free enquiry, the spirit of looking at things objectively, freedom from reverence to the past and a more humble attitude towards our own history.

Secularism, like democracy, has come to mean different things to different people. According to Chambers Dictionary,"secularism is the belief that the state, morals, education, etc., should be independent of religion". Some scholars equated secularism with atheism, for some others secularism means non-intervention of the state in religious affairs, for some others it means treating all religions equally.

The philosophy of secularism is based on certain principles and values. Apart from those principles and values, it loses its significance. There are some thinkers who consider secularism merely as a political concept applicable to the nature and functions of the state. However, secularism as a philosophy of life, can be applied to all aspects of human life. The practice and application of secular values, secular attitude and secular approach not only enrich peoples' understanding of socio-political problems in their day-to-day social activity, but also provide proper guidance to them to think and act in a morally good or justified manner. Furthermore, the practice of secular values by the members of a social system immensely contributes for an ideal social life.

Secularism, as it is understood and practiced in the West, was alien to India. Like many other political and social concepts, such as democracy, socialism, equality, etc., it has come to India from the West. Even though secularism was not in practice either in ancient or in medieval India, for many centuries "religious tolerance" had in practice in the Indian society. The spirit of religious tolerance is one of the distinctive attributes of Indian civilization. The spirit of religious tolerance fostered by Indian society for many centuries was the foundation of a secular state in India.

The Western system of education and the use of English language enabled the first generation of the Indian intellectuals, to get themselves acquainted with secularism and the Western system of liberal thought. The need for secularism and the relevance of a secular state have been recognized by Mahatma Gandhi and Jawaharlal Nehru when they assumed the leadership of the freedom movement under the banner of the Indian National Congress. They have realized the fact, rightly so, that in a pluralistic society like that of India, the policy and practice of secular principles and values, must be an essential aspect to preserve and protect the age old composite culture of the society. The rise and growth of Muslim and Hindu Communalism during the period of independent movement compelled the leaders of the Indian National Congress to adopt the policy of secularism. Consequently, the Indian National Congress, at its Karachi session in 1931, adopted a resolution which stated that "the state shall observe neutrality in regard to all religions". Thus, the Gandhi-Nehru model of secular state in India was grounded on the necessity of certain values and aspirations.

At the time of framing the new constitution, one of the important considerations before the Constituent Assembly was whether Indian polity should be secular or otherwise. However, by and large, the consensus was in favour of a secular state, which alone can allay the fears of the minorities and reassure them of the security of their cultural and religious identity. Constitutional safeguards were provided to minority religious communities concerning religious, cultural and educational rights to enable them to live with dignity. However, the word "secular" finds its place in the preamble along with "sovereign democratic republic" only after the adoption of the 42nd Amendment to the Constitution of India, which came into operation on the 1st September, 1976.

Nehru was an ardent lover of democracy, socialism and secularism. His faith in and commitment to secularism remain unshaken till his last day. Even his intense critics never doubted his commitment to secularism. The family environment in which he was brought up, his educational training at Harrow, Cambridge and London, his exposure to the new horizons of sciences, all contributed in shaping his approach and outlook towards life. His aversion to religion and religious dogmas made him to move towards rationalism and scientific approach, which are based on an open-minded approach to understand things and tries to reach truth by experiments. As a rationalist, he viewed all human problems with an open mind, examined and analyzed the situations in a systematic and objective manner and found a remedy or a solution which appeared as best to him.

A living philosophy, for Nehru, must answer the contemporary problems of individual and social life. Philosophy, as Nehru understands it, avoided many pitfalls of religion and encouraged thought and enquiry. However, it lived in its ivory tower cut off from social life and its day-to-day problems. He felt that philosophy is concentrating more on ultimate purposes of human life and failing to link them with the practical life of man.

Religion, in the form of a set of dogmatic beliefs and supernatural influences, did not appeal much to him. Explaining his discomfort towards religion, Nehru observed: "Religion, as I saw it practiced and accepted even by thinking minds, whether it was Hinduism or Islam or Buddhism or Christianity, did not attract me. It seemed to be closely associated with superstitious practices and dogmatic beliefs and behind it by a method of approach to life's problems which was certainly not that of science."[1]

Even though Nehru was quite aware of the influence of religion on the Indian masses, he was totally against to make use of religion for political purpose. He was critical of those persons who exploit religion as a means to achieve political ends. He equally denounced the communalist policies and approach of the Muslim League and the Hindu Mahasabha to achieve their political goals. Nehru's non-religious approach to politics may be distinguished from that of Muhammad Ali Jinnah's approach to politics through Islamic religion. Ever since he joined the freedom movement, Nehru sought to make Indian Politics as secular and rational as possible. He fought against communalism, the communalism of both minority as well as majority. He put larger responsibility on the majority community and said, "...... it is the dominant community and it is its responsibility not to use its position in any way which might prejudice our secular ideal".[2]

For Nehru, casteism was as dangerous as communalism. He was highly critical of casteism and the role and influence of caste in Indian politics. "A caste-ridden society", for Nehru, "is not properly secular".[3] He felt that divisions based on caste were bound to affect the social structure of the state. The caste divisions, which were based on a hierarchical order in the society, prevent people from realizing the idea of social equality.

A secular state, for Nehru, does not mean irreligion or something opposed to religion. It means equal respect for all faiths and providing equal opportunities to all creeds without attaching to one faith or religion. In other words, the state can remain independent of any particular religion. Thus, Nehru's model of secular state does not mean absence of religion, but putting religion on a different plane from that of normal political and social life.

Indian society is a pluralistic society. Indian culture is a composite culture. People belonging to different religious, cultural and caste groups, live side by side in the same state, and are governed by the same laws. A pluralistic society like India has no other option but to be a secular state. Indian secularism is not a negative materialistic secularism but a positive secularism sympathetic to the phenomenon of religion. Explaining the notion of Indian secularism, Dr. S.Radhakrishnan asserted that "Secularism does not mean opposition to religion. It does not mean disrespect to religion. It only means that the state as such is not identified with any particular religion, but tolerates every religion, appreciates every religion, respects all religions . . . . . ."[4]

Nehru's approach to the problems of human life was more or less scientific. He believes that the scientific outlook discloses the right direction to man to fulfil his desires and achieve his goals. It was his firm opinion that the application of science is inevitable and unavoidable to the modern man. Hence, he felt that scientific approach and scientific temper must be a way of life, a process of thinking and a method of acting to every person living on the earth. He was very much impressed by the achievements of science and technology and observed that the technical capacity of science made it possible to transform an economy of scarcity into one of abundance. It lessened the drudgery of man, and life became easier for millions.

Nehru had an inordinate confidence in science and scientific method. He asserts that science has brought many changes in the life of humans and the most vital change that it has brought has been the development of the scientific outlook in man. He believes that the scientific method alone offers hope to mankind and provides solutions to the agony of the world. He was critical of those people who still live mentally in the pre-scientific age and betray scientific approach in their thought and actions. The findings of science may change from time to time, but the method of science does not change, and it is to that one must adhere in his thought and activities.

Nehru was an agnostic and a humanist. He was more concerned of human life related to this world rather than life after death. He wrote, "I am afraid the next world does not interest me. My mind is full of what I should do in this world and if I see my way clearly here, I am content. If my duty here is clear to me, I do not trouble myself about any other world."[5] Referring to the imaginary aspect of human mind, Nehru agreed with the famous saying of Voltaire that "even if God did not exist, it would be necessary to invent Him". He thought that too much dependence on supernatural factors might lead to a loss of self-reliance in man and deaden his capacity and creative ability. He asserted that, "as knowledge advances, the domain of religion, in the narrow sense of the word, shrinks. The more we understand life and nature the less we look for supernatural causes."[6]

As a matter of religious faith, Nehru did not believe in a supernatural agency or a life after death or *karma* theory of cause and effect or other worldly things. Essentially, he was more concerned and interested in this world and in this life, than in some other world or a future life. Religious beliefs and dogmas, as Nehru grasped them, drifts away a person from to think rationally and scientifically and takes refuge in irrationalism, superstition and unreasonable and inequitable social prejudices and practices. He expressed the view that many of the social evils, which are capable of removal, are attributed to the original sin, or to the unalterableness of human nature, or to the social structure, or to the inevitable legacy of previous births.

Nehru's aversion to religious dogmas, irrationalism, superstitions, etc., on the one hand and his fascination to rationalism and scientific outlook on the other attracted him towards Marxist philosophy. He developed a great respect for the insight of the Marxist thought, but he did not subscribe uncritically to any of its dogmas. In general, he accepted the philosophical outlook of Marxism. He was very much impressed by its monism or non-duality of mind and matter, the dynamics of matter and the dialectic of continuous change through thesis, antithesis and synthesis. The practical achievements of Soviet Union exerted a great influence on his mind and helped him "to see history and current affairs in a new light"[7]. He was greatly inspired by the achievements of Soviet

Revolution in the advancement of human society and the foundations it had laid for a new civilization in the world.

Nehru recognized and acknowledged the positive contribution of different religions in the development of humanity by laying down certain values, standards and principles for the guidance of human life. However, he was very much displeased with the attitude of religions, which imprison truth in set forms and dogmas and encourage ceremonials and practices. He complained that instead of encouraging curiosity and thought, the religions preach a philosophy of submission to nature, to the established churches, to the prevailing social order, and to every thing that is in practice. The followers of religion are supposed to accept various dogmas attached to it without doubt or questioning. Thus for a religious man the reason is replaced by faith.

The method of religion, as Nehru conceives it, is the very opposite of science, because it relies on emotion and intuition. If we survey the history of religions, we notice that it is full of dogmatism, intolerance, fanaticism, bloodshed and with many unspeakable horrors and cruelty. The people belonging to each religion make absolute and exclusive claims about the truth of their own religion and condemn those of other as false and dangerous, deserving to be eliminated. Hence, arise conflict and opposition, resulting in communal riots, bloodshed and wars and attendant suffering and sorrow. Organized religion, according to Nehru, has always helped the exploiters against the exploited by preaching that poverty and suffering are inevitable in this world. It tends to close and limit the mind of man and produce a temper of a dependent and unfree person. Every religion promises its followers a happy life in the heaven or paradise, not in this world and not in this life, but in the other world and in the next life. Therefore, man must die with all hardships in this world, in order to get happiness in the next world.

Nehru's rational approach was quite evident in his attitude to religion and science. He looked upon science as a great step ahead from barbarism to civilization. He was convinced that proper use of science and technology could liberate man from eternal misery and could give greater meaning to human life. The scientific knowledge in general liberates one from the shackles of dogmatism, fanaticism and intolerance and makes possible to understand and assess things rationally and objectively.

Critical Evaluation

For an objective and impartial assessment of Nehru's contribution to secularism and scientific outlook, one must answer satisfactorily the following questions—

1. Does a secular state operate in a non-secular society?
2. Is the Indian tradition conducive for working of a secular state?
3. Why the word "Secular" is not included in the preamble of the Constitution of India till 1976?
4. What has gone wrong with Nehru's dream of building a secular India?
5. Why the process of secularization initiated by Nehru did not lead to its logical conclusion?

A tradition-bound, caste-ridden and authoritarian society cannot provide a nourishing soil for secularism to strike its roots. As long as we remain caste-oriented, secularism cannot make any headway in India. Caste system, which is basic to Indian life and thought, is a major factor which is preventing the growth of secular values in India. Indian democracy is working on a skilful manipulation of caste and communal interests. In India the caste system is highly organized, rigid and philosophically justified, which led to social discrimination and inequality. Casteism has been increasingly distorting the secular values and the socio-political goals of our social system.

The "caste-based theory of social justice" resulted in consolidation and strengthening of a kind of casteist fundamentalism in our society, which is serving the interests of casteist politics of some political parties. The practice of "caste-oriented theory of social justice" not only caused creation of more and more caste consciousness among the members of the society, but also resultant in polarization of castes into opposing groups in society.

The policy of our Government identifying "backwardness" of the people with caste and sub-caste is fundamentally anti-secular. So far no genuine attempt is made by the Government to find out who are really backward and who really need a helping hand irrespective of whether they belong to this caste or that caste or other socio-religious groups. The presence of poverty, ignorance, illiteracy, ill-health, etc., are to be found in every community. Our government's assumption that a man must be well off because he belongs to a particular community or that another must be badly off because he belongs to the Government-designated backward community is unrealistic, unscientific and irrational. Indeed, there are well-to-do *Harijans*, and there are poverty-stricken Brahmins in our society. Thus, there is a profound contradiction between Government's objective of a casteless society and its policy and method of elevating the backward on a caste basis.

For centuries together, Indian Social system is working on the Principle of "mutual co-existence" and a "communal mode of cooperation", which constitute a fundamental basis to the process of social life. The principle of "mutual co-existence" and "communal mode of cooperation" is an in-built mechanism devised for harmonious working of a pluralistic society. This kind of mechanism, indeed, is a marked attribute of "unity in diversity" of the Indian Society. The caste-based discriminatory approach of the successive governments and the vote-bank politics of our political parties in post-Independent India, are responsible to a major extent towards growth and consolidation of casteism in Indian society. In this process, both caste and communal politics, moved ahead hand in hand and the secular values of our democratic system have been gradually deteriorated year after year without any check on them. Speaking at the inaugural function of the South Asian Interfaith Harmony Conclave at Delhi, Former Prime

Minister Manmohan Singh deplored the tendency of some political parties to exploit religious sentiments for political ends. He observed that "attempts to divide society along religious lines deserve to be condemned with comtempt".[8]

Indian society is basically anti-secular in its character. Religion has been a powerful factor in the making of Indian culture. Every aspect of human life, from birth to death, has been covered by religious conceptions. The Nation-State in India has grown out of the multi-caste, multi-religious and multi-lingual social structure. Secularism in India appears to be primarily a political aspect rather than an overall process of social life. Hence, it is necessary to inculcate secular principles and values as a philosophy of life and conscious activity. A breakthrough from traditional social structure is an essential element in the process of secularization.

The participation of state representatives in religious functions and the state sponsored celebrations of religious occasions are preventing the growth and consolidation of secularism in India. The Indian State, "apart from encouraging communal politics", P.C. Chatterji observes, "the practice of VIPs visiting temples and mosques is leading to the denigration of the concept of secularism to which the Government is committed-on paper. The public see their behaviour as hypocrisy and for a lot of people secularism has become synonymous with hypocrisy".[9]

The Indian State as it established under the present Constitution, with many discriminatory aspects between one individual and other on the basis of caste, religion and sex, cannot be secular and to describe it as such is nothing but misusing the term. The government as well as the opposition parties in India, instead of promoting the growth of secularism, prefers to reflect on the prejudices of the vested interests of different castes and religious groups to avoid alienation of these groups and consolidation of votes cast by them at the time of elections.

The constitution makers had realized the difficulties involved in varied personal laws to different religious communities stood in the way of realizing a true secular state. Article 44 in the Directive Principles of the State Policy lays down, "The State shall endeavour to secure for the citizens a uniform civil code throughout the territory of India". Although the British rulers successfully introduced a uniform criminal law to all the citizens in colonial India, the successive governments at the centre, in post-Independent India, failed to bring a uniform civil code based on secular principles. The existence of separate personal laws is inconsistent with secularism. There is no justification for the law being different for different groups of citizens on the basis of religion. The absence of a common civil code contradicts the very principle of "equality before the law".

The Supreme Court Judgement in Mohammad Ahmad Khan *vs*. Shah Bano Begum delivered on 23rd April, 1985 by a five Judge Bench headed by the then Chief Justice, Y.V. Chandrachud, underscored the importance of a Uniform Civil Code as a Constitutional goal under Article 44 of the Constitution, which according to the bench has "remained a dead letter".[10]

A simple judgement of the Supreme Court in the Shah Bano Case evoked a nationwide controversy and split the Muslim community into two groups — conservatives and progressives. The orthodox Muslims refused to make any change in Muslim Personal Law. The Government introduced the Muslim Women Bill (Protection of Rights on Divorce Act 1986) in the parliament. This bill came under severe criticism during the introduction stage itself in the parliament and many intellectuals of India, both Muslims and Non-Muslims, opposed the bill. By passing the Muslim Women Bill, the Indian State has not only flouted the fundamental constitutional right of equality to Muslim Women, but also tarnished India's image as a secular state. Thus, the Indian Muslim Women were being sacrificed for the vote-bank politics of the Government.

The following factors, which are diametrically opposite to secularism, perhaps responsible for undermining the consolidation of a secular state in India.[11]

(a) Separate personal laws for each religious community.

(b) Provision for special privileges to some groups on communal classification.
(c) Undue state interference in Hindu religious institutions.
(d) Provision for state subsidies to the educational institutions run by religious organizations.

Human life consists of two realms of existence — the sacred and the secular. No average human being is truly secular in his character and no human society is genuinely secular in its nature. A vast majority of people in our society are concerned with both secular and sacred aspects of life. Hence, it may be appropriate to attribute the principles of secularism to the Indian state — if it is so chosen — but not to the Indian society as it stands today.

Nehru, like his political teacher Gandhi, did not succeed in his attempt to build a secular India. He failed in his attempt to bring Hindu-Muslim unity or in the suppression of casteism in India. The intensity of religious conflict does not seem to have declined. Nevertheless, Nehru tried honestly and earnestly to lay the foundation of a secular state in India. No one can doubt his commitment to non-communal secular nationalism. The history of humanity reveals that one cannot expect radical changes in human societies or in social and political institutions within a short span of time. Perfections in human societies or in socio-political institutions may take hundreds of years. Since human history is advancing to higher and more rational forms of human society, let us hope, Nehru's vision of secular India may be realized, if not immediately, in the years to come.

REFERENCES

1. Jawaharlal Nehru, *The Discovery of India* (Bombay, Asia Publishing House, 1974), p. 26.
2. Sarvepalli Gopal, (Ed.), *Jawaharlal Nehru* : An Anthology (New Delhi, Oxford University Press, 1980), p. 327.
3. *Ibid.* p. 327.

4. Dr. S. Radhakrishnan, *Our Heritage* (Delhi, Hind Pocket Books, 1973), pp. 148-149.
5. Jawaharlal Nehru, *Glimpses of World History*, (New Delhi, Oxford University Press, 1996), p. 38.
6. Jawaharlal Nehru, *The Discovery of India* (Bombay, Asia Publishing House, 1974), p. 514.
7. *Ibid.*, p. 29.
8. *The Hindu* (Newspaper, Visakhapatnam, April, 22, 2007), p. 8.S
9. P.C, Chatterji, *Secular Values for Secular India* (New Delhi, Manohar Publishers, 1995), pp. 305-306.
10. *The Times of India*, Newspaper, New Delhi, April 24, 1985.
11. *Cf.* Donald Eugene Smith, *India as a Secular State* (New Jersey, Princeton University Press, 1963), pp. 496-498.

3

Indian Culture and Technological Society : A Philosophical Perspective

R.C. Sinha

In this chapter there is an attempt to address three issues: First, technology in itself is value-free, but assumes value when linked with cultural activities. Secondly, technology is not logically incompatible with Indian culture because Indian culture is integral in nature. It integrates technological society with cultural values and thirdly, it also gives ontological basis to secular values of technological society. I have understood technology as applied science. By scientific society, I mean technologically advanced society. By Indian culture, I mean a set of values dear to Indians.

The expression "technological society" needs a little clarifications. The expression does not refer to any particular society of any scientifically advanced country. It refers to the scientific phenomenon. It refers to the attitude and the frame of mind which characterize the present day civilization. The present civilization of India has its roots in science and technology. It views techniques above other things. It seeks for the most efficient and result oriented means in every field and in every walk of life. The expression 'scientific society' has not been taken to denote 'machine society'. In the nineteenth century, the European industrial society understood 'scientific society' as a machine society. But in our Post-modern context 'scientific society' is more than 'machine society'. In the industrial society, machines became source of alienation. In a 'technological society' *technique integrates machines* with society. Machine may *alienate; technology is liberating*. Thus, the expression 'scientific society' refers to that mental attitude of the post-modern man which has been influencing the life style of people of different places in varying degrees.

The expression 'Indian culture' denotes a set of values dear to Indians. Values have two dimensions. One is spiritual and the other is secular. Spiritual value is a set of goals or ideals. Secular values refer to interest, preference and choice, which are essentially changing. When we talk about Indian culture, people may consider it as Indian moral values. Values are not necessarily moral. Indian culture transcends morality on higher planes of existence. In practical realm of existence it concentrates on secular values.

The expression 'culture' refers to values of life and society. Culture is not concerned with particular value but it is concerned with value as such. Culture is known as science of values. Values are useful at every step of human existence. The activities of individual and society should be in accordance with certain values or ideals. Man is essentially a value conscious and value pursuing being. Individual as well as society cherish some ideals or values. Human beings cultivate faith in values and also create new values. This fact has inspired us to give Philosophical analysis of Indian culture and scientific society.

The present human society is faced with a paradox. The paradox is due to the fact that if human society is scientifically advanced, it is faced with evil; and if it is scientifically backward, it is also faced with evil. Scientific advancement causes evil because man loses his meanness. Scientific backwardness also causes evil because man suffers and lives in poverty. It goes without saying that insufficient progress of technology is evil because it causes backwardness. The prime object of the invention of new technology is to get rid of backwardness. So naturally, we have to choose technology as an instrument in order to ameliorate conditions of the suffering humanity. But there is an opposite view also that considers technological progress to be a great source of present evils prevailing in the society. But inspite of laudable achievements, a man of philosophic temperament cannot deny the social evils of the past few decades. It is true that technological society is responsible for dehumanization and degeneration of culture. Technology has managed to throw relations into disorder and chaos. On the other hand, communication technology has made it quite easy to develop relationship with other nations. Science has changed human society and its values. It has been used for well-being of human society. In order to get rid of economic evils, we have to develop science and technology. Alvin Toffler observes, "To turn our back on technology would be not only stupid but immoral".[1] Recent nuclear explosion in Pokharan has established India as a nuclear power. The technology can be used for self defence and development of the country. Our late Prime Minister Lal Bahadur Shastri uttered the slogan *"Jai Jawan, Jai Kisan"*. The former Prime Minister Sri Atal Bihari Vajpayee added *"Jai Vigyan"* to the original slogan. He demarcated a new dimension and uttered *"Jai Kisan and Jai Vigyan"*. This throws ample light on our choice of science and technology since India has chosen to become Nuclear.

In scientific society, technology determines the direction of the development of society and its values. But science and technology in itself are not value loaded. Science is ethically neutral and value free. The benefits of science are mainly the use to which it is put by man. It is neither good nor bad. The use of technology determines its values. We cannot pass any value judgement relating to scientific society, whether it is a good society or bad society. Mahatma Gandhi, the great champion of '*Swadeshi* culture' does admit in his famous book entitled, *Hind Swaraj* that India can import technology and life saving drugs from foreign countries. It does not affect our *swadeshi* ideology since life saving drugs and necessary technology are linked with the well-being of India. So, it is possible for *"swadeshi culture"* to import technology and then try to assimilate it in *swadeshi* culture. We can try to position imported technology in our own cultural fabric.

The Indian mindset is culture bound. We are quite rich in culture. Indian cannot cope with the great power of scientifically advanced society. There are many questions related with Indian culture and scientific society. The conflict between Indian culture and scientific society and the influence of technology upon the course of social and cultural life of Indians have been a great source of controversy. The main objective of this chapter is to discuss the scientific society and its bearings on the cultural identity of India. We are preparing to enter into twenty first century. In this century, man can not live without technology. In twenty first century life and society will be governed by technological relations.

Technology advances rapidly. The technology which is useful today may not be useful tomorrow. If we do not prepare the new generation to adopt new technology and new values of life, the new generation will lag behind. Mahatma Gandhi was a critique of modernism and technological society.

Though science is value free yet science creates conditions for new ways of life and its values. Values do change in accordance with the change in technology. We think that technology is an instrument in the service of humanity. By the phrase value free, I mean that technology is neither evil nor good in itself. It is a means and not an end. Its use makes technology either good or bad. The new technology facilitates to coin new words and assign new meanings. Technology creates new values. It also formulates new language. It gives new meanings to words. Technology affects our value system and thus affects our culture. For example, Russell considers that "efficiency" and "speed" have emerged as new values with the growth of new technology. It also makes a distinction between values and moral values. Efficiency is a value but it is not moral value. Efficiency and speed are amoral. Efficiency and speed are values because they are valuable in life. With the change of technology, cultural values do change. B.D. Nag Choudhary observes, "Values erode, values change. A society adopts new values".[2] This means that cultural and human progress are in one sense determined by the scientific progress and advancement. Technology does affect culture. In this regard, it may be mentioned that Leslie White has introduced the most important theory of "technological determinism". According to White not only technology determines the direction of cultural development, but it also determines the need for building social foundation.[3] Scientific society presupposes technological determinism. Technological determinism assumes that technological innovation is the driving force behind social change imposing its own logic. Talcot Parsons enumerates that "...... technology is a king of capability on the part of the organization for a more effective control and necessary change in the physical environment in favour of human needs and demands."[4] To say that technology is meant to change the society is just like saying that technology causes change in our value system. It is true that technology is the product of society and values are also product of society. The Indian technological society owes its present position to Indian cultural patterns.

The social development leads to the question of science and culture. In ordinary parlance development is synonymous to economic development. In Indian society, development cannot be equated with economic progress. Development is a multi-dimensional process. It includes economic, social, political and cultural spheres. Development is an important factor for economic well-being. Technology has not been created in isolation. The introduction of new technology is also a cultural phenomenon. Technology directly affects cultural values and also behaviour of human beings living in society. Technology is responsible for new ways of life and culture. It is true that the society which consumes more and exhausts nature is considered more advanced. This society is known as consumer society. Technological society in one sense is consumer society. In Indian context, development is not simply economic. It is integral development. Integral development means social, cultural and economic developments taken together. Development is a historical change. The society moves from one historical stage to another. In fact preparing the society for development is a historical necessity. The transfer of science and technology can be effective in the progress and development of Indian society. Technology should be in harmony with the cultural conditions of Indian society.

The development is not a sapling which may be brought from one nation and transplanted in another nation. Culture can depend on scientific technique and not on technology. "We can survive without technology, we can't survive without technique."[5] To say that technology and culture are not logically incompatible is to say that technology and culture are independent. Culture presupposes scientific techniques. System of scientific technique is technology. "Thus, there can be no technique without culture, no culture without technique."[6] The logical assumption would be that every culture has relied on a corresponding system of scientific techniques. Scientific technique is nothing but the permanent and dynamic expression of an individual culture. Cultures can only express themselves or survive through scientific technique. "Thus, the so called potter wasp is known for its technique in constructing what we human beings culturally recognize as pots, however, the small vessels are conclusions of technique, without it, there would be no pot, no propagation and, therefore, no survival."[7]

Technology introduces change in society. It is a positive device in the service of humanity. It is a means which can be properly used for the welfare of human being. By applying the latest laser technology, we may help cure the cataract. However, laser could be used to guide a bomb. We can use satellites for education and cultural progress. We can also use them as a means to spread the destructive cultural and ideological patterns. Science and technology is a means in the service of human beings. It can help us to utilize natural resources in a better way. It can also play a positive role in safeguarding the cultural identity for survival of the nation. Ramakant Sinari observes, "Science and technology have invested man with power they have fructified his 'will to power'. Man can use this power, either to better and to prolong his survival or to annihilate himself."[8] Man is always trying to develop new techniques. Therefore, our culture necessitates evasion of extremes in using the natural resources. The appropriate use of technology should be made so that we would not be affected with its negative outcome. Gabriel Marcel has called this "technological mentality". The very birth of technology represents the rise of urge for full freedom in human consciousness. The growth of technology enhances man's ability to release himself from nature oriented evil. Safeguarding Indian culture and its identity does not mean to go away from the current science and technology. It is inevitable for human existence to accept the realities of the present scientific society. "Technologically advanced societies have solved many of the problems, e.g., hunger, disease, poverty, epidemics, illiteracy, physical discontent, lack of means of communication, and movement."[9] In one sense technology protects cultural identity. Technology constitutes the reality of time. Our goal must be to protect our cultural identity by using the gifts of technology. We should not sacrifice the culture for the sake of technology. We also cannot ignore the benefits of technology. If one looks at technology as a machine and the principle of work then it is value free. But if one looks at the minute details of human activities which take place in life with the use of technology, the answer will be that technology cannot be completely value free. Technology is a part of life. It is a part of culture.

Arnold Pacey believed that people use technology in its concept and sometimes with its limited meaning. When technology is presented in a limited way, the cultural values and the organizational factors related to it assume for it the shape of an alien factor. In this case, technology is known in its complete technical sense. If technology is taken as a part of life, then we cannot sway that technology is value free. We think technology has direct and indirect impact on values, traditions and the human life. Technology actually transforms cultural values. Technology is a means for change in our civilizations. "The twentieth century technological culture has compelled a change in our view of the individual, he is looked upon as a function, as a mere 'one of them' as one not necessarily with an *atman* or a human face."[10] A direct relation exists between culture and technology and both of these affect the other in a sequential manner. In advanced societies which are the birth place of technology, it is attempted that social and cultural organizations be put in line with technological development. Here we have tried to relate culture with the present day scientific society. To a critical philosopher, this attempt may sound obscure. Indian culture which is grounded in spirituality cannot be compatible with technological society. It is difficult to bring Indian culture close to technological society. We simply uphold that culture whether Indian or Western is not incompatible with technology. The present study is initiated with the conviction that technology is a part of Indian culture. The present day values in India are largely shaped under the influence of technological society.

The absence of logical incompatibility between the values cherished in a technological society and those endorsed by Indian culture can be worked out in two ways :

(1) By showing that there is some kind of compatibility between science and culture.
(2) By demonstrating that Indian culture can, in its own way, lessen to some extent the negative effects of science and technology.

This is a fact that science and technology occupy a vast place in modern Indian society. The problem is how Indian culture can accommodate technology without going astray. How Indian culture can at one and the same time satisfy Indian tradition and technology? This brings into the consideration as to under what conditions scientific society can be integrated into Indian culture without destroying its inner harmony. In traditional societies like India, the situation is more complicated because technology will be made an alien entity which appears an independent system in the face of existing cultural system. Culture determines the way in which individuals identify and recognize one another within their own social spheres of action. Indian culture and its value system constitute the factor of social harmony of Indian pluralistic society. Indian value system gives a special cultural identity to Indian society. In the process of social evolution and change which emanates from the introduction of value and models of foreign technologies, the Indian cultural system in its entirety is attacked upon. Therefore, the main risk lies in the endangering of Indian cultural identity which is rooted in tradition. The development of commnication technology, the ability to record and transmit sounds and images over any distance have changed the value system. It has changed the face of contemporary Indian culture. With the enormous development in communication technology, the culture has enormously changed. The mass media is not culturally neutral. They reflect the thinking, the idea, the value. Communication technology serves as the channel of transmitting values or ways of life.

The promotion of technology in India is not fully indigenous activity. India has three options in the face of modern science and technology :

(1) The first option is total acceptance of foreign technology without taking into account tradition bound Indian culture.
(2) The second option is total rejection of any type of foreign technology.
(3) The third option is selection of relevant technologies which have greater conformity with the socio-cultural and economic conditions of India, i.e., the selection of appropriate technology.

India, by making proper and positive use of technology, has succeeded in bringing about a fundamental change in the ways of the people's mentality. Technology is being employed for fulfilling specific human need. It is forcing man to continuously adjust to its impact. "Instead of technology being developed to meet the design of a society, it is shaping the organization and structure of a society and human relations in it."[11] Science and technology has brought change in our society. The media technology has brought change in our educational system. It has helped to popularise family planning. The T.V. has promoted health care in villages. It has created understanding among different nations.

Now, we are in a position to say that there does exist some sort of compatibility between the value endorsed by Indian culture and cherished by scientific society. In Indian culture secular values and spiritual values are not opposed. In Hindu tradition, *dharmashastra* and *mokshashastra* are not incompatible. The secular values are relegated to worldly status. But this is quite clear that even in secular culture, the spiritual attitude pervades. The Vedanta philosophy is the bedrock of Indian spiritual culture. Aurobindo's Vedantic culture is not dehumanizing. Sri Aurobindo has propounded Integral Adventism. It does not make cleavage between secular and spiritual culture. The secular culture refers to technological society. The spiritual culture gives on ontological basis to secular or technological culture. The secular culture or scientific society assumes a general spiritual dimension or ontological basis. On technological level, Indian attitude can be summed up as the attitude of impersonality. It is an attitude of the man rising above his own person. The value which emerges in a technological society is the value of impersonality. There is a basic character of the functioning of technique, and these, in turn, lead to impersonality.

The tendency towards impersonality sets in a process of dehumanization The dehumanising effects of science and technology are taken as the negative effect of the scientific society. Dehumanisation is taking away from a man his manness. It reduces man to the status of machine. It stifles creativity. Technological society makes life mechanical and artificial. The process of dehumanization upsets the person of a man. In Vedantic spiritual culture, man has to transcend his ego. It is also a kind of superb dehumanization when man transcends himself. But Indian philosophers and critic may point out that it is not proper to describe the process of transcendence as superb dehumanisation. In transcendence man does not negate man but sublimates himself to higher plane of existence. In Vedantic culture, the lower aspect of man is suppressed and transcended. The technological process of dehumanisation takes away from man his manness as such. The dehumanised individual is merely a bundle of reactions. The Indian spiritual culture gives creativity of full play. The spiritual process attempts to realise the essence of man. Technological culture robs the essence of man. Techniques eliminate creativity. In technological society technique tends to determine everything. In Indian culture, the human existence has been given an ontological foundation. The cult of spiritualisation is not negative. But in technological society dehumanisation is negative.

A philosopher may point out that any attempt to draw a line of compatibility between science and culture is far fetched because they belong to two different dimensions of human existence. This objection requires a little consideration. Science and culture both are concerned with man and society. Both attempt to contribute in social development. Social development has two aspects, i.e., one is economic and other is cultural. Science takes care of economic development. Culture is rooted in value system. But this is a misconception that science and culture operate at different levels. Technological development causes change in our value system. Moreover, spiritual values and secular values are not separate. Spiritual values give ontological dimension to scientific society.

Indian culture is integral in nature. Now, the integration may be turned outward or may turn inward. These two ways are not mutually exclusive. It is possible to emphasize either the outward character of integration or the inner character of integration. Social integration is integration turned outward. Self integration is integration turned inward. Technology integrates society. Culture is self integrating. Technology is concerned with man's world, and therefore, its aim is to have integrated social reality. The integration that it attempts is social. Indian culture is spiritualistic and the integration that it values is self-integration. Thus, it can be argued that it is not proper to say that Indian culture is far removed from the technological ways of the modern times. Margrett Chatterjee observes, "Indian has her own scientific traditions without which the people could not have survived over centuries and of which we have evidence today, for example, in indigenous system of medicine which have a long ancestry."[12]

Here we can make an attempt to demonstrate that Indian cultural values can be relevant for the technological society.

Philosophers and social scientists have spoken about the negative effects of technology. Technological society is characterised as full of environmental pollution; deterioration of the quality of life, threat to the beauty and balance of nature and effects of technological society. But we are here concerned with the technological effects at the level of human sensibility, because it is at that level that Indian culture can be relevant. Technology persistently causes alienation and estrangement. It upsets the established order and uproots man from his moorings. This is apparent also in developing countries like India where lure of industrialisation, urbanisation and computerisation have upset the life styles of the Indian society. It has led to the disappearance of privacy and of personal human relationship. Technology is causing social and psychological tension. The life is becoming more and more mechanized. The man has lost zest for living. Man created technology but in course of time man became dependent on technology. When technology is controlled and utilised by man for social well-being then, it is useful. But when technology becomes, the master of man then it is bad. There is a need to overcome the sense of being overwhelmed by science and technology. Here Indian culture can be of great help. Indian culture can help man to get rid of dehumanisation. Indian culture being spiritual in nature attempts to shift its importance from technique to man.

In technological society man leads a mechanical life. Man is under bondage of technology. The negative effects of technological society is a tragic sense of estrangement. Technology has taken away from human being his sense of humanness. Scientific society does not know how to get rid of dehumanisation. Indian culture can save humanity from estrangement and dehumanisation. The life becomes meaningless in the wake of mechanical life style. The Indian culture can give meaning to human life by sublimating man's existence to higher plane. The integral culture of India can harmonise between spiritual and secular and other worldly and this worldly values.

REFERENCES

1. Toffler, Alvin, *Future Shock*, Bantom Book, New York, 1971, p. 428.
2. B.D. Nag Choudhary, Technology, Language and Homo Indicus', in B.D. Nag Choudhary (ed.), *New Technological Civilisation and Indian Society,* Shimla, 1990, p. 8.
3. Leslie White, *The Evolution of Culture,* New York, 1959.
4. Talcott Parsons, *Societies,* New Jersey, 1966, p. 150.
5. H. Selin (ed.) *Encyclopaedia of the History of Science, Technology and Medicine in Non-Western Cultures*, Kluwer Academic Publishers, U.S.A., 1947.
6. *Ibid.*, p. 946.
7. *Loc.* cit
8. B. D. Nag Choudhary (ed.), *op. cit.*, p. 11.
9. *Ibid.*, p. 12.
10. Ramakant Sinari, Science, Technology and the Hindu Weltanschauung, in B. D. Nag Choudhary (ed.), *op. cit.*, p.18.
11. *Ibid.*, p. 29.
12. M. Chatterjee, 'Preface', in B.D. Nag Choudhary (ed.) *op. cit.*, p. IX.

4

Morality and Political Obligation

Y.V. Satyanarayana

Civil disobedience, in recent times, has been a central issue in the field of political philosophy. The most important moral question concerned with the problem of political obligation relates to the limits of obedience of a citizen owed to the state. The problem of political obligation raises the questions such as:

1. To what extent the citizen has an obligation to obey the laws of the state?
2. Is the citizen of a state, whether democratic or otherwise, under an obligation to obey the unjust laws of the state?

There are two different positions or viewpoints concerning the character of the obligation to obey the laws of the state.

1. The first position states, "one has an absolute obligation to obey the law and, therefore, disobedience to the state law is never justified".
2. The second position asserts, "one has a *prima facie* obligation to obey the law, but this obligation can be overridden by conflicting obligations. Hence, disobedience to the state law can be justified in the presence of outweighing circumstances".

Socrates and the Problem of Political Obligation

Why does the citizen have an obligation to obey the laws of the state? Socrates, one of the greatest philosophers of ancient Greece, considered this question well over two thousand years ago and thereby he provided a basis for a philosophical debate. Socrates was convicted and sentenced to death on charges of atheism and for corrupting the youth of Athens. His friend Crito visited Socrates in prison and informed him that an escape could be arranged for him and offered a number of reasons to justify that escape. However, Socrates regarded such reasons as insufficient to warrant his escape and countered with his own reasons. He offered the following reasons in support of his respect to the laws of the state.

1. Since he always taught respect for the law, it would be unprincipled and hypocritical of him to disobey it.
2. His disobedience to the law may lead to sanction of general disobedience of the law by the public.
3. The citizen's agreement to abide by the state law was a binding obligation on him.
4. Hence, disobedience to the law is an expression of ingratitude and a violation of the principles of Justice.

Since Socrates was convinced that the state is entitled to obedience, rather than to escape from a death sentence, he wilfully submitted to the penalty with equanimity and cheer.

Social Contract Theory and the Problem of Political Obligation

Another argument put forward in favour of political obligation is Social Contract Theory, which claims that individuals, as the citizens of the state, are under an obligation to keep their promises that they have made to the state. The argument appeals to the following considerations.

1. The individual, as a citizen of the state, has given an explicit or implicit promise to obey the laws of the state.
2. The state provides certain benefits and privileges to the citizen.
3. In return to the benefits and privileges he gets from the state, the citizen has to obey the laws of the state.
4. Disobedience to the laws of the state is bad citizenship, because the citizen receives benefits without performing his duties to the state.

The social contract theory makes an attempt to justify political obligation on the basis of an implicit promise made by the citizen to the state. One of the classic arguments of social contract theory was presented by Socrates in the Plato's dialogue in "Crito".

> "Although we have brought you into the world and reared you and educated you, and given you and all your fellow citizens a share in all the good things at our disposal— on attaining to manhood and seeing for himself the political organization of the state and its laws, is permitted, if he is not satisfied with us, to take his property and go away wherever he likes."[1]

Socrates' argument provides the following reasons for one's obligation to obey the laws of the state.

1. In return to the benefits he gets from the state, the citizen promises to obey the laws of the state.
2. If any citizen feels that the laws of the state are unjust, he can make an effort to convince the state of its mistake by following certain procedures.
3. If any citizen believes that the contract with the state is not producing benefits to him or that the laws of the state are unjust, he is free to leave that state at any time.

4. So long as the citizen continues to stay in the state, he ought to obey the laws of the state as promised by him.
5. Hence, one is free either to obey the laws of the state or leave that state and go elsewhere.

The argument offered by Socrates or the social contract theory enters into a difficult situation with regard to the contract made between the citizen and the state. The contract is not valid unless it fulfils the following conditions.

1. The clauses of the contract made between the citizen and the state must be appropriate.
2. The contract must not be made under duress.
3. The contract must contain escape clauses.
4. The contract must be based on moral acceptance of both the contractors.
5. The state must abide by its contract obligations.

In fact, any contract made between two parties equally places responsibilities and obligations on both the contractors. The failure of one party to carry out its obligations retracts the moral obligation on the other party.

The Conflict between Legal and Moral Obligations

Socrates' position concerning "one's obedience to the law's of the state" is not acceptable to many people. To mention a few among the many well-known persons – Henry David Thoreau, M.K. Gandhi and Martin Luther King Jr. – have chosen a different position in relation to a citizen's obligation to obey the laws of the state. They insist that in addition to the political criteria, the system of laws must meet moral criteria as well. They refused to consider an unjust law as a law. It is not simply enough to sanction a law by the state, but that law must have adequate justification. Therefore, to have an obligation to obey the law, the law must be morally justified. Making a distinction between a just and an unjust law, Martin Luther King Jr. observed:

> "A Just law is a man made code that squares with the moral law or the law of God. An unjust law is a code that is out of harmony with the moral law".[2]

Many moral philosophers regarded that the legal version of "one's obligation to the laws of the state" is not sufficient. They argued that *prima facie* the citizen has a primary duty to obey the laws of the state, but at the same time he has a right to break the law if it seriously violates fundamental moral principles. In the name of law, if the state creates situations such as discrimination of its citizens or violation of individual liberties or any other such injustice, then, the citizen has a moral duty to violate such laws.

John Locke regarded that the citizen's obligation to the state holds good only if the state does secure justice. If the state acts unjustly or if the state is not a means to a moral end, it loses its right to be obeyed. The Utilitarian Philosophers held that if the state is harming instead of promoting the common good, it loses its right to obedience. Thus political obligation is not absolute and the citizens are not obliged to obey anything that the state will decree. If any individual citizen thinks that a particular law is unjust or harmful to the common good, he is morally entitled to disobey such law. Thoreau's classic treatise on 'Civil Disobedience' adopts this approach and justifies disobedience. Thoreau held:

> "The only obligation which I have a right to assume, is to do at any time what I think right – There will never be a really free and enlightened state, until the state comes to recognize the individual as a higher and more independent power, from which all its own power and authority are derived and treats him accordingly."[3]

John Rawls in his essay on "Civil Disobedience" admits that

one does have a right to disobey, if one is subjected to deliberate injustice which violates the liberties of equal citizenship.[4]

The Nature and Content of Civil Disobedience

Civil disobedience is a form of non-violent protest against unjust laws of the state. It is an instrument of struggle against evil and injustice. The action of a person becomes civilly disobedient if he deliberately violates the laws that have been sustained by the highest legislative and judicial bodies of the state. The civil disobedient regards the dictates of the conscience as superior to the commands of the state. He violates the unjust laws of the state in order to bend the government to the will of the people. Explaining his idea of civil disobedience Gandhi said, "civil disobedience is civil breach of unmoral statutory enactments. . . . It signified the register's outlawry in a civil, i.e., non-violent manner. He invoked the sanctions of the law and cheerfully suffered imprisonment. It is a branch of *satyagraha*".[5]

Civil disobedience can be defined as an *intentional* act of a citizen who violates a *valid law* for the purpose of registering a *moral protest* against the state. The emphasis on the words *intentional, valid law* and *moral protest* distinguishes civil disobedience from other acts of law breaking. Unlike other people who break the law out of greed or a desire to subvert government, the civil disobedient breaks the law to register his moral protest. Thus, the act of civil disobedient differs from the act of both the criminal and the revolutionary by his different motives and objectives. The criminal is interested exclusively in personal gain, not in justice for citizens in general.

A civil disobedient generally supports the legal system of the state and disobeys only some selective laws or judicial decisions that he regards as unjust. He breaks the law in order to register his moral protest. The revolutionary, in contrast, regards the entire legal system of the state as corrupt and advocates complete overthrow of the system. Since the purpose of the state is to provide justice to all its citizens, the act of a civil disobedient who is pointing out an unjust law or policy of a state in civil procedure must be considered as a good citizen, but not as an ordinary law breaker. Martin Luther King Jr. made a distinction between the law breaking of a non-violent civil disobedient and clandestine law breaking. He observed:

> "One who breaks an unjust law must do it openly, lovingly, and with a willingness to accept penalty. I submit that an individual who breaks a law that conscience tells him is unjust, and willingly accepts the penalty by staying in jail to arouse the conscience of the community over its injustice, in reality expressing the very highest respect for law".[6]

The technique of civil disobedience, Gandhi says, is intended to replace all brutal methods of violence used to resolve social and political conflicts. It aims at the conversion, but not the embarrassment of Government. The success of the civil disobedience is essentially based on the cause as well as the means employed to resolve it. Since civil disobedience is a powerful method of bringing change in the policies of the state, it must not be used unless all other remedial methods such as negotiation, discussion, arbitration, etc., have been exhausted.

A civil disobedient should give due publicity to the unjust laws or policies of the state to educate the public on the issues as well as to rouse consciousness of the sufferers. Before launching the civil disobedience movement, he must give due notice and fullest possible time to the state so that the state can correct its wrong policies. Civil disobedience movement includes different methods of agitation such as — peaceful marches, breach of laws, picketing, courting of arrests, non-cooperation with government, etc.

The Appeal to Conscience

The problem of disobedience is closely connected with "one's duty to one's conscience". The civil disobedient often claims that he disobeys the laws of the state on the basis of his conscience. Many ethical philosophers thought that simply an appeal to conscience alone is not sufficient for one's disobedience to the law. Claiming something as *right* on the basis of one's conscience, is not sufficient to make it *right*. We must rely on reason for justification of such claims.

Justification of Civil Disobedience

Many philosophers and thinkers regarded that the justification of civil disobedience is necessarily based on certain conditions. Unless the following conditions are satisfied, it is difficult to justify an act of civil disobedience:

1. *The act of civil disobedience must be open and public.* The law breaking of a civil disobedient is a political act of a good citizen. In the case of clandestine law breaking, the lawbreaker tries to go undetected. Breaking the law openly and publicly is what distinguishes the civil disobedient from the thief in the night or a clandestine law breaking directed against the state.
2. To establish justification for the law breaking of the civil disobedient, *the issue or the cause related to the protest must be genuine, just and clear.*
3. Resorting to civil disobedience is never morally legitimate unless *all other methods of remedying the evil complained of are exhausted.*
4. *The civil disobedient must necessarily accept the legal sanctions and punishments imposed by the laws.* The protest should focus on the unjust laws or policies of the state, but not an attack on the state itself. His willingness to accept penalty indicates that the person is neither at war with the state nor with his fellow citizens.
5. *The protest must be based on the philosophy of non-violence and peace, both in its form and activity.* Violence

does not promote peaceful atmosphere for a public debate or re-examination of its policies by state. The civil disobedient must avoid hardship or harm to his fellow citizens, who are not directly responsible for the situation created under protest.

Critical Evaluation

The problem of political obligation is as old as the civil society. There has always been a clash between the claims of political authority and the claims of individual conscience and autonomy. One of the most important questions in the field of social and political philosophy is – what is the nature and extent of one's obligation to obey the laws of the state? The problem of disobedience is closely related to the nature and limits of the citizen's obligation to obey the law, of the rights and duties of the citizen against the state, of the relation between the authority of the citizen's conscience and the authority of the state. These questions have an important relevance to the political condition of man in the contemporary world.

Is the Citizen under an Obligation to obey the Unjust Laws of the State?

The citizen is not under an obligation to obey the unjust laws of the state. One ought to do what is morally right and so one ought to follow the rules or orders of the state when they are morally right. Besides legality or even justice, there are other values in the world and in certain cases, the *prima facie* obligation may be overridden by a higher ethical principle. If the state simply requires obedience on the ground that it is having sufficient power to make its subjects obey, then the commands of the state would lose all their moral legitimacy. Therefore, the argument of legal absolutists like Jeremy Bentham and John Austin — "one is never justified in violating any law in any circumstances" is unsound, unreasonable and unconvincing.

The violation of a law entails upon the person the obligation of justifying it. Moral justification for violation of a law is a matter of reason, but not of conscience. There must always be reasonable justification for the violation of rules. The person who breaches his political obligation to obey the laws of the state merely on the basis of his conscience is not enough. The voice of conscience may appear loud and clear. But, it may conflict at times not only with the law but also with another man's conscience. Conscience is neither a special nor an infallible organ of apprehending moral truth.[7] The reliability of conscience need support from an external source, not simply to be self-certifying. Therefore, conscience without conscientiousness or conscience which does not cover the process of critical reflective morality, is likely to be a prejudice.

Is Civil Disobedience a Legitimate Act

The justification of civil disobedience depends on the following special conditions :

1. When certain laws, policies and actions of the state are unjust.
2. When there are no meaningful political channels for the legitimate expression of individual's dissent.
3. When the state authority is too powerful or indifferent to the appeals of the people.
4. When the state violates or suppresses the rights of the individual citizen.
5. When the state becomes corrupt and fails to deliver the goods to all its citizens.

The act of civil disobedience gives an opportunity to the individual citizen to make a moral appeal to his fellow citizens that the policies and practices of the state have violated the rights of some people. It is used as a means for seeking a redress of grievances. The state is forced to re-examine its policies and ever vigilant against such injustice situations. Genuine civil disobedience strengthens the state rather than undermining it. Thus, the civil disobedient performs the role of a catalyst for bringing reforms in the policies of the state. Moreover, a state constantly challenged is more likely to be a just one. Hence, a civil disobedient should not be considered as an enemy of the state, but as a good citizen of it.

There are some risks involved in the process of civil obedience. What is begun as civil disobedience may be perverted by the extremists into uncivil disobedience, which alienates a large number of people who have supported the cause of civil disobedience. Hence, Gandhi cautioned the civil disobedient and said "disobedience without civility, discipline, discrimination and non-violence leads to destruction".[8]

Is Civil Disobedience in a Democratic State Justifiable?

Civil disobedience seems to have a central place even in a democratic system. Civil disobedience in a democratic society must be understood as an appeal to the principles of justice. It expresses disobedience to law within the framework of fidelity to law. If the appeal against injustice is repeatedly denied, then the civil disobedience may be justified even in a democratic regime. Since, we cannot frame a procedure for enactment of only just and effective legislation, it may be possible to pass unjust laws and enforce unjust policies by the government even under a just constitution. For the practice of democracy, we need some form of the majority principle, but at times the majority may be mistaken, more or less wilfully in what it legislates.

Civil disobedience, Gandhi believed, is an inherent right of a citizen. Any action of the state to put down civil disobedience, he considered as, an attempt to imprison conscience of the citizen. When the state resorts to unjust laws or unjust practices, it is the sacred duty of the citizen to protest such laws and policies. He regarded that civil disobedience and non-cooperation as efficient and acceptable means to bring pressure on the government and turn it to the will of the people. Thus, Gandhi held:

> "Cooperation with a just government is a duty; non-cooperation with an unjust government is equally a duty– I do not consider non-cooperation to be unconstitutional, but I do believe that of all the constitutional remedies now left open to us, non-cooperation is the only one left for us."[9]

In a democratic state if a citizen believes that a particular law is against to the will of a section of the people, he may campaign against that law. Political protest as such is not a problem in democracy because the very ethos of democracy supports and permits political protests. Moreover, in a democratic set up the dissent and opposition acts as the oxygen of a free society. Thus we may conclude with an observation that unreasonable obedience to any law and unreflective violation of laws at the behest of individual conscience are morally wrong. If the repressed emotions of the dissenter do not come out in non-violent ways, they will come out in ominous expressions of violence and this is evident from the facts of history.

REFERENCES

1. Plato, "Crito", trans. Hugh Tredennick, in *The Collected Dialogues of Plato* (New York, Pantheon Books, 1961), pp. 36-37.
2. Martin Luther King Jr. "Letter From The Birmingham City Jail", in James Rachels, *The Right Thing To Do*, (New York, Random House, 1989) p. 242.
3. Henry David Thoreau, *Civil Disobedience* (Boston, Ticknor & Fields, 1866), pp. 125, 151.
4. *Cf.* John Rawls, "The Justification of Disobedience" in James Rachels, *The Right Thing To Do* (New York, Random House, 1989), pp. 264-65.

5. M.K. Gandhi, *Satyagraha* (Ahmebabad, Navajivan Publishing House, 1951), pp. 3-4.
6. Martin Luther King Jr, *op. cit.* p. 243.
7. *Cf.* Sidney Hook, "Social Protest and Civil Disobedience" in *Moral Problems in Contemporary Society* (ed.) By Paul Kurtz, (New Jersey, Prentice-Hall, I.N.C., 1969), p. 166.
8. M.K. Gandhi, *op. cit.* p.173.
9. M.K. Gandhi, *op. cit.* pp.159-160.

5

Non-Violence, Sovereignty and Security : Gandhian Thought in the Modern Context

L.G. Chincholkar

Introduction

Consideration and evaluation of Gandhian thought in the context of sovereignty and security of the state and their relevance in the light of his concept of non-violence as a supreme political value deserves objective study. The world of today—ridden with almost universal terrorism and clash of social, economic, religious and political interests—appears to question the very principle of non-violence as a stabilising force in the human society.

Could non-violence arrest the ongoing clashes of interests among the states? Could it compromise the sovereignty of the state? Does non-violence guarantee the security of the people who are ingredients of the state? If the concept of state implies that it must protect its sovereignty and ensure security of its people, and if relevant measures of the state for the purpose imply and sanction reference to violence, would it be inconsistent with the responsibilities of the state? Is violence under such circumstances antithetic to Gandhian concept of non-violence? If so, how could the state discharge its responsibilities without endangering its basic liabilities? How would Mahatma Gandhi help us solve such problems? These are some of the issues which this chapter hopes to consider and strive for a realistic evaluation of the various aspects of the subject in the context of Gandhian concept of non-violence and the concept of sovereignty and security of the state.

Before we proceed to consider various related issues, it would be helpful to be acquainted with the concept of non-violence, specially the concept of non-violence of Gandhi.

Concept of Non-Violence

The concept of non-violence is not new to Indian thinking. It has been there throughout the evolution of Indian thought. Indian philosophical literature has not only recognised it but has also been advising its translation into human life. The philosophical quest in India, which implied generally spiritual training at a preparatory stage, accepts non-violence as a virtue to be practised by a spiritual seeker. It was not merely an intellectual pursuit.

What is non-violence? It is an abnegation of violence. What is violence? It is to cause death or pain to the other knowingly and deliberately.[1] It is also said to be an action leading to death. If an action causing death is violence, then does it mean that causing pain to others—other than death—is permissible in non-violence? It does not. The reason is that violence is not limited to bodily death. To cause pain deliberately to the minds of others is also violence. Thus, violence is not limited only to the causation of death of anybody, but it is also to cause any type of pain including psycho-physical pain to others.[2] Jainism and Buddhism were also no exceptions. On the contrary their insistence on non-violence as a way of life was significant.

However, for Gandhi, non-violence meant not only a personal virtue to be practised, but a system to be incorporated in life. The Gandhian non-violence is a logical corollary of the monistic Vedanta of Shankara. As Vinoba Bhave—esteemed and ardent follower of Gandhi—points out, monism (*Advaita Vedanta*) and non-violence are inseparable. If we subscribe to the principles of *Vedanta* which believes in ultimate identity of all, violence cannot be justified; for then, violence would mean violence against oneself.[3] Besides, non-violence is equivalent to Truth and Truth, is equivalent to God.[4] As Gandhi points out, Non-violence and Truth are inseparable.[5] Thus Non-Violence is Truth and Truth is God. He asserts that, "I believe that no other path but that of Non-Violence will suit India."[6] He is confident that self-rule based on non-violence will awaken the people to their duties and not to their rights.[7] Thus, it is to be noted that Gandhian concept of non-violence is not limited to any specific virtue to be practised in an individual life but a social system to be adopted in socio-individual life whose ultimate purpose is to seek identity with God who is identical with Non-Violence and Truth.

Non-Violence is not a negative concept. It implies fearlessness, love, co-operation, constructive work and faith. It means to recognise the cord of identity amongst the people.[8] Vinoba Bhave points out that celebacy and unwavering mind are the chief bases of non-violence.[9]

With all this background of non-violent approach to various socio-individual problems a society faces, how are we to conceive the state of Gandhian model? What would be the structure of Gandhian concept of state based on non-violence? It has to be made clear that the state conceived by Gandhi is not the state with any coercive power over the people living therein. What then would be the structure of such a state?

Gandhi's *Swarajya* or Self-Rule is based on *Satyagraha*, Self-confidence (*Atmabala*) or *Karunabala*, and it requires adoption of *Swadeshi*. He was against the English civilization but not against the Englishmen.[10] His concept of state basically differed from the modern concept of state. His "state" consisted of people settled in small villages imbued with co-operative spirit.[11] His concept of state was the concept of *Ramarajya*, which consisted of prosperous, happy and self-contained village-communities.[12] His concept of village economy was based on non-violence. He rejected "Factory civilization" based on "exploitation" and "violence."[13] Actually he visualised a stateless society. Vinoba categorically declared that some of the Gandhians say that "State would always be there—it may be minimal, decentralised, good, but it would be there. . . . . . I submit that this is not Gandhi's thought". Vinoba held that stateless society was Gandhi's ideal and he, too whole-heartedly subscribed to it.[14] Quite naturally then, in this context, Gandhi – (1) denounced the state, (2) Disapproved the parliamentary democracy, (3) appreciated *Ramarajya*.[15] A question may be asked how to defend such a state and how the conflicts therein to be resolved? Gandhi is clear that "Non-Violence will have the sanction of the village community. Conflicts will be resolved through non-violence, i.e. *satyagraha*. Individuals and groups will resort to *satyagraha* whenever necessary. And what about the defence of such a state? He continues that it will look after its own defence. It is important, as defence has been one of the important functions of the state. Autonomy will be virtually lost if the village is not capable of defending itself. Secondly, all villagers will participate in this task. There will be no separate standing militia. Government will be conducted by a *Panchayat* of five persons. They will be elected annually. Their period of working is thus short. Voting will need certain prescribed qualifications (i.e., manual labour, etc.).[16]

What would be the structure of non-violent state of Gandhi? How would it work? Gandhi himself is not very clear on this issue. He believes that, in the course of time, the non-violent state will itself develop its own technique.[17] He could not say what the non-violent state would be like. It is a process. It is in the process of evolution. He points out that "Just as violence has its own technique known by military science, which has invented means of destruction unheard of before, non-violence has its own science and technique. Non-violence in politics is a "weapon" in the process of evolution. Its vast possibilities are as yet unexplored. The exploration can take place only if it is practised on a big scale and in various fields."[18] Thus, whatever be the circumstances, non-violence is the only Gandhian way out to tackle any situation including any attack by the invaders. His concept of *sarvodaya* aims at spiritualisation of politics.[19] It is neither necessary nor possible here to elaborate fully the concept of state by Gandhi. It is, however, clear that his concept of state rules out any defence by violence. All types of defence must be non-violent in nature like non-cooperation, *satyagraha*, fast (either for the change of heart of opponent or self purification), etc.

Concept of State

Before we proceed to know how and if the Gandhian non-violence would be able to tackle the problem of protecting and retaining the sovereignty of state, it would be helpful to understand, briefly, the concept of state and its sovereignty especially in the modern context.

In political theory, state has four essential elements :

(i) Population,
(ii) Territory,
(iii) Government, and
(iv) Sovereignty.[20]

However, such a concept of state is—comparatively—a modern phenomenon. Greeks had city states. For Aristotle, state is an "Association of families and villages for the sake of attaining a perfect and self-sufficient existence."[21] This appears to be the proximate Gandhian concept of village "states", though Gandhi's insistence on non-violence was not therein. Socrates was administered poison for his supposed crime of "way-laying" youngsters in the then city state. Actually, the concept of state is abstract in nature. It is intangible while the people who constitute it are concrete. Besides, it is "Difficult to separate the purpose of political life from the purpose of life itself."[22] Why should I obey the state? What is the purpose of state? These are the basic questions which any political theory has to address itself. In case of Gandhi, however, the state implies a "Village state" or at the most collective "Village states" prone to socio-individual realisation of God which is possible only through non-violence, co-operation, inclusive and collective responses of the people through *swadeshi*. This means that an atheist is inconceivable in the Gandhian plan. Why, should Gandhi ignore the atheist—who could equally be an ardent seeker of Truth—remains unexplained. Possibly his faith superseded the attempts at the possibility of unbiased and yet variegated quests of Truth.

As we have known previously, sovereignty constitutes an important aspect of all the concepts of state, specially in the modern era. The essential characteristics[23] of sovereignty of the state are stated to be :

(i) Absoluteness,
(ii) Universality,
(iii) Permanence,
(iv) Inalienability, i.e., the essential attribute of the state cannot be alienated, sovereignty is the very essence of personality of the state, and
(v) Indivisibility.

It could not be nominal or real, legal or political, *de facto* or *de jure* or popular sovereignty.[24] Thus, the sovereignty of the state is of utmost value to the people of that state because it also ensures their security and freedom. As Mr. Blackstone says, "Sovereignty is the supreme irresistible, absolute, uncontrolled authority in which the highest legal powers of the state reside."[25]

However, the concept of sovereignty appears to have suffered noticeable change in the modern concept of international law. It is bound and affected by various international laws and mutual contracts. The circumstances have changed to such an extent that sovereignty of many states—especially of the small and non-nuclear states—has remained almost practically nominal U.S.A. and Russia, China and India are not the same as Sri Lanka and Bangladesh, though all of them claim to be sovereign powers. The interdependence is unavoidable.[26]

As we have now known, the concept of sovereignty of state

has now been subjected to qualitative change to such an extent that it has remained neither absolute nor supreme. Friedmann talks of the present "Transnational society" (represented by increasing co-operation amongst various states) and "super national society" (in which the activities and functions of states or groups are combined in permanent international institutions, supported by international treaties and agreements).[27] Quite naturally then, the concept of sovereignty of a state has undergone considerable change in the present international scenario. Jean Bodin's concept of sovereignty in which the sovereigns are not subject to any laws and commands[28] is no more operative. The international law has been trying to "domesticate sovereignty" of the state.[29]

There is also an awareness that military alone cannot solve the various problems facing the modern states.[30] We live in a multi-cultural world. As seen earlier, the concept of sovereignty of state has undergone remarkable changes. Strangely, even the traits of legal positivism appear to persist. Sovereignty of the state is yet sought to be protected and revered.

Gandhi, however, was against the concept of such a state. He was, in a way, an anarchist. He visualises, "a classless and stateless democracy of autonomous village communities based on non-violence instead of coercion, on service instead of exploitation, on renunciation instead of acquisitiveness and in the largest measure on local and individual initiation instead of concentration."[31] Thus, he denounced both, the prevalent concept of state and its sovereignty. He was not a democrat. He rejected parliamentary democracy because majority vote does not—by itself—justify the "Rightness" or "Wrongness" of any action. Value is supreme, not the vote. The rule of majority is not a criterion for security also.[32] He knew that Hitler was a product of democracy. Possibly he also entertained the thought that democracy is prone to degenerate into ochlocracy. In this respect Gandhi—interestingly—approximates the position of Benito Mussolini's denunciation of democracy.[33] However, other differences amongst them are basic, many and remarkable. Gandhi's insistence on non-violent techniques—even in the context of the invaders' attacks on the security and sovereignty of the state is so remarkable that he appears ready to abandon them, i.e., sovereignty and security of the state. He does not allow even a fist to be raised against the armed invader and would prefer death of the soldier without malice for the invader.[34] He could not enlighten General Cariappa—the first Commander-in-Chief of the Independent India—on how to train Indian soldiers in non-violent methods without "subordinating their main task of preparing themselves effectively to be good soldiers."[35] He had reiterated the same view of being in the "dark" on the issue when William Stuart Nelson met him in August 1947.[36]

Thus, it would appear that Gandhi was wavering between the "Darkness" born of absence of clarity on the issue and his faith in "Non-Violence" as a supreme value. He was candid enough to admit this. However, his "Non-Violence" appears to have an upper edge. He never sided with violence even as defensive measures.

It follows then that, according to Gandhian Non-Violence, no state is allowed to take recourse to violence even against a terrorist or secessionist activities for the protection of its sovereignty. Such a state has to follow the non-violent measures only. Similarly, there is nothing like "just" violence or "just' war. Violence is violence. Change of nomenclature does not transform its basic characteristics. Therefore, violence, in whatever form and for whatever purpose, is unjustifiable. Whether the invader state is powerful or weak, whether the invaded state is strong or imbecile—whatever be the circumstance—the violence has to be rejected. Gandhi advised non-violence even at individual level when confronted with violent attack by the assailant.[37]

Gandhi preferred violence to cowardice, but did not recommend violence at any cost. This is also applicable in case of the states. To defend the state through non-violence is no cowardice. No powerful state is entitled to play with the sovereignty of any weaker state. The non-violence of the weaker state—under such situation, i.e. if it defends itself non-violently and genuinely—is no cowardice. On the contrary, such a non-violent defence is praiseworthy. It is wrong to believe that non-violent defence by a weaker state is—by itself—a sign of weakness or cowardice.

Gandhi is very clear on this issue. Actually he had advised England to fight Hitler with the "weapon" of non-cooperation (not with arms) which is a non-violent way of protest to defeat the invading army of Hitler.

It has to be noted that concept of state as envisaged by Gandhi is basically different from such a concept embodied in political theories. Actually, he visualises stateless village-based, socio-economically self-sufficient system wherein all the members form a defence force, a force to combat violence with non-violence. In such a state the sovereignty would not be there because sovereignty of the state implies a coercive force, a distinction between the ruler and the ruled, which Gandhi rejects. His state would be a co-operative state based on Gandhian ideal of self-rule, *swaraj*.

Is the Gandhian concept of non-violence applicable and effective to protect the sovereignty of the state? How could, if at all, it be protected without taking recourse to violence? Are either cumulative death of people or slavery of the invaders for the survivors offering non-violent protests the only alternatives for the "*satyagrahi*" state? If all the measures of non-violence fail to change the hearts of the wrong-doers, then is to suffer non-violently the only alternative for a *satyagrahi* even for a "just" cause? If "justice" is a socio-individual value and if it is to be respected, then is it not denied to one who faithfully follows Gandhian methodology under such circumstances? Does non-violence supersede all other human values? If the security, freedom of the people, etc., are the primary duties of any welfare state and if by defending its sovereignty—if necessary violently—a state performs its duties, could it be condemned only because it had no other alternative than to use violent means to be true to its duties?

Gandhi did not enunciate any "practical" solution to such problems. Many have pointed out such a limitation of his point of view. He was oscillating—as we have now known—between "darkness" and his faith in "Non-Violence". He was candid enough to admit it. It is not without reason that his own disciples and followers—when they were constituents of Government of India after independence—totally ignored him alongwith his ideology.

They knew well that to defend the sovereignty of the state was their prime responsibility and it could not be done non-violently in the Gandhian way. Therefore, they disregarded him. Gandhi did not realise—or chose not to take into account—the limitations of non-violence. Though this does not justify violent means of whatever category, it does point to the fact that not all situations in the socio-individual human life are fruitfully responsive to the non-violent measures.

Despite the problems his concept of non-violence has to confront in the "factual" world—for which he had no ready and effective solution—his vision strives to ensure a peaceful, co-operative, healthy and integral human society where Non-Violence, truth and God would form a constituent Trinity. He was a visionary of the twentieth century. He strived to "socialise" "non-violence" which—appears to have—so far, remained only an individual virtue. Above all, he was an ardent, transparent Truth seeker whose character, life and thoughts have left an indelible print on the annals of human history. World would scarce believe, as Albert Einstein said, that such a man ever walked on the earth.

REFERENCES

1. Cp. "*Maranoddeshyakatve sati maranukula vyaparah himsa*" in *Siddhanta Muktavali*, pp. 519-521, Nirnaya Sagar Press, 1933. Also "*Sakshat maranakula vyaparah himsa*".
2. "*Ahimsa apeeda praninam*" —Shankara-Commentary on *Gita* (10.5) also (16.2) "*Praninam pieda varjanam*", Ashtekar & Co., Pune, 1929.
3. "*Ahimsa –Vichar Aur Vyavahara*" – Vinoba Bhave, Gram Bhavana Prakashan and Gandhi Shanti Pratishthan, First Edition. September, 1970, pp. 8-9.
4. *Ibid.*, p.7
5. "*Ahimsa* and Truth are so intertwined that it is practically impossible to disentangle and separate them" in "*Socialism of My Conception*" by M. K. Gandhi, Editor & Publisher – Anand T. Hingorani, Bhartiya Vidya Bhawan, Bombay, 1967, p. 2 (F.N.).
6. "*Young India*" 8 January,1925; *Ibid.*, p.105.
7. "In *Swaraj* based on *Ahimsa*, people need not know their rights but it is necessary for them to know their duties", *Ibid.*, p.142.

8. "*Ahimsa –Vichar aur Vyavahara*" – Vinoba Bhave Gram Bhavana Prakashan and Gandhi Shanti Pratishthan, 1970, pp. 22-23.
9. *Ibid.*, p. 73.
10. "*Swaraj*" by Gandhiji. Navjeevan Prakashan Mandir, Ahmedabad-14. Translator : Amrutlal Thakurdas Nanavati, p. 87, published in 2001.
11. "Society based on Non-violence can only consist of groups settled in villages, in which voluntary co-operation is the condition of dignified and peaceful existence" by M.K. Gandhi in *Harijan* dated 13.1.1940, Vol.7, pp. 410-411. Q.F. "Gandhian Theory of State" by Dr. Parag Cholkar, p. 151 (A thesis).
12. "Now for Ramarajya. It can be religiously translated as Kingdom of God on Earth; politically translated, it is perfect democracy in which, inequalities based on possession and non-possession, colour, race or creed or sex vanish, in it land and state belong to the people, justice is prompt, perfect and cheap and the Press — all this because of the reign of self imposed law of morale restraint.

    "Such a state must be based on Truth and Non-violence and must consist of prosperous, happy and self-contained villages and village communities. It is a dream that may never be realised. I find happiness in living in that dreamland ever trying to realise it in the quickest way" in *The Collected Works of Mahatma Gandhi*, Vol. 80, p. 300. Published by The Publications Division, Ministry of Information & Broadcasting, Government of India, New Delhi, September, 1970 (*The Hindu* dated 12/06/1945).
13. "Non-Violence" is not a cloistered virtue, confined only to *Rishi* and the cave dweller. It is capable of being practiced by millions, not with full knowledge of its implications, but because it is a law of a species. It distinguishes a man from the brute. But man has not shed the brute in him. He has to strive to do it. This striving applies to the practice of non-violence, not to the belief in it. . . . . . You cannot build non-violence on a factory civilization, but it can be built on self contained villages. . . . . . Rural economy as I have conceived it eschews exploitation and exploitation is the essence of violence". By M.K. Gandhi in *The Collected Works of Mahatma Gandhi*. Vol. 70, p. 296. Published by the Publications Division, Ministry of Information & Broadcasting, Government of India, New Delhi, September, 1987 (*Harijan* dated 4/11/1939).
14. Report of the Eighth Sarvodaya Sammelan, Kanchipuram, 1956; Sarva Sewa Sangh, Wardha, 1956, p. 137.

    Q.F. *Gandhian Theory of the State* by Dr. Parag Cholkar (A thesis) p. 186.

15. J.C. Johari in *Principles of Modern Political Thought,* Sterling Publications Pvt. Ltd., First Edition, New Delhi-16, p. 811.
16. Q.F. *Gandhian Theory of The State* by Dr. Parag Cholkar (A thesis) p. 162.
17. "I have purposefully refrained from dealing with the nature of government in a society based deliberately on non-violence. All society is held together by non-violence. Even as the Earth is held in her position by gravitation. But when the law of gravitation was discovered the discovery yielded results of which our ancestors had no knowledge. Ever so when society is deliberately constructed in accordance with the law of non-violence, its structure will be different in material particulars from what it is today. But I cannot see in advance what the government based wholly on non-violence will be like". What is happening today is disregard of the law of non-violence and enthronement of violence as if it were on eternal law. The democracy, therefore, when we see at work in England, America and France are only, so called, because they are no less based on violence than Nazi Germany, Fascist Italy or even Soviet Russia. The only difference is that violence of the last three is much better organised than that of three democratic powers". (*Harijan* dated 11.2.1939) by M.K. Gandhi in *The Collected Works of Mahatma Gandhi*, Vol. 68, pp. 389-390 published by the Publications Division, Ministry of Information and Broadcasting, Government of India, New Delhi, January,1977.
18. In *The Collected Works of Mahatma Gandhi*, Vol. 66, p.269 (*Harijan* dated 12.10.1937) published by the Publications Division, Ministry of Information and Broadcasting, Government of India, New Delhi, October.,1976.
19. "Principles of Modern Political Science" by J.C. Johari, Sterling Publications, First edition 1989, New Delhi-16, p. 834.
20. *Ibid.,* p. 54.

    Cp. T. E. Holland – "The State is a numerous assemblage of human beings occupying a certain territory, amongst whom the will of the majority or of an ascertainable class of persons is by the strength of such a majority of class made to prevail against any of their number who oppose it". (Q.F. *Ibid.,* p. 60)

    Also Cp. Robert Philimore – "State is a people permanently occupying a fixed territory, bound together by common laws, habits and customs into one body politic, exercising through the medium of an organised government, independent sovereignty and control over all persons and things within its boundaries capable of making war and peace and of entering into all international relations with the communities of the globe". (Q.F. *Ibid.,* p. 60)

21. Q.F. *Ibid.*, p. 60.
22. C. L. Wayper in *Political Thought,* The English Universities Press Ltd., 102, Newgate Street, London, 1958. In "Introduction", p. vii.
23. Cp. Herold Lasky in *An Introduction to Politics* (New Edition prepared by Martin Weight) p. 89, George Allen & Unwin Ltd., Ruskin House, Museum Street, London, 1958. "Broadly speaking, before reformation, democracy, public opinion, the will of the state lacked any sovereign character. It was regarded as inherently limited by the Law of God and the Law of Nature. Any enactment of the state contrary to their principles was uncertainly void of effect".
24. J.C. Johari in *Principles of Modern Political Science,* Sterling Publications, First edition, 1989, New Delhi-16, pp.145-149.
25. QF *Ibid.*, p. 143.
    Also Cp. "Sovereignty is the strongest power and supreme authority than a state, which is unlimited by law or anything else, since otherwise it would neither be strongest nor supreme". Donald F. Russel. (Q.F. *Ibid.,* p.143).
26. Max Beloff in "International Integration and the Modern State". (A Paper) in "The New International Actors"). The United Nations and The European Economic Community (Edited by Carol Ann Cosgrove & Kenneth J. Twitchett, MacMillan, St. Martin Street, 1977, Britain, p. 93).
    "For practical purposes the value of maintaining the pure doctrine of state of National Sovereignty must depend upon circumstances. What is plausible in the case of United States or Soviet Russia is less plausible in the case of Canada or Poland. In other words under modern conditions both from the point of view of the people's livelihood and from the point of view of defence, interdependence today is a much common experience than independence".
27. Wolffang Friedmann in *A Changing Structure of International Law,* pp. 36-37, published by Vakils Feffer & Simons Pvt. Ltd., Hague Building, 9, Sprott Road, Ballard Estate, Bombay-1, 1964.
28. *Modern Political Thought* by Dr. Surinder Suri, Sudha Publications Pvt. Ltd, 48/4, East Patel Nagar, New Delhi-12, p.31.
29. Charles D.E. & Visscher in *Theory and Reality in Public International Law,* translated by P.E. Corbett, published by Prinston University Press, 1968, p.104.

30. *The Right of The People* by William O. Douglas (Associate Judge of Supreme Court, U.S.A.) Pyramid Books, 444 Madison Avenue, N. Y. 22, NY, 1961.
"It is a great and dangerous weakness to take the attitude that military can solve our important problems. Yet that is growing trend in the nation". p.140.
31. G.N. Dhavan in "The Political Philosophy of Mahatma Gandhi, p.3; Q.F. *Principles of Modern Political Science* by J.C. Johari, p. 811.
32. Cp. New Heinrich von Treischke in *Politics*. "The rule of the majority, then, which is a necessary adjunct of democracy is most certainly no security for political liberty. Each citizen is given the right to make his voice heard in the national decision, but if he does not go with the majority he must just put up with it, and hope that his turn will come some day". "One half of freedom is alternatively to rule and be ruled" as Aristotle said long ago. (from "*Modern Political Thought – The Great Issues*" – William Ebenstein, Second Edition, Oxford & IBH Publishing Co., New Delhi, 1970, pp.346-347).
33. In *The Political and Social Doctrine of Fascism* (1932). "Fascism controls the whole complex system of democratic ideology, and repudiates it, whether in his theoretical premises or in its practical application, Fascism denies that majority, by the simple fact, it is a majority, can direct human society, it denies that numbers alone can govern by means of a periodical consultation ..... Q.F. *Ibid.,* p.346.
34. Prof. Bodharaj Sharma in a paper on "The State in Gandhian Philosophy". published in "*Gandhian Concept of State*". Edited by B.V. Mujumdar, published on behalf of Bihar University by M.C. Sarkar & Sons Pvt. Ltd., 14, Bankim Chatterjee Street, Calcutta-12, 1957.
"On the 5th of November, at the prayer meeting at Delhi, Gandhiji read a letter which rebuked him for having dared to advise Churchill, Hitler, Mussolini and Japanese to adopt his advice on non-violence. But he did not give the same advice to the Congress Government when it sent armed assistance to Kashmir. Gandhiji's reply was that he had no influence in the matter over his friends in the Union Cabinet. He held on his views on non-violence as firmly as ever but he could not impose his views on his best friends. He said that he did not approve of the use of arms by the Union Government for the aiding of Kashmiris. Non-violent assistance could be sent from the Union without stint. He wished that the defenders had died at their

posts of duty without malice and without anger in their hearts against the assailants and without the use of any arms, including even their fists. That would have been an exhibition of heroism perhaps unknown to history". p.147.

35. "It is relevant to quote the conversation between General Cariappa, the first C-in-C of India and Mahatma Gandhi reported by Mr. K. Subrahmaniyan, ('Evolution of India—Defence Policy—1947-64' in *A History of Congress Party*, Delhi-AICC & Vikas Publishing House), 1990.

    General Cariappa sought a clarification from Gandhi just a month before his death. "I cannot do my duty well by the country if I concentrate only on telling the troops of non-violence, all the time subordinating their main task of preparing themselves effectively to be good soldiers. So I ask you, please give me a "Child's guide to knowledge"—Tell me, please, how can I put this over, i.e., the spirit of non-violence to the troops without endangering their sense of duty, to train themselves well professionally as soldiers", he asked. Gandhi replied, You have asked me to tell you in a tangible and concrete form how to put over the troops the need for non-violence. I am still groping in the dark for the answer. I will find it and give it to you some day".

    (Q.F. Col. J.K. Deosthale in his paper on "Human Rights, Humanitarian Law and Armed Forces" (A Paper) published in a "Special Issue of National Seminar on Human Rights and Terrorism" by Institute of Human Rights, Jaripatka, Nagpur-14, Editor Dr. P.L. Joshi. pp. 87-88, (Vol. V, No.1, June, 2002)

36. In a paper on "Tradition of Non-violence and its Underlying Forces" in *Gandhi – His Relevance For Our Times*. Editors G. Ramachandran and T. K. Mahadevan. Published by Gandhi Peace Foundation, 1967, Second Edition, p. 3.

37. Gandhi was asked the following questions. His replies clarify his views on the subject.

    (1) *Question* – "Can a woman be advised to take her own life rather than surrender?"

    Gandhi's reply – " A woman would most certainly take her own life rather than surrender. In other words, surrender has no room in my plan of life" (*Harijan* 9-2-1947).

    (2) *Question* – "If a choice is between taking one's own life or that of the assailant, which would you advise?"

Gandhi's reply – "When it is a question of choice between killing oneself or the assailant, I have no doubt in my mind that the first should be the choice" (*Harijan* 9-2-1947).
(From "Communal Unity" by M.K. Gandhi, Navajivan Publishing House, Ahmedabad, 1949), p. 393.
Presented on 27/11/2004 at the seminar organised by Akhil Bhartiya Darshan Parishad held at Ahmedabad (Gujarat) in its Golden Jubilee Session.

6

Relevance of Gandhian Measures in Tackling Terrorism

L.G. Chincholkar

The recent Beslan tragedy in Russia wherein hundreds of school children—along with their parents and others—were mercilessly and inhumanly scorched to painful death by the Chechen terrorists has once again forced the global attention on the problem of terrorism in the world. It is not the case that the terrorism is a new phenomenon. It has been there throughout the history of the human race in one form or the other, the stronger bullying the weaker into submission or death for the fulfilment of either personal, political, religious or ideological perceived interests. The problem came to be widely acknowledged now after the Islamic terrorist on 11/09/2001 attacked the World Trade Centre and other buildings in U.S.A. in which thousands of innocent people were killed. The destroyed buildings can be built again but not the destroyed precious lives of the innocents.

Terrorism has assumed varied and destructive dimensions with the newer technological advances and enormous destructive power they possess. It is not only the persons or the group of persons who indulge in such activities for personal gains, but even the states are found to initiate, harbour and encourage terrorism, which they believe to be in their interests. The attack on Indian Parliament by the Islamic group—which owned the responsibility for this act of terrorism—grounded in Pakistan is only one such incident. Thus, it is not only the persons, but even the states are under the shadow of terrorism throughout the world in greater or lesser degrees despite the most modern protective shields available to some of them. Thus, it is not the persons—as individuals—but the states, the government of the states also face the danger of being overpowered by or subjugated to the arbitrary wills of the terrorists for whom human life has no worth.

India has been facing Pakistan-sponsored terrorism for the last more than 50 years not only in Jammu & Kashmir, but also in various parts of the nation killing thousands of innocent men, women and children, destroying property worth crores and crores of rupees. The Indian soldiers also are dying in thousands. Monetary loss to the nation is also incalculable. And yet the dance of death goes on. Is there any remedy to remove this evil of terrorism? Could Mahatma Gandhi—the unique leader of the independence movement—lead us with the kindly light. What would be his strategy to counter and if possible to arrest such occurrence? How would his methodology help us to arrest the wrong and establish the right under such circumstances with his non-violence oriented approach to life and its problems? Are his measures relevant in this context. What would have been his reaction under such circumstances? This chapter intends to understand, elaborate and evaluate Gandhian approach in this context. It would be helpful to be acquainted with the concept, quality and types of terrorism before we proceed to view it in the light of Gandhian Measures.

Terror means "extreme fear". "Terrorist" means "one who favours or uses terror inspiring methods of Government or of coercive government or community."[1] "The ingredients of terrorism are stated to be as follows:

(1) A cause,
(2) Popular support for the cause,
(3) Financial support,

(4) Training,
    (a) Military,
    (b) Explosives and sabotage,
    (c) Radio and communication, and
    (d) Operational planning and execution, and
(5) A safe sanctuary to hide, recoup and plan next act."[2]

Accordingly terrorism does not operate without any support. It requires men, money, material and support of at least group of sympathetic persons and relevant training for the purpose. Thus, it is a systematically organised group of persons trained for the purpose of carrying out its activities. Terrorism, in the modern context, is far more dangerous and destructive. It could go to the extent of eliminating even nation if it is sufficiently equipped with disastrous weapons of formidable quality. Unfortunately the innocents are the worst sufferers. The basic question, in this context, is what prompts terrorism? "Is intolerance of other point of view the cause? Is aggressive tendency – said to be inherent in a human being – responsible?" Is it a basic psychological trait in all? Is it an expression of the wrath against the supposed suppression of justice denied to the people? Is it an indication of the egoistic superiority prevalent in haves against havenots? Is it a way to secure justice for those who have been denied it socio-politically with no hope to secure the same lawfully? Is it an expression to fulfil any exclusivist religious faith or is it only a politically motivated phenomenon to score victory over the opponents? Questions are many. They are pertinent. They do require realistic elaboration and consistent explanation.

It appears that the concept of terrorism could be broadly classed into three types, i.e., Religious terrorism, Political terrorism and Personal terrorism. All these types have a factor in common, i.e., they all thrive on the fear of death or any type of loss to the other side to be caused by the methods employed by the terrorist. It has to be noted that all these three types are not exclusive of each other. They could be inclusive depending upon the circumstances. Let us try to understand them.

(1) Religious Terrorism

It stems from the religious faith that to convert others to one's religious faith is a religious duty. That a religion—other than his own—could not be a true religion. Therefore, a terrorist normally "faithfully" puts forth two choices before the people belonging to other religions, either accept "my" religion or be prepared for death, or at the most, for slavery. All the semitic religions appear to be entertaining this attitude. When Mohammad Bin Kasim invaded India in 711 A.D., he had two aims at his heart, i.e., to loot and to convert.[3] The war of Crusades between the votaries of Christianity and Islam—started in 636 A.D.—went on for hundreds of years.[4] The religious faith of Christianity that it alone is entitled to salvation.[5]—whatever it may mean—and of Islam's concept of *Jihad* are such faiths. The *Holy Qur'an* is very clear about it.[6] When Prophet Mohammad was asked which was the best action according to Islam, he replied that the best action was *Jihad*—the holy war against the non-muslims—for the cause of *Allah* is the best action in Islam.[7] The Judaism also chose not to think differently. There are commands of God to slaughter Hittites, Amorites and others.[8] If the religious faiths are exclusive then naturally cordial relationship with other religious communities becomes strained and at times untenable.

In India, which has been the cradle of many religions, such attitude was absent. The concept of *Syadvad* of Jainism is significant in this respect. So are the Buddha's teachings. Hindus always respect different points of view religiously. Hinduism, Buddhism, Jainism, Sikhism and the sub-sects, despite their differences and earlier mainly intellectual clashes, remained appreciative and respectful of each other because of the inclusive attitude of all of them which insisted on virtuous living and not on any formal conversions. Any faith in formal conversion is antithetic to socio-religious amity amongst different religious groups. It is also disastrous because it has political implications as well. It is similarly inconsistent with the concept of equality of religions. The religious consciousness is not the product of any specific religion and does not bring about the assured "certainty of God's grace."[9] The virtuous and vicious persons are there in every religion. Therefore, to entertain any such exclusivist attitude in the name of religious faith is to be blind to the higher ascensions of the human mind. If such a religious faith could be outgrown and if possible eliminated, one of the basic causes of the prevalent religious terrorism could be rooted out.

(2) Political Terrorism

This implies terrorism to further the political interests of a nation. It emanates from the lust for power of territory: economic, strategic, defence interests and some such other interests. "The two world wars of the twentieth century were triggered by territorial ambition, the perceived humiliation by Germany in the aftermath of the treaty of Versaill's and Hitler's most diabolic and outrageous antisemitic obsession which resulted in the horrendous killing of six million Jews, the worst ever genocide and ethnic cleaning."[10] Mr. S.M. Zafar, the former Law Minister of Pakistan, acknowledged in 1996 that "Everything is done by Pakistan in Kashmir. Kashmiri movement is the official jargon for an armed violence and terrorism in the State."[11] Political terrorism is of different hues, takes different forms and is often justified in the name of justice and honour.

The bombing of Vietnam and recent attacks on Iraq by U.S.A., the enslavement of Tibet by China which forced Dalai Lama to flee to India, the Russian interference in Poland and Czechoslovakia, U.S.A.'s recent attacks on Afghanistan, its machinations in Cuba, Pakistan's perpetual sponsoring of gangsterism of various forms in India are all examples of political terrorism. The political terrorism, however, need not always be extra-territorial.

The emergency clamped in India in 1975 to frustrate all the politico-judicial processes when the Allahabad High Court invalidated Indira Gandhi's, the then Prime Minister of India, election is an incident of intra-territorial political terrorism resorted to retain her political power. The elimination, assassination of political opponents in Russia and China after Stalin and Mao ascended to their respective seats of power are the instances of the political terrorism basically genocidal in nature.

There are various aspects of such terrorism. Pakistan sponsored attack on Indian Parliament on 13/12/2001 is only an incidence. Kidnapping, hijacking, drug trafficking, psychological warfare, political or ideological propaganda, radio, television, economic investments in their nations could have political implications to further terrorism. Creation and circulation of fake currency, economic sanctions or economic allurements could also have political motives. They are not always merely criminal acts, but terrorist acts. A question may be asked then how are we to distinguish between a terrorist act and a criminal act. A terrorist act is necessarily a criminal act, but all criminal acts are not necessarily the terrorist acts. The motive and other relevant circumstances have to be looked into to decide upon the type of action.

(3) Personal Terrorism

This type of terrorism is normally involved in an attempt to acquire objects of personal gratification through means antithetic to the accepted standards of morality and law in a given society. One of the main reasons for the prevalence of this type of terrorism is the failure of the law and order system in a society. When the offenders go unpunished, when the oppressed or the victims sulk waiting for the justice which they believe would possibly never be awarded to them, when the offenders cleverly manage the political system—steeped in corruption—to escape the consequences of their offences, when the mighty and the wealthy, as a rule, escape the claws of law, when the judicial system—in its tower—based aloofness and nonchalance—fails to respond to the just, effective and prompt aspirations and hopes of the wronged, personal terrorism—tends to creep in effectively in the fabric of the society.

The Virappan episode, which had been infesting the South India for the last more than three decades is such an example. Why the Akku Yadav, who was accused of habitually molesting women in some areas at Nagpur and who always remained free to carry on his nefarious acts under the police "surveillance" was lynched to death recently by the agitated women at Nagpur? Why the women of Nagpur, again, had also lynched to death two such other persons for the similar reasons?

The answer has to be sought in the failure of the executive and judicial systems in India along with prevalence of corruption at almost all levels. The demand for the 'protection money' from the wealthy, threats to voters and others during election, the 'booth capturing' etc., the success of such goons in getting elected to the legislative assemblies and the parliaments are the sad commentary on the prevalent parliamentary system in India. This also affords breeding ground for the personal terrorism and endangers the very basis of a welfare society.

We have very succinctly strived to outline the different types of terrorism. As pointed out earlier, they are neither exclusive nor the only types. They are believed to point to the general trends. Is it possible to deal with this problem effectively under the Gandhian plan? What would be the Gandhian approach to tackle this problem? Is it dispensable or would it remain an ingredient of the human society? In this context, it would be useful to know of the general outline of the Gandhian view of life and state and the type of the society he envisages.

Gandhi was a staunch votary of non-violence. His conception of the society and the activities therein rely on the basic principle of *ahimsa*, i.e., non-violence. But the concept of non-violence is neither solitary nor independent. Non-violence is equivalent to truth and truth is equivalent to God. Thus, non-violence = truth = God. This is his confirmed formula. He says, "This society must naturally be based on truth and Non-violence which, in my opinion, are not possible without a living belief in God, meaning a self-existent, all-knowing, living force which inheres every other force known to the world and which depends on none and which will live when all other forces may conceivably perish or cease to act.

I am unable to count for my life without belief in this all-embracing living light."[12] Thus Gandhi is a theist, a staunch believer in the existence of God. His conception of the non-violent society is inconceivable for an atheist. A socialistic society is not merely a society based on conceived "socialistic pattern" as a constitutional measure. One who believes himself to be a socialist must have a pure heart. He must be truthful. He must be non-violent in his approach.[13]

Explaining the philosophical basis of the concept of non-violence, Vinoba Bhave—the acknowledged and most prominent disciple of Gandhi—points out that Vedanta, the monistic view of truth is the base of non-violence. That no one should kill the other—whatever its category—or be violent against anybody is not merely an altruistic attitude. It is a logical consequence of the philosophical doctrine of monistic *Vedanta* that all are ultimately and inherently identical. Truth is the ultimate identity of all. Therefore, this being the case, non-violence against any category is consistent with the basic accepted philosophical structure. Vinoba Bhave points out that Gandhi only substituted Truth for the word *Vedanta.*[14] Therefore, to be violent is suicidal. It is being violent against oneself.

Besides, even the struggle for independence in which Gandhi participated was not a struggle for Indians alone. It had wider implications for the world over because India was a constituent of the world. It could not be happy if the world elsewhere were unhappy. The entire humanity for him is a unity. For him *ahimsa* and 'truth' are so intertwined that it is practically impossible to disentangle and separate them. They are like the two sides of the same coin, or rather a smooth unstamped metallic disc: Who can say which is the obverse, and which is the reverse."[15]

Now, with this position of non-violent, truthful approaches how would Gandhi tackle the "ills of the world"? How would he react to the situations apparently unjust, violent and antithetic to human dignity and sense of honour especially when terrorism has been rampantly, constantly and continuously threatening the peace all over, killing the innocents under the various garbs of ideology or personal vendetta world over? What would be his reply to the acts of terrorism whether they are state-sponsored or ideology-oriented? And what would be his methodology to counter the same? To seek answers to these and such other problems it will be fruitful to be generally acquainted with the measures which he had been recommending to face such or similar situations.

What are the general measures Gandhi had adopted himself or would recommend to be adopted by one committed to tackle any such situation non-violently and truthfully? They can be generally enumerated as follows:

(i) Non-cooperation,
(ii) *Satyagraha*,
(iii) Fast (for self purification),
(iv) Fast for change of the heart of the other party,
(v) Self-denial,
(vi) *Hartal*, and
(vii) Suicide (in exceptional cases especially when the honour of a woman is involved).

All these measures are not necessarily exclusive of each other nor is it claimed that they are the only methods for the purpose. But one thing is very clear. For Gandhi, a *satyagraha* has to be a model of truth and non-violence. He points out that "*Satyagraha* differs from passive response as North Pole from the South Pole. The latter has been conceived as a weapon of the weak and does not exclude use of physical force or violence for the purpose of gaining one's end, whereas the former has been conceived as the weapon of the strongest and excludes the use of violence in any shape or form."[16] It is quite consistent that Gandhi should condemn terrorism because for him it is "self destructive."[17]

The problem is how the Gandhian measures would non-violently resist the terrorism? How would his measures stand up against such acts without compromising non-violence or truth? It is interesting to note here that Vinoba Bhave believes that—in the case of India—Russia or U.S.A. would never attack India because they have ample land to settle upon and if any nation—having less land—invaded India to grab the land here then we would gladly, peacefully and non-violently pass it on to such a nation. If any nation attacked India it can be only Pakistan. That would be then a fight between the brothers and not the enemies, he pointed out.[18]

Now how could a *satyagrahi*, or any of the Gandhian methodology face the terrorist. If such a *satyagrahi* were at World Trade Centre at New York or at the terrorist-ridden Kashmir Valley, or at Parliament House in New Delhi which was attacked by terrorists, or at Mumbai in 1993 in the other infamous bomb-blasts killing hundreds of people or at Beslan in Russia or at any such place devastated by the acts of terrorism in the world around or in India itself how could he 'non-violently' face such situation? It may be that the *satyagrahi* himself would not be alive to resist non-violently in such a situation. The methodology of non-violence and other Gandhian measures could at least try to convince by reason and an action the opponent if he were discernible. But the terrorists are not 'open enemies'. They are almost always disguised. They hit and run. The victim is uninformed and often unarmed. It is not the persons or the group of persons alone who are terrorists, even the states sponsor terrorism to secure their interests. How is a devout Gandhian to respond to such a situation?

It is very clear that Gandhi was not only against terrorism, but against any type of violence. His methodology to combat terrorism or any type of violence including invasion of the nation was not often deemed practicable. Romain Rolland believed that "Some of the suggestions of Gandhi for the use of *ahimsa* in the world of diplomacy appear unrealistic and unconvincing to me."[19] What was Gandhi's reaction to the failure of non-violent methods even during his life? William Stuart Nelson refers to his meeting with Gandhi in August, 1947 and points out that Gandhi accepted that he was in the dark in respect of the efficiency of the non-violent technique in group relations.[20]

It is possible that the type of global terrorism prevalent today was not discernible during the life of Gandhi. At present the political terrorism is sought to be justified in the name of peace. The recent invasion of Iraq by U.S.A. in the garb of securing a nuclear-free state points to a formidable type of terrorism by a nuclear power. How would Gandhi's measures arrest such eventualities? "The doctrine of nuclear deterrence today as practiced by the ruling elites of the nuclear weapon nations constitutes the ultimate extra-polation of terrorism. Consequently, terrorism has been sought to be legitimised and sanctified. The communication between the legitimisation of the doctrines of nuclear war and the rise in international terrorism is obvious. Indeed they are the two sides of the same coin."[21]

Would Gandhi's advice to England during Second World War "Not to fight Hitler with arms" and allow Hitler's army to march in England and then offer "perfect non-cooperation" with them from every Englishman,[22] be practicable? And what if Hitler wipes out the entire English population to secure his ends so that there could be no scope even for "non-cooperation"? Professor Cole has raised the similar question. Miss Raith Bon asked, who would, whether a saint or a commoner, allow the terrorist to kill the innocent children at the altar of non-violence?[23] Gandhi, however, insisted that terror must be fought with non-violent means and not with violence because he believed that ultimately non-violence alone succeeds.

Elaborating salient features of Gandhi's non-violence, Mr. Johari said, "It would be an action of non-violence to beat and kill a person who runs amuck and may kill anyone with a sword in his hand. So, a country has every right to beat the foreign aggressors by force of arms.[24] This understanding of Gandhi is inconsistent with his concept of non-violence whereby he advised England—as noted earlier—not to fight with Hitler and defeat him through non-cooperation. Mr. Johari has not quoted any reference in this respect. His view is that of *Manusmriti*, the work of the Indian law-giver Manu and not of Gandhi. During the aggression of Pakistan in 1947, Gandhi had advised Government of India not to face the aggression with force of arms. He very clearly stated that

"He had no influence in the matter over his friends in the Union Cabinet" and that he "Held on to his views on non-violence as firmly as ever, but he could not impose his views on his best friends, as they were, in the Cabinet.[25] Thus, it would be evident that Gandhi was consistent in his insistence on facing the violence with non-violence—with the variety of measures in the context of prevailing circumstances.

Having now strived to know Gandhian measures, his insistence on non-violence and truth and God, his application of various measures to combat actions opposed to justice, honour, freedom and such other values which he sought to justify and translate into human life—including in his life—the applicability and practicability of his measures to tackle terrorism, it becomes apparent that Gandhi tried to bridge the gulf between the "ought" and "is", "value" and the "fact", and in his unalienable trust in non-violence and its corresponding measures chose to be not influenced by inherent limitations of the socio-individual and collective human personality.

For example, what Lord Rama whose wife was abducted by Ravana, according to epic *Ramayana*, should have done if Ravana refused to return Sita? What type of *satyagraha* or non-cooperation should he had adopted? What type of fast either for self-purification or for the change of heart of Ravana would have become effective? Would *hartal*—in Lanka, the place of Ravana—or elsewhere or any type of self-denial could be meaningful to get Sita released from his custody? Would suicide have solved the problem? Actually Rama tried various 'non-violent' means to persuade Ravana to right the wrong, to secure "justice" both for himself and Sita. What would be Gandhi's remedy in such a case? Or should Rama and Sita forever suffer injustice?

Besides, is not Rama entitled to 'justice' as is anybody else? If to secure justice, non-violence failed to evoke any "change of heart" of the opponent what would be the remedy? Ethically speaking, if Rama and Sita are also entitled to justice and if it is not possible through non-violent methodology, should they suffer injustice forever including recourse to death for none of their fault

Does such a course not only morally, but politically and jurisprudentially also shake the foundation of socio-individual relationship sought to be built up for the welfare of the society? In such cases then non-violence would be not only a disadvantage it would frustrate the very purpose of the Gandhian ideal of social equilibrium. This not only applies to individual aggressors but terrorist activities by states also. Is submission to violence the best way of securing and establishing non-violence? As noted earlier, Gandhi was completely in the dark about the steps a non-violent *satyagrahi* should adopt under such circumstances. In his conversation with General Cariappa also he honestly acknowledged it. His advice to face "non-violently" the aggression of Pakistan in Kashmir in 1947, however, was disregarded by his own disciples. All this points out to the fact that Gandhi chose to remain undecided on all such issues which stare at human relationship so poignantly. He honestly acknowledged this. This, however, does not belittle him. He was a visionary, a saint, a crusader for truth which, for him was only a synonym for God. His faith in non-violence was supreme and unadulterated through which he set forth to embark upon the quest of truth. He, however, either did not or chose not to think of the limitations of the non-violent measures in the world ridden with human weaknesses. This resulted in his erstwhile followers forsaking him when stark realities of life confronted them.

He was a crusader for peace, not only national, but international peace, not only for humans but even for non-humans. His methodology to actualise his conceived values may appear less effective in the terror-stricken world of today but the measures he advocates tend to be more relevant today at least when the nuclear volcano stares to annihilate the entire life itself on this globe.

For him non-violence has no instrumental value. It is an absolute value over-riding all other values, it appears. Thus in priority, it is supreme. Its value must not be measured through its consequences. In this context, he is not a utilitarian. Relevancy of Gandhian measures lies in its emphasis and trust to effectuate catharsis of the hearts of the terrorists, for, as he said, terrorism is self-destructive and counter-productive and does not solve basic problems. Despite the perceived difficulties in always adopting such measures as already pointed out, it has to be noted that they strive to effectuate healthy and just human relationship, peaceful coexistence, mutual cooperation amongst states and the peoples in the world through such means and thereby constitute a veritable and triable contribution to the methods of tackling terrorism which is worrying the world today.

REFERENCES

1. The Concise Oxford Dictionary, 4th Edition, Oxford, 1952, Revised by McIntosh at the Clarendon Press, England.
   Also"A terrorist is a member of clandestine or expatriate organisation aiming to coerce and establish the government by acts of violence or terrorism against its innocent subjects". According to the Oxford Dictionary as specified by Lt. Gen. V.M. Patil in his paper on "Changing Face of Violent Conflicts", "*Journal of the Institute of Human Rights*", Jaripatka, Nagpur, Vol. 5, No.1, June, 2002, (p. 95), Editor Dr. P. L. Joshi.
   *Also*According to *Mitakshara* 2/21—One who sets on fire anything arbitrarily, one who administers poison, one who attacks with a weapon, one who forcibly occupies land and one who abducts anybody's wife are the terrorists.
   Whether a person is your teacher or a child or an old man or an erudite brahmin, anybody who is a terrorist has to be killed.
   According to *Manusmriti* there is no sin in killing terrorists (9/278)
2. Wing Commander R.N. Parasnis (Retired) in "Rooting out Terrorism", p.111 (A paper), *Ibid.*
3. "The Muslim invasions were not undertaken merely out of the lust for loot or conquest. There was another object behind them .....But there is no doubt that striking a blow at the idolatary and polytheism of Hindus and establishing Islam in India was also one of the aims of the expedition." (Of Mohammad Bin Quassim in 711 A.D.) Dr. B.R. Ambedkar in "*Thoughts on Pakistan*", p. 49, Thakur Co., Bombay,1941.
4. Arnest Baker in "The Crusader" (A paper), pp. 40-76 in "Legacy of Islam" edited by late Sir Thomas Arnold and Alfred Guillaume, Oxford University Press, London, 1931.

5. (i) Jesus said to him (Thomas) "I am the way or the truth, and the life. No one comes to the Father except through me". (John 14/6) (p. 1093).

   (ii) "Nor is there salvation in any other. For there is no other name under heaven given among men by which we must be saved". (Acts 4/12) (p.1108) (M. *Holy Bible*—The New King James version, Thomas Nelson Publishers, Nashville, Canden, New York,1980) Printed in India by Thomas Press.

6. (i) Cp. "But they who disbelieve, and deny our revelation, such are rightful owners of the Fire. They will abide therein".

   (ii) "Lo ! Those who disbelieve and die while they are disbelievers, on them is the curse of *Allah* and of Angels of men combined." (*Qur'an* 2/161) (Translated by Pickthall—Published by Muslim Reform Society, Rampur (UP), 1970.

7. "Fight against those who disbelieve in *Allah*, make holy war, do not embezzle the spirits". (*Sahih Muslim*, No. 4294) (Q.F. "*Jehad*—The Islamic doctrine of permanent war" By Suhas Mujumdar, *Voice of India*, New Delhi, 1994, p. 31.

   Also

   Refer Sayyad Qutb (of Egypt) "In Islam lawful *Jihad* is only one and that is to continue war till the entire world accepts the supremacy of the *Allah*."

   (Q.F. : "*Muslim Manacha Shodha*" by Sheshrao More, p.392), 127 Vivek Nagar, Nanded.

8. *The Holy Bible*—Old Testament "Deuteronomy" (20/10) (Revised standard Version, Catholic edition—Catholic Trust Society, Publishers of the Holysee, 1966, p.170).

9. Cp—William James in *Varieties of Religious Experience,* Collins Fountain Books, 1977, (p.283).

10. C.G. Raghwan in "Terrorism and Human Rights—An Overview" (A paper) in "*Journal of the Institute of Human Rights*". June, 2002, Jaripatka, Nagpur, Editor P.L. Joshi.

11. P.M. Kamath in "India's War Against Terrorism : Issues, Challenges and Enduring Strategy", p. 34. *Ibid.*

12. M.K. Gandhi in *Socialism of My Conception*, Edited and Published by Anand T. Hingorani, Bhartiya Vidya Bhawan, 1957, pp. 148-149.

13. "Only truthful non-violent and pure hearted socialists will be able to establish a socialistic society in India and the world. To my knowledge there is no country in the world which is purely socialistic." (*Ibid.*, p.3)

14. *Ahimsa—Vichar Aur Vyavahara,* Vinoba Bhave, Gram Bhavana Prakashan Tatha Gandhi Shanti Pratishthan, First Edition, September, 1970, pp. 8-9.
15. *Socialism of My Conception*, M.K. Gandhi, p. 2, (footnotes).
16. Q.F. : *The Principles of Modern Political Science* by J.C. Johari, Sterling Publications Pvt. Ltd., First Edition 1989, New Delhi, p. 822.
17. "Gandhi condemned terrorism and questioned the doctrine that it can ever lead to achievement of any worthwhile goal. Terrorism is counter-productive and self-destructive. In the Gandhian framework, neither terrorism nor nuclear deterrence has any place. To Gandhi, even the exceptions to non-violence have to be non-violently arrived at. Volitional violence diminishes man. On the other hand non-violence in practice helps the limited individual to extend its limit itself and break down walls between the self and others to be the basis of group actions, human system and international institutions." (J.D. Sethi in "*Gandhian Values and Twentieth Century Challenges*", Patel Memorial Lectures, Publication Division, Ministry of Information and Broadcasting, Government of India, 1994, p. 46).
18. "Ahimsa – *Vichar Aur Vyavahara*", Vinoba Bhave, Gram Bhavana Prakashan Tatha Gandhi Shanti Pratishthan, First Edition, September, 1970, p. 211.
19. In *Mahatma Gandhi* P. 81, Q.F.: *Principles of Modern Political Science* by J.C. Johari, p. 819.
20. In a paper "The Tradition of Non-violence and its Underlying Forces" in the book, "*Gandhi – His Relevance for Our Times*", Editors G. Ramchandran and T.K. Mahadevan, Publishers Gandhi Peace Foundation, New Delhi, Second Edition, 1967. "My Final Conversation with Gandhi was in Calcutta in August, 1947 when riots raged between Hindus and Muslims, and the Hindu now in authority, being the aggressors.

    I raised the question of the efficacy of the non-violent technique in group relations. He declared that on the subject he was at the moment in darkness. He had spent almost a lifetime teaching that non-violence was a weapon not of the weak, but of the strong, or those who are able to strike back, but will not. He realised then that his people do not understand. This is one of the most difficult aspects of non-violence to fathom and accept and the explanation for violence to fathom and accept and the explanation for the failure of so many efforts in its name"(p.18).

21. J.D. Sethi in *Gandhian Values and Twentieth Century Challenges*, pp. 45-46.
22. J.B. Kriplani in "Gandhian Approach to World Peace". Q.F. *Principles of Modern Political Science*, By J.C. Johari, p. 243.
23. Ref: Introduction by Shri Mahadeo Haribhai Desai, to *Hind-Swaraj* (New Edition) by M.K. Gandhi, Navjeevan Trust,1949, Ahmedabad Translated by Amrutlal Thakurdas Nanawati pp.19-20.
24. In *Principles of Modern Political Science*, p. 814.
25. M.K. Gandhi in "*Communal Unity*" (p. 850) (*Harijan* : dated 16/11/1947), Navjeevan Publishing House, Ahmedabad.

7

Social Justice : A Vedic Perspective

Sashi Prabha Kumar

Social justice is relatively a new concept in the field of socio-political philosophy. The term first appeared in political debate in the early nineteenth century. It was employed, among others by John Stuart Mill and its use has since become widespread.[1] This caption emphasises on justice and justice is the first virtue of social institutions.[2] A just society is a more or less self-sufficient association of well ordered individuals who have disparate aims and aptitudes, but the shared conception of justice establishes a bond of civic friendship amongst them. The principle of social justice provides a solid foundation for social structure, it tries to establish that basically all human beings are equal and there should be no discrimination amongst them on the basis of religion, caste, colour and creed.[3] In other words, social justice is based on social equality, i.e., it envisages that no section of the society should be debarred from its fundamental rights and everybody must get ample opportunities for the development of his personality. It is an accepted fact that inequalities are inevitable in the basic structure of any society, but for a mutually cooperative and balanced society, the principle of social justice is very relevant. It does not mean that there will be no disparities at all or the persons of higher capabilities should be degraded from their positions, but that all efforts must be made to upgrade those who are weaker and less privileged than others.[4] In this respect, social justice demands social security also.[5] It means that social structure should be such in which every member gets a fair share according to his capabilities and necessities and none is deprived of basic living facilities. This is the ideal of society laid and depicted in the Vedas. Hence an attempt has been made here to present a brief account of social justice in the Vedic perspective.

Vedas are the oldest source books of Indian culture. The ancient moral, spiritual as well as social norms of life are rooted in them. Vedas inculcate the ethics of collective living through mutual love and promote social harmony by upholding social virtues like fidelity and friendship.The justice of a social scheme depends essentially on how the imposed inequalities are minimised and the optimum economic and social conditions are created for the various sections of the society. From this point of view we can study three aspects of social justice in the Vedic perspective namely. Gender Equality, Class equality and Economic equality, since these are the three main parameters of social justice.

The equality between man and woman is the cornerstone of social justice and the Vedas distinguish themselves from all other Indian literature by the high regard in which they hold woman. It will, therefore, be very interesting and useful to look at the glorious status which a woman was accorded in the Vedic society. "What they call a wife is the half of a man", this assertion of the *Shatapatha Brahmana*[6] atonce states categorically the rights and role of a woman in the life of society. The Vedic people never underrated her capacities and wants for ever imputed religious disability to her. On the other hand, there are references to show that a person who did not marry was considered to be incompetent to perform a sacrifice.[7] The Vedic word *pathi*[8] itself connotes a sense of equality and justice which are due to a woman. In the, Vedic age there is ample evidence to show that woman not only studied the Vedas, but also figured among the authors of Vedic hymns.[9] According to the *Taittisiya* and *Shatapatha Brahmanas*, a woman was required to be initiated along with the man, before the start of a sacrifice. The *Rig Veda* describes man and wife performing equal and selfsame functions in the sacrifice.[10] Sacrifice was the most important affair of the Vedic family and in that the woman had been accorded a dignified and equal position with the men. There is no doubt that they were equally regarded in the routine and normal conduct of everyday life. The *Rig Veda* in fact considers wife as the very essence of household.[11] The honourable position of the woman in the Vedic society has been described in the *Brihad Aranyaka Upanishad* which survives as a pattern of ideal womanhood even to this day.[12] It was the conviction of Vedic sages that life becomes perfect whole with the joining together of two complementaries. This can be very well gathered from the exemplary attitude of the Vedic people how they regarded and adored woman as an equal half in all the functions of life. Even in the *Sutra* period the position of woman was of reverence and respect.[13]

Class Equality

Social justice demands that the different classes of society should be treated equally and there should be no discrimination between man and man on the basis of class or caste. Believing in the united collective life, the Vedas uphold the comprehensive view of society. It can be clearly inferred from various Vedic expressions that there was no classes and castes: the whole Vedic society was a classless one (Besides the same amount of views prescribed for each, irrespective of sex, testifies to the classless society during this period).[14] In the tenth *mandala* of the *Rigveda*, a well integrated concept of society is given by splitting up the common people in to two groups, (a) the *Vaishya* i.e., the farmer and the trader; (b) the *shudra,* i.e., labourer. It is said that the Brahmana, Kshatriya, Vaishya and Shudra are respectively the head, arms, thighs and feet of the body of *Purusha*—the supreme being, who sacrificed himself (i.e., his absoluteness) in order to be manifested through creation in nature and in the society of men.[15] This social concept is the basis of justice and it has two implications—one, that four main functions must be performed by a society in order that it may survive in the struggle for spiritual, political and economic existence, another that each of the four functionaries has a divinity about him (being a manifestation of *purusha*) and the functions are equally sacred. The *Brihadaranyaka Upanishad* explaining this four fold Vedic division of society says that these functions can be successfully performed when all the four are performed side by side and in accordance with *dharma*, i.e., social justice.[16] Thus, according to the Vedic concept, no society can survive in the struggle for existence unless it organises four types of work. A society without the Brahmana would be as bad as one without the Ksatriya or without the Vaishya or without the Shudra. But it should be noted that this Vedic idea of functional cooperation is different from that of the federation of tribal and occupational groups of later ages known as the caste system. It took a long time before this social division of labour hardened into hereditary caste, not only through the multiplication of functions, but also through the accession of various tribal and racial units into the society. The strength of the Vedic society, however, lay in the differentiation of functions without dividing the people into exclusive social groups.[17] It was in the scientific and balanced arrangement of these different occupations and trades as well as their thoughtful distribution in the different sections of the society that the whole idea of justice evolved so that the most effective and fruitful results of common welfare were enjoyed by all without any conflict. It is also worth mentioning here that in later times there developed the theory, opposed to the *Veda*, that the Shudra is the servant of other classes. But the *Veda* does not say so. It recognises the dignity of manual work skilfully done by the Shudra Describing the work in the corn field the *Veda* speaks of the field labourer as *Kavi* or the creative worker. Similarly, the chariot maker has been described as a '*Manishin*' or 'wise man', another term for the Vedic seer.[18] The *Atharva Veda* invokes the deity presiding over harvest gathering and associated him with Shudra labourers by saying that "He dwells in the homes of those who do not sacrifice".[19] The Vaishya-merchant seeks splendour like the spiritual and the kingly man by pursuing his own vocation, "the winning of wealth through wealth",[20] Another *Yajurvedic* prayer shows an equal attitude to all four types of workers.[21] There came to be developed a theory in *Puranic* times, that the Shudra cannot be permitted to hear the *Veda*. But in *Vedas* it is made only too clear that the *Veda* was preached to one and all and in the list of social groups the Shudra was sometimes mentioned before the Vaishya., e.g., in So may, I speak the sacred word to the masses of the people to the Brahmana and the Rajanya (Kshatriya) to the Shudra and the Vaishya, to our own men and to the stranger.[22] In the Vedic society, the basic occupations and resources of life were agriculture, plough culture was already a serious social concern in the *Rigvedic age*.[23] This country, India, even in the fag end of the twentieth century remains to be primarily dependent on the cultivation of the soil. Complementary to agriculture, cattle breeding, with special attention to cow and her progeny was an engaging occupation of the Vedic people. Besides these, there are more than sixty expressly named professions which enumerate the diverse callings of the society. Various are the thoughts and diverse the callings of man, the carpenter seeks what's broken; the physician, the diseased; the priest some profession.[24] But the more important aspect of Vedic society is that the men of all professions had the same status, more or less. It is a well recognised fact that in the Vedic society there has never been any competition or strife between the different classes in the matter of their professions. Among various other profession of the *Rigvedic* period may be mentioned those of the tanner (*Charmamna*).[25] the Barber (*vaptri*)[26] and to women are ascribed sewing the plaiting of mats from grass and reeds and the weaving of cloth. What is noteworthy in this connection is that those who practised these arts were not in any way regarded as inferior members of the community in the Vedic society.[27] A poet of the *Rig Veda* very frankly says, "I am a poet, dad is a physician, my mother throws the corn upon the grinding stones, having various occupations and desiring riches we remain (in the world) like cattle (in the stalls)".[28] Rare description expressly shows that in the Vedic society, each member of the family had freedom to choose his vocation according to his aptitude and that is possible only when there is an atmosphere of social justice prevalent in the period. Elsewhere it is said in the *Rigveda* that variety is the natural form of society—two hands are alike but their work is not alike, two sister cows do not give milk alike, of two twins the powers are not similar and two kinsmen are not equally pleasing.[29]

Economic Equality

A social structure, if it is said to be just and conducive to the general welfare, must depend on a very sound and solid foundation of social economics. This economic foundation must be completed without any seeds of conflict between the different classes constituting the community: The Vedic seers, who were great social philosophers gave a very serious thought to the basic principles which contributed to the evolution of an unshakable structure of social justice. There is whole hymn in the tenth *mandala* of the *Rig Veda* which is titled support the needy, where it is said that he is not a friend who does not give to a friend, to a comrade, who comes imploring for food, let the rich man satisfy one who seeks help and let him took upon a larger pathway, wealth revolves like the wheels of a chariot, coming now to one now to another, he does not cherish a comrade or a friend. He is all sin who eats alone.[30] The plain implication of these words is that it was considered to be the duty of every citizen to see that all members of the society were fed as well as himself. The Vedas have declared that whatever a man partakes after feeding his fellow beings is *amrita*, which makes him immortal, but what he eats alone, without sharing, is a sin or poison which kills him.

Administration of Social Justice

It is also worth mentioning that the head of the state, namely the king, was considered to be the protector of social justice. In *Rig Veda* he has been called the protector of the society.[31] In "the ideal of protection of social justice", emphasis was not merely on the physical protection from some external aggression but mainly on the maintenance of social order between different professions and vocations of classes and communities. This was considered to be one of the primary functions of the kind, namely the maintenance of social equilibrium.[32] The *Atharva Veda* clearly says, "O king! You are sitting in such a high place of authority that we want you to distribute the wealth equally and impartially amongst your subjects".[33] In another place the king is assured that all the gods and deities will back him if he performed with devotion and determination his function of right distribution of wealth among his subjects.[34] This is enough to indicate how high was the sense of equity and impartiality in the minds of the Vedic philosophers and kings who gave the lead to the nation. That famous verse in the *Chhandogya Upanishad* also has bearing upon the economic conditions of the society where the king Amvapati declares that there were "no thieves in his kingdom, no misers, nor any beggars."[35]

Even in the later Vedic tradition of the *Smritis,* the king was deemed to be the foundation of justice. Manu personifies the administration of justice as *Dharma* incarnate, by representing that when justice is administered the dart of *adharma* or falsehood by which *dharma* is pierced is taken out from the body of the *dharma.*[36] Yajnavalkya declares that the impartial administration yields the same rewards as solemn Vedic sacrifices do.[37] The kings court of justice was called *dharmasthana, dharmasna* or *dharmadhikarana.*[38] This clearly shows the high sense of justice prevalent in the Vedic society.

It is clear from the above that the Vedas represent a fair picture not only of social justice but also of social integrity and cosmic harmony. The idea of justice or *dharma* took the place of very ancient conception of *Rita.*[39] In the *Rig Veda, Rita* denotes the supreme transcendental law of the cosmic order by which the universe and even the gods are governed and which as ultimately connected with sacrifice.[40] This idea of cosmic harmony envisages a equilibrium not only amongst men, but amongst all elements of cosmos.

In fact the Vedic concept of society is very characteristic and much higher than the so called social justice of today which is mere lip-service of some politically motivated, selfish persons. The *Veda* believes in a mutually cooperative, integrated, harmonious society. The Vedic prayers are not for individual happiness, but for the collective well-being of the society. In a Vedic prayer five things are wanted for the society (a) That there should be active pursuit of knowledge and spiritual interests, (b) that the society should be ruled and defended in accordance with *Pita* or *Dharma*, (c) that the people should be well nourished and strengthened, and (d) that aggression should be effectively resisted. Even today this will appear to be a fairly complete view of social life if we compare this Vedic view with the socialist objectives of modern political theory.[41] The famous *Samanvaya* hymn of the *Rig Veda* gives the secret of united social life.[42] It states that the integration of aims and of emotional as well as the intellectual interests leads to a well integrated social life.[43]

Hence, it may be concluded that although there is no clear term like 'social justice' used in the Vedic literature yet we find an ideal and inspiring concept of a just society where everybody is free for his own upliftment but complementary to others, there is equality among all human beings and welfare of the whole mankind is prayed for. There seems to be no place for unequalities and disparities in the Vedic society: in fact it presents a harmonious homogenized and unified view of life not only for all the human beings but also for the whole world. To sum it up, it may be said that the Vedic philosophy does not advocate social justice but social concord which is much more meaningful and essential for the development of the society.

REFERENCES

1. Miller, David. *The Blackwell Encyclopaedia of Political Thought*, New York, 1987, p. 26.
2. Rawl. Jolm. *A Theory of Justice*, Oxford, 1972, p. 3.
3. *Encyclopaedia of Social Science*, Vol. XV, pp. 131-133.
4. Foerg Joel. *Social Philosophy*, p. 99.
5. *Encyclopaedia Britannica* (1855 Edition), Vol. XX, p. 893.

6. '*Ardho ha va esa almano yat jaya*', *Shatapatha Brahmana,* 5.2.1.10.
7. '*Ardho ha va esa ye apatnikah*'. *Ibid.*, 3.3.3.1
8. Ashtadhyayi, Panini, 4.11.3.
9. *Great Women of India*, Advaita Ashrama, 1983, p. 26.
10. *Rigveda*, 8.37.8.
11. *Ibid.*, 3.53.4.
12. *Brihadaranyaka Upanishad*, 1.1.3.
13. Mitra. Priti. *Life and Society in the Vedic Age*. Calcutta. 1966. p. 69
14. Chakrabarty. Haripada. *Socio Economic life of India in the Vedic Period.* Calcutta 1986, p. 1.
15. *Rigveda.* 10.90.12.
16. *Brihadaranyakya Upanishad*, 1.4.11-14.
17. Bose. Abinash Chandra, *Hymns from the Vedic*. Delhi. 1966. p. 47.
18. *Atharva Veda*, 3.17.1.3.5.6.
19. *Ibid.*, 3.21.2.
20. *Ibid.*, 3.15.
21. Yajurveda, 18.18.
22. *Ibid.*, 26.2.
23. Ghurya. G.S., *Vedic India*, Bombay, 1979. p. 226.
24. *Rigveda.* 9.112.1.
25. *Ibid.*, 8.5.38. *Yajurveda.* 30.15.
26. *Ibid.*, 10.142.4. *Atharvaveda.* 8.2.7.
27. Bhargava, P.L. *Indian in the Vedic Age*, Lucknow, 1971, p. 253.
28. *Rigveda*, 9.112.3.
29. *Ibid.*, 10.117.9.
30. *Ibid.*, 10.117.4-6.
31. *Ibid.*, 1.25.10. 54.7.7.30.1. *Yajurveda*, 20.17.
32. Hardas. Balshastri and Apte. S.S., *Glimpses of the Vedic Nation* Madras, 1967, p. 617.
33. *Atharvaveda*, 3.4.2.
34. *Ibid.*, 3.4.4.
35. *Chhandogya Upanishad*, 5.11.5.
36. *Manusmriti*, 7.12.14.
37. *Yajvavalkyasmriti*. I. 359-360.
38. *Naradasmriti*, 1.34.
39. Kane, P.V., *History of Dharmashastra*, Vol. III. p. 245.
40. *Rigveda*, 1.68.2, 1.105.12, 1.136.2. 142.7. 1.164.11, 2.28.4, 4.23.8-10.
41. Ebenstein William, *Great Political Thinkers*, Oxford, 1969, p. 77.
42. Rigveda, 10.191.2.
43. *Ibid.*, 10.191.4.

8

Secularism : An Imperative for Indian Society

S.A. Shaida

One of the controversial themes in Indian polity is that of secularism, We not only debate what secularism means, but also whether this is the best form of our society and state. Of course, the former is done explicitly, but the latter is done surreptitiously. Publicly, of course, not many take an anti-secular stance as openly as some would like them to do. Instead of publicly decrying secularism, some people express their reservation by equating it with atheism while others have coined and use the pejorative term 'pseudo-secular' to downgrade many of those beliefs and tenets which are essential for the secular policy of Indian society. Recent happenings have clearly shown that there is great urgency to understand and appreciate what is secularism and if there are several forms and senses of secularism, what form of secularism will suit our conditions. Majority of our people share the view that for peace, progress and development of the nation in socio-economic field, secularism is the only available way of life which most appropriately suits the Indian character.

In a country like India, with its beautiful mosaic of multi-cultural, multi-religious and multi-linguistic – people, the secular character of the state is inevitable. And above all, a democratic set-up in modern Indian society cannot function smoothly without, being founded on secular principles.

But first of all let us briefly see, what does secularism and how best it can be interpreted to be in conformity with genius of the Indian people. Lest I may not be misunderstood prescribing any specific or new meaning of secularism, I would only make an attempt to mention various available meanings of secularism and would present one or a combination of several of these which come closest to what we have been practicing and what founding fathers of our Constitution had in mind when they drew the blue-print of the constitutional framework.

It is often argued that secularism is a western notion—a product of post-renaissance and post-Industrial Revolution in European culture which found it necessary to separate the Church from the state. This is also a guiding principle in the U.S. since most of these events never occurred in India or they did not occur the way they did in Europe, it is an illegitimate grafting of alien notion in the climes of Indian polity which would never take its roots on Indian soil. Hence, many of us who swear by *swadeshi* values and attitudes think it to be a futile exercise. Sometimes it is mistakenly argued that secular society and secular state can be established in those places where religion has lost the battle against atheism and only a godless people have to fall on secular ideology. India, on the contrary, maintains great regard and respect for religion which governs important aspects of our life. Therefore, for some it runs contrary to our way of life. Besides, secularism also implies polity, morals and education must be independent of any religious beliefs or divine sanctions. There are other views as well, which indeed make 'secularism' a fuzzy notion. This makes it imperative to seek greater clarification.

The original meaning of the word 'secular' has indeed the sense of being this—worldly, temporal or profane as contradistinguished from divine, sacred or other-worldly. But unless its operative field is delineated, it can be misunderstood for plain and simple atheism which it has never meant even in Western hemisphere. The plea to separate the Church from the state was only aimed at keeping their respective domains mutually non-interfering. Nowhere it was meant that people should give up Church or harbour disbelief in their religion. (I am of course referring to the western capitalist society and not to the communist countries. Present day commonwealth of Independent States of the erstwhile Soviet Union is also largely heading towards some such state though it is far too complicated and it would be premature to put them, in any particular category). What was advocated is that a secular state should have no official religion and the state policies should show no bias for or against any religion. Thus, a complete separation between politics and religion was stressed. But since politics manifest social aspirations and values, it was also assumed that secularism, like modernization would also percolate through our social activity. In the West, all attempts at modernization of society was mostly seen as its secularization. (However, it should be kept distinct form 'dereligionization'). It was an attempt to move the society away from traditional values and to goad it towards impersonal and utilitarian values. The epitome of such a venture was seen in acquiring scientific knowledge with a view to promote technological development. This may be seen as a corollary of the rise and development of the capitalist society. In the west it led to the fragmentation of the social institutions. Society was denuded of the cohesiveness which pre-modern institutions and values could offer.

Now turning to India, what we find is that till 1976, the need to formally declare India as a secular state was not felt though many of the acts and provisions of our constitution did favour a secular approach. The forty-second amendment to the Constitution included the word 'secular' before 'democratic republic". Apart from any other political gain which might have been intended, it was only a formal declaration of what was already in practice. The Indian brand of secularism has or can have some of the features stated above but above all it is equality (and I will add 'respect') of all religions—*sarva dharma samabhava*—coupled with the express policy that state would have no religion. The operative definition of secularism may of course find some deviations in practice but these are either out of personal beliefs or out of political expediency. The point concerning the separation of the state from the Church has never been so crucial in our country as from early days the Church never interfered with the state in any significant manner. Of course, there have been examples where some archaic or parochial social practices and prejudices sanctified by religion have been encouraged by state but these have been limited to a few social practices. On the whole there has been a secular approach in inter-religious matters. Most of the Muslim rulers and the British government also maintained a secular stance in most of their legal and political decisions.

In the post-independence era the need to adopt secularism as state policy became more pressing for various reasons. The more important being the need to evolve and develop the awareness that all citizens irrespective of their caste, creed, religion and language are equal and together they enjoy all the freedoms guaranteed by the Constitution. In a vast country with world's second largest population and with many castes, communities, religions and languages the state has immense responsibility to foster secularism and democracy. As long as secularism is not confused with atheism, it may not sound paradoxical to assert that greater the religiosity of the people, greater is the need to promote and inculcate secular values. If religious beliefs govern many departments of our day to day life, there is always the risk of our polity being infected with particular religious biases. What is required is the proper understanding of the universal and humanistic values of all religions with the realization that our religious differences need not be condemned but sympathetically understood and appreciated. But at the same time it should be seen that such differences remain confined to our private life and are not allowed to influence state policies. Education was and still remains the most potent instrument of creating the right kind of approach by secularising the text books and other reading materials meant for school-going children. But the government failed in its task of maintaining strict vigil in this regard. Some state governments deliberately participated in communalising the reading materials in order to misguide and misinform the too impressionable boys and girls who, with their natural innocence and credulity, absorbed the untruths or half-truths propogated for vested political interests. Such an attempt may appear to be profitable from a narrow point of view but in the final analysis it is not only an intellectual sin but also very damaging for our future generations. History of a people becomes a universal legacy which is always subjected to objective scrutiny. That travellers like Al Beiruni, Ibn-Batuta or Fa Hein came to India and have left precious accounts of India of their times shows universal interest of historians in other peoples' culture and their way of life. Our deliberate distortions of historical facts will in future be evaluated against many other parallel accounts provided by world historians and our future generations will be put to shame when they would discover that they have been fed with untruths or distorted versions about their own past. At least all those who would have regard for truth and objectivity would live under the shadow of guilt and remorse like the people of Argos in Sartre's Flies. Truth may not always be victorious or prevail, but it can never be totally suppressed. A sound education on secular lines is our greatest hope for the unity and integrity of the nation in spite of the fact that our educational enterprise so far has also bred prejudices and misunderstandings. It is an unfortunate thing that in the drive against secularism the educated greatly outnumber the uneducated and even the illiterates. The point can be illustrated by the fact that till recently communal harmony and amity have not left our soul. By 'our soul' I mean our village people who constitute 80 per cent of our population. Anti-secularism and communalism have been predominantly urban phenomena while in most of the villages people accepted with due regard those of other faith notwithstanding the awareness of their mutual differences. It may look an over simplification to hold that the virus of communalism or anti-secularism has infected the urban population simply because wrong sort of education has been provided to them. Large scale movement from villages to the city, sub-human living conditions in the slums, loss of identity and a sense of ennui born of being uprooted from traditional values, the sharp difference between haves and have-nots and many other sociological factors create an explosive situation which a political match stick: easily ignites. Hence, the need for a sensible socio-economic policy is inevitable to make democracy and secularism a viable policy for social organisation. A sound educational programme will still be a very important component of such a drive. Coupled with this we need a sound secular ethics within a comprehensive utilitarian framework: embodying the notions of justice: fraternity and equality. The greatest responsibility for working towards social cohesiveness and understanding lies with our political leaders who exert tremendous influence on public but unfortunately most of our politicians have selected this profession as a last resort and are only governed by the sole objective of coming to power by whatever means it is possible. And the easiest ways that they have chosen are criminalization and communalization of politics. Gandhiji's concern for the purity and rightness of means has been completely banished from any consideration of what they ought to do. Their 'ought' has lost all its association with moral considerations.

To conclude, I will once again assert that if we want to maintain the democratic set-up with the ideals of universal justice and equality enshrined as guiding principles, a country like India has no other choice except to develop secular values and attitudes in social and political action.

9

Secularism and Contemporary India

Dharmendra Goel

Introduction

I shall present in this chapter "Secularism and Contemporary India" some consideration for discussion which, according to my mind are both important and interesting for both clear understanding of the contemporary Indian life and society, as well as, profitable for articulating a feasible and satisfactory perspective for (a) avoiding total bigotry, communalism and attendant political mess that they have caused to our polity all through the twentieth century; (b) to sort out the correct relation between relevant modernization and its scientific ideology viable without plural and somewhat compulsive stereotypes of mutually incompatible traditions; and (c) some issues relative to the place of spirit and transcendence of man in the context of dominant technocratic economism of western industrial cultural nemesis today, engulfing us also willy-nilly. I shall also attempt to formulate my own reflections of what could be a rational feasible policy for our times. I hope our discussion would sharpen it. On my own, of course, I have been reflecting and thinking for last many years on some of these ideas and have published them, on several occasions, earlier, I on some of these lines.

With my decidedly very limited capacities, but I assure the reader one thing, i.e., my genuine sincerity and utmost. concern for making a minuscule humble participation in modernizing process of my people. I also observe that the time and occasion for this discussion is most opportune and could not have been delayed any longer without serious damage to already thin reputation of our academic community's colossal apathy in the context of this deep crisis that the entire sub-continent faces in India, Bangladesh. Pakistan and Sri Lanka waves of revivalistic bigoted fundamentalism coupled with suicidal cultural chauvinism of Kin, Kindred and Sect. These need to be eliminated to liberate this sorry mankind from the curse of its past. Let me straight forwardly summarize the imbroglio that our twentieth century poses for most of traditional societies first. We know for a fact that there are very many serious gaps and disparities in wealth, knowledge and civilization and technology skills amongst different social formations around the globe. We are no less unequal among our world community, today, than probably we were in more rude and unenlightened ages of the past. Yet, we are witness to several destabilizing revolutions, I mean those of transport, media and modern technology of mass annihilation that force our contemporary world into a collapsing neighbourhood of ever escalating danger of mass conflict and its horrendous consequences. Here our knowledge of what some people elsewhere have cornered for themselves, and the knowledge that no amount of sentimental piety on their part is ever likely to offer equality to the wretched of this world causes deepest 'scars' of bitter suspicion, rancour and hatred. To know all this is centainly not today to excuse all.

In this volatile environment of supicion and fear, insecurity and hatred, this new information and media innovations are providing equal wind to passions for wild revanchism and arousing burning ambitions in the hearts and minds of those who are being made to see all others only as their exploiters and oppressors. Violence, is now legitimized, ever more.

We witness globally; at present, a state of confrontation between states, races, nations. having inter-societal inequities and in every complex society some intra-societal alienation, as well to some extent latter being reinforced by the former. What is true of the globe as a whole that is sudden realization of inequities, and consequent distempers amongst simultaneous but certainly non-contemporary cultures, today. We, in our own sub-continental society are progressively and inevitably experiencing this family of confrontations increasing with the advent of being forced to take note of dispersed and atomized regional, tribal and local communities sitting cheek by jowl unequal but peaceful placidity without mingling or cross-fertilizing with each other for aeons, right close up our ten times, the end of the nineteenth century I maintain further that modern Indian society with its present conflicts and distempers. Therefore, is the creation of colonial domination and other innovations followed by wilful attempts of modernizers to get hurriedly on to the band-wagon of industrialization, democracy and socialism in last few decades, after decolonisation. The situation roundabout, now is fairly disturbing and bleak but it calls for utmost clarity and freedom from cant to get a clear perspective over it in the first instance, before one suggests any policy prescriptions for remedial inventions.

Before I proceed in my discussion at this stage, I propose to make a couple of brief clarifications about 'Multi-religious Indian Society' and 'Secularism'.

Let me state that widely believed stereotypes of Hindu, Muslim, Sikh, Christian, Buddhist, Jains and host of atomized tribal animism do not fully articulate the plurality and complexity for religious demography of modern India, diversity of faiths, institutions, rituals and practices and scriptures and churches do not get sorted into the neat categories of being a Hindu, a Buddhist, or a Muslim. No doubt in the last few generations after British consolidation of their imperial authority different local communities for purpose of constitutional bargaining delivered themselves to such rubrics and the sorry political culture of last two generations is the consequence of such earlier sectarian mobilization of population which, according to that great student of Man's History Karl Marx, was atomized living out in Autark villages rutted to primitive and stagnant Asiatic mode of production, sans dynamism (One need not have to agree to all Marx had to say on India or for that matter on anything else to appreciate this historical insight). I only insist that we note that two-way of myths and rituals from the macrotraditions to local tribal cultures and local tribal gods being metamorphosed into universal idioms of higher religions (This is true of every variety of Hindu sects tribal religions. Islam and Christianity besides other religions like Buddhism, Sikhism or Jainism). But it could never make a militant church like one of medieval Europe.

Till the arrival of communal politics of Twentieth Century the multi-religious communities of India, except at the elite level of feudal power was placid and tolerant of each other's faith as far as the common people were concerned. True, Indian society was never egalitarian. Yet even under the period of Sultanate and the period of imperial Mughals common categories of conflict were not religious crusades for some Muslims Pathans did side with Rajputs against Babur and some Rajputs fought against both Maharana Pratap and Shivaji for Aurangzeb. In that sense Indian Society had generally been secular in as much as it has, if not in word and ideology; at least in actual practice separated spheres of state and that of the church. Earlier, that the event of Islam and temporal authority of the rulers never interfered with the autonomous tidings of spiritual and religious experiments, made in the sub-continent. Indeed, when a particular transition would establish itself amongst the people the rulers would adopt it. Cases of rulers like Bimbisara, Ashoka, Kanishka, Pulkeshin, and Harsh illustrate an immediate change of state, patronage from Vedic to Buddhist and Jainism and subsequent transitions to revived Brahmanical sects of *Vaishnavas* and *Shaivas* and *Shaktas* along with newer cults of occult *Varna-margis* and *Tantras* cutting through the categories of Hindus and Buddhists and others. Much of these practices were also crystallizations of local cults and beliefs that survived. Hindus and Shramanas, Jains contributed to Sanskrit and Pali ideology of Brahmins and the *Shramanas*, later Islamic *Sufis* also joined these. *Anekantavada*, in real sense, emerged out of these encounters, without hatred.

Sarva Dharma Samabhava as advocated in our contemporary

ideology of secularism, refers to our late classical and medieval period of civilization where power, economy and transport and channels of diffusion of information were extremely limited and confined to oral precepts with minimal documentation. Society had no history and lived as it were in a timeless present face to face with myth, legend and real contemporaries. Facts of the present age do not allow this catholic spirit to prevail. We want certainty and quick positively stated instructions for specific private and community decisions which can no longer be left to be open-ended or to settle down slowly by their inherent strength as in leisurely times of medieval India. A Muzahid, A Roshania, A Chistia, A Kalandari, could peacefully come to see the virtues of a Ramanand and a Tulsi, a Gaurang, or a Mira, Kabir and Nanak echoed and reechoed this hoary spirit of ancient wisdom in newly emerging idiom of *Sant-Bani* of their age. A pan-Indian reconstruction of this is to be seen in the land of Nanak in the project of secularism of the *Adi-granth* composed as a lexicon of extent excellence of spirit of those times (of course, I can imagine similar effort among great Tamil Sangam literature and Vaishnavism of Eastern India of birth of this very sensibility of Maharashtra and Gujarat). Now, we must face it, after submergence of the atomized cultures of local and regional varieties forced by military, political and economic conquest as well as domination by the west in eighteenth and nineteenth centuries it is not possible after the end of the colonial epoch to go back to India on the establishment of those three forts - William (Calcutta), George (Bombay), and David (Madras) of East India Company in sixteenth and seventeenth century unless the gains of education, rule of law, contemporary science and modern industrial production are nothing and we wish consciously to revert to the glories of Ruhellas, Khalsa Raj, Maratha Shahi, Nababis, Peshwais and Nizamshahis, Pindaris and Thugee. Howsoever, agonizing it may be, like Dr. Sunyat Sen or later Mao the two makers of China we ought to see without fear of shame that Indian society despite all its creativity in several dimensions of mind such as its great forays in poetry, Philosophy, liberal arts, some architecture, linguistics and mathematics could not standardize its insights for effective defence and trade making either viable mobilization of India's mineral and energy resources or manpower for historical progress. It was because of those persistent and recurring failures that India's recorded history from the times of Alexander's invasion to East India Company's conquest betrays that pathetic flabbiness that led this society to succumb to successive invaders even by handful of upstarts who were joined in easy conscience by ever willing mercenaries locally gathered freebooters. It is one patent sorry tale of collective political disgrace. Modern multi-religious society of twentieth century of India has just one future a secularization of public life. We must advocate it and promote it self-consciously.

In this connection, I wish to offer the following arguments, that there should be liberation from the repetitious cant of India being a classic instance of unity of diversity, composite culture and equal respect for all sects and attendant multiple identities nurse and nourished on such sectarian mentality. What was once valid for the unhurried synods of saints and religious conclaves cannot be true of indigent populations, now, those who are facing diminution of their agricultural lands, denudation of forests, white-slave traffic of their girls. This is the sorry lot of all the disadvantaged poor, *harijan*, tribal and minorities not excluded. In the name of exclusive cultural an religious traditions can we allow discriminatory asperities to be perpetrated and continued by willy operators of cults are orthodoxies. Without in the least trying to obliterate richness of long cultural experience, we must confront ourselves with the question as to what is living in our traditions and what merely, now has become the dead ritual in our heritage, wherein the change, adaptation and rejection is called for consistent with emerging ecology and compulsions of economic political society of Pan-Indian character as against the narrow confines of a tribal face-to-face world even of the elite Brahmins of Nadia, Kanchi or Varanasi. All of India, nay of the some-continent, need to recognize this public reorganization of collective solidarity on the new consciousness of Modern world order which we do not creatively respond to it is threatening to swallow us once again as it did in the wake of breakdown of the Islamic supremacy in the eighteenth century.

Days of Theocratic states are gone. Khomeni or no Khomeni. The great Imam or the Saudi-Wahabis have neither learnt to fraternize with poor Druises, Kurds or Palestinians of the Islamic society nor to discipline their own irresponsible, king, elite, Amirs and Sheikhs to acquire wherewithal of modern civilization which is very different than squandering away their oil royalties in metropolitan ecology of jets and five-star cultural filth of Paris, New York and London.

Second, India and its neighbours are too poor and none else (either U.S. or remnants of dissolved Soviets or China) can either feed them even if someone manages to dominate them by intrigues and religious manipulations of tribals, *harijans* or minorities their credulities and their myths. The answer lies only in self-sustain programmes to meet the revolutions of rising expectation of those young millions who are coming to demand their Rights to have a place under the Sun for the first time in our history.

Let some of us who are no longer so young appreciate these vast rumblings that lie under the deceptive rubrics of tribal revolts (like Naga, Mizo, and Jharkhand) or sectarian and ethnic riots in Kashmir, Punjab and Assam and elsewhere, *Dalit* panthers in Maharashtra and communal and caste riots in U.P., Bihar and elsewhere. All these point out that religions and sectarian identity is only a cloak to mobilize widespread distress, fear and insecurity of the younger people to wrest power from the present rulers, who have trifled with time, flitting about the near-non-development of Indian economic and industrial system. This system is bedevilled by Tokenisms and establishment's several ingratiating collusions with entrenched reactionary vested interests (local, regional, national, multinational), that do not permit either effective mobilization of available resources (both material and human) nor energetically promote creative enrichment of skills, training and organization of surplus manpower till date. The religious, tribal, cultural linkage is being mercilessly exploited by all sorts of sundry elites and their pimps to hoodwink their captive constituents to enable our irresponsible elites to go on playing the unsavoury weird power-games at the cost of those very poor men and women unsuspecting Mundas, Muriya, Nagas, Assamiya, Tripuraris, Tamils and *Harijans*, Sikhs and Muslims. Can enlightened social science develop a secular ideology to counter these games? Secularism., in the twentieth century India, has to rise above the apathetic indolent doctrine of westernized enlightened smugness of the rich class, variety of metropolitan urban educated elite that is based and disengaged with the far from graceful life-styles of ordinary Indian masses. It should not be a mere rehearsal an imitative enterprise of those brilliant phrases or what Russells, Poppers, Shaws, Wells or Laskis have said or not said in London School of Economics or Cambridge or what Lenins have spoken of in the second international to this or that pontiff of Marxism (those unending polemics) or to the sailors in Petrograd on the Mom of Bolshevic revolution? No aping. Howsoever, all or some of these things may have fascinated our colonial psyche. What I am insisting on the recognition of the need for forging in the sub-continent an effective life design for planned reconstruction of life, for the deprived. It must come participatively through making a modern ideologycal it secular humanism of Muslims, Buddhists, *Harijans*, of landless peasants, Women, Tribals Naga, Mizo and others), Sikh or Hindu unemployed young man in Calcutta or Madras and Bombay or Patna and Delhi. Ahmedabad not be excluded, either. It is only such people's secularism, based on appreciation of the down to earth needs of majority of the destitutes that can hope in time to dismiss our present generation of jokers and performing clowns that pass for public servants and spokesmen of communities and pedlars of effete cant of Gandhian, Nehruvian or Marxian vintage in India.

Traditional leadership or tribal and caste lines is reinforced owing to the very restricted exposure and insular communication amongst our Indian disaggregated and atomized oppressed victims, at present, Those of ruling classes along, communicate where convergence of information, skill, power and solidarity of vested privilege has made them resourceful. They often use religious tokens for their pyramidal leadership roles of their respective folks is clear, of course, they hold on other secular modernizing elitist role postures as well among the elect group of our rulers, shamelessly. This sham-modernity of privilege and exploitative secularism has to be unasked and eradicated of its vicious tentacles by a ferment and genuine pedagogy of the oppressed who should be made to see: this perverse ugliness of religiosity and captive. vulnerability of this vast oral segment of India's millions to the dirty tricks of these; ruling cliques. Such a sham version, effective secularism has to eradicate, soonest.

In the final analysis, I do not in the least reject the spiritually creative dimension of human psyche and I cannot abdicate man's quest for values for what perceptive American intellectual, Herhert Marcuse called one dimensional man. I do not think the mind of creative analytic scientific temper and historic humanism. I am suggesting is an appendage to mindless aping of consumerist idiocy of atrophied minds of industrial robots of western capitalism and its unsuspecting consumers. No, it violates human dignity and manipulates their tastes and outlook. Secularization and vulgarization should not be equated, as many traditionalist and obscurantist publicists play on these misidentifications with (and seek to gain legitimacy for themselves) obviously lurid abominations or distempers of alienated gross materialism of industrialized west.

Conclusion: I conclude by reaffirming

1. It is my considered view that we ought to go beyond this inert and ineffective doctrine of *sarva-dharma-samabhava* because it fails to wage a very important struggle against obscurantism and blunts the edge of rational criticism against sheer traditionalism as against nourishing one's being from roots in one's culture.
2. It is important that modem India's commitment to bring justice fair-play and elimination of disparities should reassert its radical and revolutionary edge against the short-

run tactics of political manipulators, who wish to befuddle real progress with holding on to gimmickry using popular morbidities. Much of this perverse caste, cult and tribal chauvinism that appears such inviolable sacred cow for all political activists need to be simply thrown over board by affirming and thereafter bold dissemination of realistic historical interpretation of our contemporary plural society and by being determined to chop off all the dead wood from its ideological kit.

3. Science and humanism can adequately serve as the sheet-anchor for forgoing a practical contemperary rational ideology that would reason and refine pursuit of values without falling back into uncritical received gospels of conventional cults. Finally one need not necessarily go to Marx either.

If all these are agreed to, secularisrn can lead the march of contemporary India to a progressive democratic future.

I have presented a long note on Concept of Tolerance and its Relevance to Contemporary Indian Culture. I.C.P.R. Seminar in March 1983, Madras University.

Besides this, I have reflected on 'Indian Cultural Perspective Contemporary Interpretations of Indian Culture. A note published in *Visva Bharati Journal of Philosophy,* Vol. XIII, No's.1-2, pp. 62-65, the same point has been more fully argued in paper, "The Idea of Tradition" published in *Journal of Medieval Indian Literature*, Panjab University, 1980, pp. 80-81.

I have also reflected on "Rationalism and the Modern Indian Mind", *Radical Humanist*, November, 1972, pp.1-6, New Delhi and "Orthodoxy and Modernization in India" *Radical Humanist*, August, 1975, pp. 47-52.

About spiritualism and mysticism I have reflected in my Quest for Authenticity, pp. 88-93, *Journal of Medieval Literature*, PU, 1982.

A long review of Late Dr. S.N. Ganguly's interesting work "Tradition, Modernity and Development' (MacMillan, 1977) was published in *Philosophy and Social Action*, 1979, pp. 57-60, New Delhi.

10

Terrorism : A Conceptual Analysis

Shiva Nath Prasad

The term "terrorism" comes from the French word *terrorisme*, it is also based on the Latin verb "*terrere*", which literally means, "*to cause any one to tremble*." It dates back to 1795, when it was used to describe the actions of the Jacobean club in their rule of Post-Revolutionary France, the so-called "*Reign of Terror*". The Jacobeans are rumoured to have coined the term "terrorists", to refer to themselves. The English word "terrorism" was popularised in English when it was used by the conservative Edmund Burke, an outspoken opponent of French Revolution in general, as well as, Terror Acts described as '*Jacobean club terrorism*', were causes of arrest or execution of opponents as a means of coercing compliance in the general public.

The exact definition of the word "terrorism" is elusive, and in the book *Political Terrorism: A Research Guide* by Schmid Alex, it has been mentioned that between 1936 and till 1981, as many as 109 definitions had been framed and by the year 2007, i.e., 26 years gap, it is not known how many more definitions would have come into existence, specially, in view of the fast spreading incidence of terrorist activities. In view of a vast array of definitions of the word, it is difficult to collect all the definitions at one place and then assess which definition covers the most important factors, explaining all the aspects of terrorism, so as to come to a most comprehensive definition.

"Due to the term's pejorative connotation, groups that are called "terrorist" by the popular media, typically do not accept that identity for themselves; instead, terms may be used that reflect ideological or ethnic struggle." For example, the terms used in this context are, *freedom fighter, rebel, separatist, liberator, revolutionary, vigilante, military, paramilitary, guerrilla* (Spanish word for "small war"), *Jehadi* ('struggler'), muzahiddeen ("one engaged in holy war") and *fedayeen* ("prepared for martyrdom"). Western media often labels "groups or individuals a "terrorist", when fighting for liberation, and the same people, "statesman" when they succeed in liberating their country. There are two examples of such persons, e.g., Nobel Peace Prize laureate Menachem Begin and Nelson Mandela. The terrorist acts India is facing for a long time from its neighbours, but Pakistani terrorists use the term "freedom fighter" or liberator of Kashmir for themselves and their own brethren on the ground that the Kashmiris are men holding Islamic religion, so the all the Indian Muslims should go with the Pakistan is so that the entire Muslim belt should merge into Pakistan side. There are also in Pakistan, camps which produce '*fedayeen*' or '*muzahiddeen*' in the name of Islam. It is a different sort of proxy-war, as it is called, from what the Indians did to liberate the country from British Rule, in which all people of India, to whichever faith they belonged to, they fought a peaceful war, without matching war machines or guns or arsenals of the other party, the Britishers, the oppressor, by *satyagraha* or silent suffering; so such of the Indian freedom fighters who fought against the British forces to librate their motherland can't be kept in any category except the liberators, liberators by facing tortures without retaliation but silent surrender the way Ganddhi led them.

In 1990, the U.S. Department of Defence framed a workable definition of "terrorism", according to which "terrorism" is "unlawful use (or the threatened use of pre-mediated force or violence against individuals or property (the property either of individuals or civilians or the government) by a group, to coerce or intimidate to achieve Political or Religious or Ideological objectives (social objectives) without express chartered permission of a specific government".

The above definition gives the following ingredients of "terrorism." *Firstly*, the above definition uses the word "unlawful use or threatened use" of force. This expression covers the *method* for all terrorist acts.

Secondly, terrorism is a "*violent act*", forceful act, instead of peaceful act. This violence is the *end-result.*

Thirdly, terrorism is a *pre-mediated* act of violence, which means that it is well thought-out, fully planned act, as against an spontaneous act of retaliation, war for war, guns for guns, slap for slap. This is about the *method or tactic* of terrorist acts.

Fourthly, this definition speaks about the motive of such terrorist acts, the guiding motive is to *coerce* or *intimidate.*

Fifthly, it is directed towards individuals, civilians or the government or even societies. This refers to the target. The targets of the terrorist, is the innocent civilians, who have nothing to do with any other person, but intentional harm is done to innocent persons to create panic in the mind of common man. The motive of terrorist act is also to destroy the government buildings, military installations etc., causing heavy loss to the government.

Sixthly, it is an "*unlawful act*", i.e., it does not find sanctions of the rule or law of the land. So, it is illegal act, acts prohibited by law, and are really violations of government rules, such acts are done without the permission of any competent authority. The intention behind all these is to spread chaos by breaking the law.

Seventhly, it has a fixed target, to destroy or damage individual or government property.

Eighthly, its aims are *Political, Religious* or *Ideological* (social). Whatever may be the other ingredients, this definition, which speaks of the use of the word "*religions*" sounds to be very queer. It does not satisfy anyone that "Religion" can be the cause for any terrorist acts, since it is in the very spirit of the word 'religion' or even its other seemingly synonymous word "*dharma*", 'to bind together' 'Rel + Ligare', or its equivalent Indian word *dharma*, also stands for what can be 'adopted', as something universally accepted principle, "*dhārayati dharmah*" or "*dhāratiti dharmah*";

and its further elaboration is that "*dharma* binds all", if *dharma* is protected, everything is protected, if *dharma* is lost, everything is lost, "*dharma eva hato hanti, dharmo rakshati, rakshitah*", and "*dharma dharayati praja*", *dharma* protects all.

Terrorist and Freedom Fighter

There are the other groups of Marxians, for whom "religion is opium of the people", yet Lenin did not encourage "terrorism" and he said, "Terrorism" is "one form of military struggle essential during certain moments of battle". Lenin and Marx rejected "terrorism" due mainly to the reason that terrorism involves violence. A question may be posed, could the assassination of either Stalin or Hitler be called an act of terrorism, as an attempt to kill, since their not being assassinated might have saved the lives of millions of people. It may not be classed as "terrorism", since in countless examples of struggle for independence, *one person's terrorist was another person's freedom-fighter*. This question immediately leads to the drawing of distinctions between a *freedom fighter* and a "*terrorist*". A freedom fighter struggles for the liberation of his country from foreign domination, oppression, which is not approved by the oppressors. The freedom-fighters are people of their own country, a "terrorist" may not be such person, they are mercenaries also, invariably doing such 'terrorist' acts for earning money, they are hired persons and have nothing to do with anyone's right claims or unrighteous claims.

There is a great difference between a '*freedom fighter*' and "*terrorist*", a freedom fighter is guided by the love of the country, who wants to remove outside interference, to remove tortures of outside agencies, it is guided by love, pity, while "terrorist" has no such aims, they are trained militarily to shower damage to common people or government, with the help of these trained mercenaries. The feeling of indifference to violence is a kind of trained act, trained in such cruel ways, that their sensibilities are totally destroyed, they have no feeling of love or pity; showering atrocity is their main aim, to create panic, chaos and create instability of the government or country. They are trained to be hard-headed, cruel and desperate, ready to kill or be killed any moment, in this sense they are, "suicide squads", "*feedayeen*". There is too much of gravity in freedom fighting for the motherland, or *desh bhakti,* and as it is said in a popular proverb "*dulce et decorum est pro-patria mori*", which means, "it is sweet and glorious to die for one's own country", or in the Hindu proverb "*Janani janma bhumishca svargadapi gariyasi*", i.e., mother and motherland are even higher, loftier than *svarga.* Terrorism is a condemnable act from every point of view, even from humanity's point of view, it is irrational act, a fanatic act without rhyme or reason.

Since terrorism is not a legally approved act, there is *a criminal intent* in all terrorist acts. It involves conflict, or clash of interests and ideologies. There are *two types of conflicts, criminals' conflict and political conflict.* A criminal conflict may arise with individuals, and it may be for psychological or economic reasons, it may start by groups or gangs as organised crime, it may arise also in the clash of interest in dealing with or selling or transporting narcotic drugs for earning money, etc. Political conflict may be initiated by either small groups with or without foreign support, again, political conflict may be initiated by large groups with or without foreign support.

The terrorists are engaged in criminal acts, but *terrorists are not the same as ordinary street criminals.* Ordinarily, street criminals commit any crime. When he/they get any opportunity, they slip away; he/they are non-motivated, self cultured, untrained and are escape-oriented. On the other side, the terrorist's objective is political, they find motivation in some sort of ideology/religious pretexts, they are focussed on a well-concerted aim, they are trained in such of saboteuring acts they face encounter, they are offensive and they do not escape even when an opportunity to escape is available or possible.

Terrorists are divided into *two categories*, so far as the *goals* of terrorism—

(a) *Traditional terrorist* have political and social goals, e.g., (1) gaining independence, (2) getting rid of foreigners,

(3) establishing a new social order, and (4) forcing concessions from governments.

(b) *New Terrorism*— (a) Its goals are non-political, (b) destruction of society, and (c) elimination of large population sections.

Terrorist Organisations are of two types

(1) Utopian Group, and (ii) Apocalyptical groups.

(i) *Utopian Groups* – Its aim is to destroy the existing order, they do not form alliance with the state, they have no political, rational approach or strategy, they endorse no traditional social structure. It is a part of their principle to hold no negotiations, no dialogues, no peace-making.

(ii) *Apocalyptical Group* – Such group of people use collective violence but are indiscriminate. Their firm belief is that they are divinely ordained to commit violent acts and engage in mass casualty and mass catastrophic terrorism, e.g., Al-Qaida, Armed Islamic Group of Algeria. The September 11 attack of World Trade Centre of America, the Al-Qaida moved from Utopian type to Apocalyptical type of terrorism, since WTC was non-military, non-government target, it was sheer attack on innocent human beings and their private economy."

The question may be asked if terrorism is an intentional act of mass-murder? Should terrorism be called only organised crime? There is some difference between the two, and though they are directly related, yet due to the fact of common enemy, they often survive together.

There are *several factors that feed terrorist acts*, they fall mainly under six heads (i) *Ideological,* (ii) *Religious,* (iii) *Nationalistic*-Separatist-Democratic, (iv) *Exotic,* (v) *State Sponsored,* and (vi) *Ethnic*. The 'Ideologistical' factors tops the list since terrorism mainly starts on ideological grounds.

Under the 'Ideological', for example, there are communist countries, there are non-communist countries; the communist countries want the rest of the countries to be converted into communist-fold, as it is said let all the communists unite and set up a whole world of communistic society. The communists are guided by their own ideology of communism, and such people want everyone should follow their ideology for creation of world communism. This is again divided into *Left Wing* and *Right Wing*, otherwise known as capitalistic and communistic terrorism. Deepak Rao and Seema Rao in their book *Terrorism* say "In every communist country there were factions who supported imperialism (by USSR) and other communist factions who wanted independence (Socialists) with right wing ideology. Both committed terrorism against the government."

"Karl Marx and Friedrich Engels (both Germans) were the founder of communism, principle of common ownership but was feudal in nature. Socialists (Socialist democratic conservatives) were supporters of equal rights for all, for independence of countries, but against parliamentary democracy, was an improvement over communism" (pp. 18-19). Left-wing terrorists were "rare intellectuals, communists, fighting for communism, common before World War-II, under support by USSR and China. Important in Europe and America—as they want to overthrow non-communists. "Right-Wing extremists want independence from feudal rule and democracy. More common, (It is) Not very important Europe and America and Governments are not seriously endangered" (p. 19). "Left wing terrorism prevailed after World War-II from 1945 to 1980, and tapered until the breakdown of USSR in 1991.

Violent Extremism/Right Wing Terrorism

Rao says about Right Wing Terrorism as any "Terrorism which does not fit into Left Wing. It is made of disgruntled unemployed frustrated youth, posing no serious threat to the government. Small time crimes, no deadly weapons. Right wing comes in the limelight only when Left Wing petered out. It developed as a reaction to Left Wing Terrorism, as violence on the streets—wanted communism (socialism), but independence from USSR, in fact wanted to expel all ruling foreign powers, were religious, believers in God and racial." (p. 22) The following fall into this category, e.g., (a) Germany—Neo-Nazis, patriotism sprang from shame following Germany's defeat in World War-I, and (b) Italy/Austria – New-Fascists.

Religious Nationalistic Ethnic (Racial/Fundamentalists)

As in India, Hindu *vs.* Muslim in J & K/Sikh. The groups in terrorism like Harat ul Muzahiddeen, Hizbul Muzahiddeen, J & K Liberation Front, Dukhtaran-e-Milat - A Women's organization.

In U.K. (North Ireland) Catholics of North Ireland *vs.* Protestants of South Ireland, they want separate united Ireland, anti-British Government rule in North Ireland. Leader Michael Collins was killed by his partner Eamon De Valera, who become PM.

Nationalistic separatist (Democratic) like Liberation Tigers of Tamil Eelam, 20 per cent Tamils want separate Tamil State from 80 percent Sinhalese population.

(b) *PKK* – Kurdisthan Workers Party in Turkey, Kurds wanting separate Kurdistan.

Exotic Terrorism

As in Peru-Columbia, etc. Apart from these categories, there are new types of terrorism known as Ecoterrorism.

Scholars have said that terrorism is ruthless behaviour which creates atmosphere of fear of violence and does not care of any human consideration of values. One of the most important part of its tactics or *rana niti* is wide publicity.

Several words like insurgency (*vidroha*), civil strife or civil war, *Guerrilla* War, intimidation are often used synonymously with terrorism, and *himsa* is a common factor in all these. It is an organised behaviour of intimidation. A terrorist is one—who according to the directions and dictations of his group or group leader use violence or violent methods making others to accept his group's intentions. A terrorist does not give prior warning, but directly use destructive means. Even if a terrorist is kept in jail or imprisoned, he does not plead for his innocence rather he/they move forcefully, ventillate his/their ideology. Though the long range aim of insurgency and revolution are similar, i.e., to overthrow the existing political organisation, but its short-range aim, tactics may differ.

There are two types of terrorism (i) those activities which are adopted against state; and (ii) terrorism which is perpetrated by the state itself. Though Hitler, Stalin, Mao, Yahya Khan, Mussolini and Franco can't be called 'terrorist', they were involved in terrorist acts of murder and violence. State-sponsored terrorist acts are based on extra-legal methods. All disruptive acts of state cannot be kept in the category of terrorism, because sometimes the state has to take resort to violent acts in order to protect the interest of the state as well as to enforce the rules and laws framed by the state in the common interest of the people of the state. Only totalitarian states engage in terrorist activities but there are exceptions to this also.

There are persons who adopt violence for personal reasons, such persons cannot be kept in the category of terrorist, since his/their acts are directed towards their personal benefit in loot, dacoity, etc., but the loot and dacoity done by the Naxalist group will come in the category of terrorism.

Intimidation and Revolution

'*Intimidation*' and '*Revolution*' are differentiated; in intimidation for ransom, usually such persons/group do not give forewarning but in 'terrorism' and 'revolution', heavy or other type of injury is caused. Terrorism is not a strife or battle or war between one person or the other, between one group or the other, but the terrorist does injury, if the person/group does not obey the terrorist directions.

According to Paul Wilkinson (1924), blackmail, forced acceptance etc., are the weapons for compelling people to accept the demands of the terrorists.

Terrorism and Mob-violence

Terrorism differs from *mob-violence*. Mob-violence is not organised, not planned, it occurs instantaneously due to incidental causes, which may have or may not have any concerted plans/ reasons, it is automatic, quick act, but terrorist act is well planned, well defined, well directed to specific purposes, its aims are to weaken the morals of man or state, its aim is destruction for creating supremacy.

Terrorism and Insurgency

There is difference between '*terrorism*' and '*insurgency*', the insurgents have greater support of the mass, but this is not necessary for the terrorist. Further insurgents are the citizen of that state who raise voice against the state, against the laws and practices, regulations of the state, they may use guerrilla tactics also, but the terrorist may or may not be the citizen of that state. Terrorist acts are done in open places, e.g., railway station, bus stand, hospitals, market, etc. to create maximum loss of life. In terrorism mercenaries are used frequently.

Some sociologists divide terrorism into *five categories*, (1) state-sponsored, (2) section sponsored, (3) crime related, (4) Narco, and (5) Issue motivated.

Revolution (Kranti) and Terrorism

It is essential to differentiate the two words '*Revolution*' which is otherwise expressed by the word *Kranti* and terrorism and this word *Kranti* is also differentiated with *Bagavata* or *Vidroha*.

The word 'Revolution' comes from the word 'revolve'; usually 'rotation' and 'revolution' are two words used in geography for earth's daily movement and yearly movement around axis and orbit.

Thus, the word 'revolve' means to 'move around'. The Hindi equivalent of the word *'revolution'* is *kranti*, which comes from the root *Kramu* which means to 'stumble', unable to stand firmly, to become shaky, while trying to stand erect etc., the Hindi meaning of the word is *ladkharana*. The word *ladkharana* also means shifting or changing stand '*movement*'. The word '*movement*' is commonly understandable by everybody and is equivalent to the word *kranti* in Hindi. Applied to our present context, revolution will refer to a state of affair or circumstances when the old system has crumbled and become ineffective, it is substituted by a new thought or ideology suited to the prevailing situations, and the change so effected must be something very outstanding, something very novel, quite different frcm the old one, a complete change. Some scholars say that change or revolution should be bloodless, some scholars say that such change or *kranti* may involve violence and bloodshed. Change is occurring to everything and at every movement, as Heraclitus had said, we cannot dip in the same stream twice in a moment. So, change is the law of the world. Even the word 'world' means in Hindi *samsāra*, and the word *samsāra* is defined as something which is rolling, moving every moment "*Samsarati samsārah*". *Kranti* or revolution does not simply mean ordinary change. It is also not development or *pragati*. *Vikasa* or *pragati* or *parivartana* is not the exact sense of revolution. Further, *kranti* or *revolution is different from social reform*, though in social reform change occurs and sometimes the change is also spectacular and quite new and novel. Sometimes, the word *'Vidroha'* or *bagavata* is also used for *kranti* and revolution, but actually there is difference between these terms. In *bagavata*, attempt is made to change the existing system, sometimes such attempts becomes successful, sometimes attempts go fruitless, but opposed to *bagavata* is *kranti*. Change of political system is essential. *Change* or *development* termed as *vikasa* or *parivartana* is gradual, in slow speed, while in revolution or *kranti*, the change is sudden. In *kranti* or revolution the aim is to change the old system and substitute it by new and so bring reform into a novel form, in *vidroha* the aim is not to make a new change, but to re-establish the traditional system. *Kranti* or *revolution* differs from *social reform* in this that reform is always partial, the whole political system is not changed. The social reform wants a change not the whole, but to make minor change even without disturbing the political system, they are satisfied, if only some of evils crept into the society are cured or removed. Natural calamities, like huge earthquake or Tsunami also cause change, but that is not called *kranti* or revolution.

Causes of Kranti or Revolution

According to Aristotle there are *three causes* which bring about *kranti* or revolution—(i) *Main cause is inequality*; (ii) *common cause* is selfish acts, fear, hatred, caste/creed bias, the desire to be superior; and (iii) *special cause* suppression of the poor by the different/wealthy people.

According to Marx, the three causes of revolution or *kranti* are : (i) Inequality *(asamanata)*, (ii) dissatisfaction (*asantushti*); and (iii) *shoshana* or exploitation. Dissatisfaction is also of three kinds — *(a) social-cultural* factors, *(b)social-psychological factors* and *(c) economic factors*. Strictly speaking, Marx emphasises on economic factors, e.g., poverty, hunger as well as exploitation of the poor by capitalist (wealthy persons) the subjugation of the proletariat, this is called *varga-sangharsha*. According to some sections, the intellectuals find no role in revolution.

According to one great scholar, the *three causes of revolution* or *kranti* are : *(a) divine causes*, *(b) human causes* and *(c) natural causes*. According to Aristotle, *kranti* or revolution is quite an uncommon event, while according to some, it is a common event and it always happens.

There are scholars who contend that revolution is limited to social sphere only, and all revolutions or *kranti* are socially related, limited to social sphere. Hymes and Moniers feel that revolution is always strong social change. But there are others like Friedrich, and Jubinel, etc., who opine that revolution or *kranti* is always related to political sphere, as political change, political revolution, to destroy the existing political system outright. Kimble Young also says that revolution is act of sudden overthrow of political system. According to Kimble Young, force or use of force is an essential factor in all revolution. According to Aurther Bauer, revolution is social change, not accompanied with force. J.P. did not speak of violent movement, but peaceful movement, movement led by non-violence, non-injury to anyone, but with self suffering, *satyagraha*, *ahimsa* and truth. According to P.A. Sorokin, "A comparatively sudden, rapid and violent change of the absolute official law of the group or the institution and the system of values it represents may be called a revolutionary change." According to Hanna Arendt, "only where change occurs in the sense of different form of government to bring about the formation of a new body politic, can we speak of revolution. In these definitions 'violence' has been shown as essential." But Eugene Kamenkg takes revolution only as a social change, which normally involves violence, and the word 'normally' may be interpreted as 'not necessarily involving violence', may include violence also, may not include violence, to quote him, "Revolution is a sharp, sudden change in the social location of political, expressing itself in the radical transformation, it has usually been believed could not normally occur without violence."

From all the above elaborations, it is now possible to express the difference of all these with "terrorism". Terrorism necessarily involves violence, violence is ingrained in the very concept of terrorism. Terrorism generally arise out of political causes, not social causes can be adduced to terrorism. Terrorism is essentially a violent act, whereby mass-killing, mass-disaster is bound to come. It is a negative approach to all norms, social, moral and humanistic. *It is a disease*, it has been called *a vile serpent* which ought to be crushed while it is very small, otherwise it would cause death without discrimination. The intention of violence is to create fear, threat, psychological and physical, show down, to break the morale of all, these are the weapons to make others to concede to their vile and malicious design. That is the main motive. It has no social ambitions, no social plans, but political aim, more so ideological and religious aims, which can be termed as fanatical fundamentalism rather than sane, rational and constructive approach. In *vidroha*, *bagavata*, the aim is not necessarily destruction, but only for eradicating some of the ills for the purpose of reconstruction, for reformation, rather than mass scale murder. To create a fear-psychosis all round so that everyone surrender before them, is the chief aim of the terrorists, and it is quite different from change, development, etc.

Terrorism and Anarchism

One more fact may be mentioned, the word 'anarchy or anarchism' is also to be compared with terrorism, for the reason mainly that the main aim of terrorist is to shake one's moral faith, shake physical strength by creating fear, threat to life and property. All these are only means to create social, political, moral, economic fear, i.e., to create chaos and confusion, so that everyone may surrender before them and accept their dictates. Thus anarchism/chaos, confusion, unrest are the means adopted by the terrorist to force people for accepting their orders, while Anarchism is a separate concept, ideological concept in the text-books of political science. It is a concept of political philosophy. Anarchism is related closely with both individualism and socialism, it is related to individualism, since in it topmost importance is given to individual freedom. Any organisation, institution which deters or hinders individual freedom is bad. Even state is according to it, is a 'necessary evil', state is an 'unnecessary evil' for individual. According to Marx, after the 'dictatorship of the proletariats', a stage will come when the existence of state would be finished. Gandhi also spoke of stateless society. The chief exponent of anarchism is Peter Kroptikin, who said stateless society is the ideal society, state is necessary evil since it forces individual to obey some rule or law. According to Dickins, anarchism is "absence of force or power of enforcement and it does not assume or propound loss of organisation". According to Huxley anarchism is such organisation where everybody is his own self ruler. According to Koker, stateless society is the ideal society. According to Russell, anarchism is such concept which is against any sort of force or 'governance', since all state/governance is hindrance to individual. This is a very old concept. In the modern age, Godwin, Proudhan, Thoreau, Gandhi, Bakunin, Kroposkin, Tolstoy, and Russell, etc., are supporters of this concept or ideology. It is against *rajnaitika satta*, or political power, religious and economic power, religious *satta* and economic *satta*. There are two groups of anarchist, one is led by mild/tolerant group or reformative and the other is staunch anarchism, who do not hesitate to the use of violence. The first group adopts the path of peace, i.e., *shanti*, the other group adopts the path of *kranti*. Bakunin's brand of anarchism, give birth to *samyavada*, Kropotteni's type of anarchists give rise to philosophical anarchism as we find in Gandhi, Tolstoy, etc. Proudham was an anarchist, who was against personal property, he said that keeping of personal property amounts to theft which is adopted by the rich. He is called a tolerant anarchist. Against this, Bakunin held that the old traditionalist anarchists are wrong. Bakunin's method was that of violence, he supported anarchism as he said, "without violence, no change in society or state is possible". Kropotkin was a pupil of Bakunin.

From the above discussion, it is apparent that there is some sort of similarity between anarchism and terrorism. We have already stated about the two groups of anarchist, one led by mild / tolerant reformative group, who decry violence as a means to attaining individual freedom, in which group, Russell, Gandhi, and Tolstoy, etc., Come and from other group, who support the view that without force or violence, there cannot be any change. Thus, when *himsa* is adopted or supported, it comes to terrorism, so far violence. The aim of both terrorism and anarchism is change. In so far as the tolerant group of anarchist, they speak for individual freedom, there is an element of morality, there is element of elimination of force from all sides, including religious force, it is peaceful method, while with the terrorist, peace or moral element is wanting. Terrorist act is far away from reformative. But, both terrorism and anarchism try to create an air of chaos, confusion, by this method the anarchists try to develop peaceful atmosphere, the terrorist on the other hand create such confusion, chaos and try to gain its criminal ends, try to gain selfish mileage, or advantage by fishing in the troubled waters. Only frustrated, disgruntled, tortured youths generally enter into terrorist acts, they are immune from any humane attitude, they are hardened by ill training, cruel hearted, they feel that they are born only to indulge in violence, not for love sympathy, etc. Both anarchism and terrorism plead against state or state interference, but the former act for better ends, the latter from greater evils, crime, slaughter and all sorts of inhuman acts. Both terrorism and anarchism are illegal acts and are subject to the rules of the state concerned.

Is Terrorism : A Philosophy

Has anarchism any philosophy? It has been said above that anarchism is a philosophical concept but what about terrorism. Is it also a philosophy? Terrorism means to attain political ends, religious ends, but anarchism is not a means in the strict sense of the term, its aim is to root out the evils of the society, to bring individual freedom, to overthrow force, to make everybody to govern himself, to root out complaints emanating from the state, from religion, from economic imbalance. It brings to man freewill to arouse his own conscience, and voice of conscience can do no wrong, as Gandhiji used to say. Wherever man is overwhelmed by his selfish consideration and think of committing any immoral illegal act, the voice of conscience at once cautions man not to engage in such acts. So Gandhi, Russell, and Tolstoy, etc., were moved towards it. It is a *positive* philosophy, while on the other hand terrorism is *negative frame of thought*, it is at once not only immoral, but also illegal and for such illegal acts, one has to face punishment as per the laws of the land. Terrorist intentionally violate law, without any human feeling, without guilt feeling, acting ruthlessly, shamelessly, and tolling other's lives as well as throwing himself to the risk of his own life. Terrorism is an act of desperation, cruel to the last extent and in so far as it is most cruel as well as heartless act, it is most unethical and immoral.

But is it correct to say that anarchism is a full-fledged philosophy. It cannot be said to be a sound political philosophy, it is impracticable, it is useless concept says C.E.M. Joad, it is purely idealistic concept, quite not feasible, it is impractical. A purely unfettered society, a purely stateless society, a purely forceless society is a contradiction in terms. There cannot be any society, where there is no fear of punishment in committing any crime.

Mohammad Bin Mohammad in his book *Anatomy of Terrorism* has made some very good observations and it is enlightening to refer to his contentions to such contentious issues like 'terrorism', which our country is facing for several decades. According to him, terrorism is a "*symptom rather than disease*." Like a good farmer who pulls out the weeds growing by the root of the trees planted by him/them, so that there is healthy growth of the tree, so also 'terrorism' has to be nipped in the bud. Terrorism is like a serpant which has to be killed before it grows. What is needed is not *ad hoc* palliatives but a radical treatment of this deep-rooted, deep-seated, dangerous disease of terrorism, an inhuman act, like the most dreaded and dreadful disease that inflicts mankind today.

It is true that terrorists are born like street animals. But in fact as the author opines that the *terrorists are not born but are created by the society.* He says, "Individual traits including biological, mental and emotional factors together with unfavourable social environment explain the anti-social human behaviour, under the extreme "pressure cooker" conditions, the individuals real breaking point. He becomes desperate and uses the only weapon available to him, the weapon of protest for, as Abraham Lincoln has said, "To go by silence when we should protest makes cowards of men." Driven to the edge, the protest may take the extreme form of inflicting death, demolition and destruction, and in its ultimate form self-destruction and suicide. "Nothing strikes more in the human heart than a brooding sense of injustice," observed Justice Brennar of the U.S. Supreme Court holds "injustice makes you want pull things down", an Algerian terrorist Frantz Fanon says, "violence is the cleansing force. It frees the native of his inferiority complex and from his despair and inaction. It makes him fearless and restores his self-respect". The same idea is expressed in an Urdu poem—

मायूसियों ने और भी सरकश बना दिया
इतने हुए जलील के खुद्दार बन गए।

Frustrations made them more rebellious. Their humiliation was so great that they became self-respecting.

The author cites, the case of America. America wanted Laden dead or alive after terrorist attack on the Trade Centre. But the question is, who made Laden so important. None other than American itself. It has been rightly remarked that "Laden was created by C.I.A. and wanted by F.B.I."

The above author cites the example of Afghanistan, where history is being repeated. Two thousand years ago Roman historian Publices Tacitus saw through the rhetoric. "They make wilderness and call it peace."

The author refers to the observation of one American Islamic scholar who spoke about the perpetrators of September 11, "*the enemies of Islam*" *non-martyrs, but murderers*. Religious zealots of any creed are defeated people, who lash out in desperation and they go after horrific things. Imam Malik said, "60 years of oppression under an unjust rules is better than one hour of anarchy." *Jehad* means "struggle against evil forces, suicide which is resorted to by *fedayeens*, is a sin, a mortal sin in Islam. Islam prohibits suicide strictly, but the *fedayeen* squads are rampantly doing this against the Islamic injunctions, and terrorists call themselves true Islamic, they say, they act for Islam, but are really violating Islamic rules of morality." *Fedayeen* attacks are being faced by our country for several decades and Sir Mohammad Bin says, that Pakistani's cross border terrorism is "perfidy under pretence of faith. His suggestion is right, when he says that we have to set our house in order and "stick to your guns and the rest will follow".

Mohammad Bin further cites the example of America's act in killing or seeking to kill Saddam in which context James Baker has once said, "Oil is our civilization. We do not want a demon (Saddam) to sit on it". This fact has been expressed by President Lyndon Johnson, "that there are two types of threats to peace : (i) the desire of most people to win better way of life; and (ii) the design of some people to force their way of life on others". The most remarkable observation of the author with respect to the strategy of U.S. in Asia is "to irritate, arrogate, ingratiate and (when defiant) devastate," by nuclear bombing in Hiroshima and Nagasaki, "Carpet bombing in Afghanistan," "precision bombing in Iraq," "humanitarian intervention in Kosovo," or "just war" against nameless enemy (terrorism)— "all done in the name of peace without justice, you shall have neither justice nor peace." He observes that "nothing happens in India without a threat and nothing is achieved without agitation." We speak of democracy we are proud of it Democracy is preferred because "it is the only social order that is admissible because it is consistent with justice". But "Man's capacity for justice makes democracy possible, while man's propensity for injustice makes democracy necessary." Some scholars have divided humanity in *three* principal categories— *(i) human angels*, *(ii) human devils*, and *(iii) human man*. The first category is law-abiding, good-natured and incorruptible; they do not need any external control to maintain their goodness. The second category is the vast majority in the middle, who behave well under some kind of control which may be called "parental force". The lot which are called terrorists far supersedes all categories of imagination.

Prof. Naqvi Imam has observed in his celebrated book, *Partition : The Real Story*, that the root of this present bitterness between the two neighbouring countries of India and Pakistan is the partition of India. He says, "partition was a surgical operation by an amateur butcher performed in the dark on the pavement...... Partition was uncalled for, unnatural, not at all inevitable and negation of all that India stood for throughout her long and chequered history spanning 50 centuries." Out of 10 crore Muslim, 6 crore went to Pakistan and 4 crore left to India. It is said that now Muslim population in India is 12 per cent whether this data is correct and uptodate or not, this figure equal, the population totalling Bangladesh and Pakistan taken togather or more than Muslims in the entire Arab world, only next to Indonesia. The main reason is that the politicians have to grind their own axe by taking them as vote bank.

The principle of *Jehad* which the terrorists understand, can be measured in terms of murder and violence. But according to

Mohammad Bin, "the biggest *Jehad* is *Jehad–e-Azam*–is fighting against one's ego in the way of *Allah* against evil temptations, animal desires, anger, hatred, jealousy and arrogance." But the choice between cowardice and violence, even Gandhi, who is the Messiah of non-violence, also preferred violence. What is called "Muslim fundamentalism" gives religious colour to terrorism and play foul forgetting the fact of self-sacrifice, the sacrifice of all evil forces for a good cause, for the welfare of all humanity at large. One has to read the voice of the spirit, the voice of conscience, which always fights when anyone commits a sinful act. Sinful acts arouse a guilt-feeling, as and when such sinful acts are committed, what is required is to correct one's consciousness against guiltful acts.

11

Terrorism : How Rajneesh takes it?

Shiva Nath Prasad

Acharya Rajneesh has thrown a floodlight on terrorism which is so very graphic, so very subtle, minute and so very heart rending that I wish to give his views to have an understanding of terrorism according to his versions and find out a solution of it in the heart. In the whole of his writings, he has thrown flood light on this topic at several places which is the burning topic of the day.

In his book *Sermons in Stone, Love is the Greatest Alchemy*, Osho cites an example, who is a terrorist, a particular man or the whole country, the so-called most powerful country, merely for resisting a small country/place not to accept their own personal choices. Cuba is a small country. The whole country became communist, it was their right to choose to become a follower of any type of ideology they like, but American poke its nose to resist their choice of self-determination. America spent two hundred millions dollars out of its secret fund to send the guerrillas, terrorists, to destroy this place for the reason that they accepted communism. America was although denying this expenditure, but later it was accepted by the American President, "Yes, that money has gone to the terrorist". The whole world knew it, all countries kept silent. A country's job is to save the people from terrorism, and a whole country is sending terrorists. What is it, when America itself became a target of terrorist attack 9/11 September, it accuses others for terrorism and pleads that the menace of terrorism should be stopped, not even once spoke about India which facing the problem of terrorism from its neighbour for decades. Why is this policy undertaken by so vast atomic power like America which has the maximum arms for the whole world's destruction.

England's Example of Terrorism

Osho in his book *Beyond Psychology* has given example of England's terrorist activity. England was a powerful state, and it was said of it, that the sun never sets in the British Empire, this means that while in one part of its Empire, people were awaking, it was day time, in other parts of its Empire, it was night and its people remained in sleep. It was a long famous saying that India is a 'golden bird' thus Pythagoras has said, Alexander had said. So many invaders had come to India, taken away its treasures, but India remained inextensibly rich even then. The English were the last. There is a holy place of the Sikhs, a beautiful garden which has high walls and only one small door out of which only one man can come out. There was a silent and peaceful meeting and the main prayer was "The British Government should change its heart and should out country". There was no revolt or revolution of any kind. It was a simple prayer. General Dyer was a Colonel then and he shot each and every person of the park, irrespective of children, women, old persons, etc. Was it the act of a government who is the ruler of the same country and killing millions of innocent people of his own Empire. It was their own country then and they have killed its own citizens. Rajneesh says that the British had been terrorists. It is no less than an act of terrorism.

And Rajneesh asks who creates terrorists, and himself that answers the governments create terrorists. Terrorists do not drop from the sky. "What can individual do when governments having all the power start destroying their individuality, their freedom of expression. They are forcing silent, simple people who have no business with violence, who are not politicians. . . . . . but if forced too much. . . . . . there is a limit". America destroyed Rajneesh's commune for no reason. He says, "President Reagon is a fundamentalist Christian, which is another name for fanatic Christian. So all the fanatic Christian and Ronald Reagon together destroyed the commune. Who creates terrorism? India is not a rich country like America, but it is spending its 75 per cent of its budget in defence, while on the other side people in thousands and millions are starving. Can one eat bombs? People have eaten leaves of trees, but eager to prepare more bombs. Rajiv Gandhi once had said, the "instinct of violence was reflected in acts of terrorism". Yet, we are begging for more of uranium. Had there been no terrorist threat, why could India go for uranium?

Religion and Terrorism

David Yallop has written a very remarkable book named *In God's Name*. In this book, he already lays out the role of the Roman Catholic Church in murder, terrorism, embezzlement, major drug-running and continual swindling of incredible sums of money; manipulation of politics in America, Italy, South America, and Poland. . . . . ." Rajneesh says, "Recently the Pope declared that the church should not take part in any kind of politics; that Christian priests, monks, bishops and cardinals should remain beyond politics. And while he was saying this; he was sending millions of dollars to political party in Poland to fight against communism".

"These people have so many faces! If you are not to take part in politics, then why should you be interested in the Communist Party not remaining in Poland? And where did you get millions of dollars to support opposition?. . . . . . from drugs.

The Example of Hinduism to Buddhism, Jainism and Mohammedanism

Buddha was against Vedic ritualism. He discarded the Vedic rituals and this enraged the Brahmins. They created great furore. Buddha was so much gifted in reasons that he could reply any offensive or any question raised by the Brahmins with much of their satisfaction.

When he died, none of his disciples had the ability to refute Brahmanism attack on Buddhism. Buddhism started to wane and in the very land of its homeland, it has decayed, while the Buddhist who went to other countries, e.g., Lanka, Burma, China, Japan, Tibet and to several countries, Buddhism is still the practiced religion of the land.

Jainism also had to face attacks of the Brahmanism and it also could not flourish in healthy conditions, as such only a small portion of the population of India are Jainists, the majority being some business class of India.

The Muslims came to India and ruled India for several centuries and they exploited the Indians. There is no book written as yet by any scholar about the history of exploitation by the Muslims, how many beautiful temples were destroyed and were given the shape of Masjids, how many Hindus were forced either to become Muslims or to face death, no history has been written how many women were raped and converted in the Muslims fold. The Hindus were also so conservative that once a woman was raped by any Muslim or if any women lived even for one night in any Muslim's house, she was ousted and she alongwith her entire family had to be converted to Muslim faith. There are more converted Muslims in India, than they had actually come from outside India. They were converted to Muslim faith not by intellectual convictions, that Mohammedanism is better religion than their own, but at the point of sword, with the argument of sword. And Rajneesh says that Pakistan has erased the Hindus completely, he also opines that raping women was out of the basic strategies to convert to other religion. Since once any woman was raped by a Muslim or even kept for a night or when the poor women who worked as maids in the Muslim, they were prohibited entry in their own home as something untouchable and this formula worked very well as automatic conversion and hence growth of their population.

One of the very ugliest examples of religious torture has been narrated by Rajneesh. He has described about one Muslim Caliph Omar who visited the world's largest and the oldest library in Alexandria, it kept most ancient scriptures from Atlantis, a continent which has sunk into the ocean and from ...., another very small continent that has gone under water. The Caliph Omar went to the library and searched out the librarian, his one hand was having the Qur'an and his other a torchlight. He asked from the librarian who was himself a very great scholar, two questions – (i) is there any literature in the library which goes against Qur'an? If your answer is yes, I am going to burn it, If your answer is 'no', then too, I am going to burn it. Because if everything in this library is consistent with the Holy Qur'an, then the only Qur'an is enough. What is the need of having such a big library? He did not wait for the librarian to answer, he himself answered, and he set the library on fire, it took six months to burn the whole big library and one of the greatest libraries of ancient scriptures was destroyed. Does it not this amount to an extremist act.

The religious people were always in favour of self fortune rather than on rejoicing. Their crime is most vital for the loss of positive attitude to life. Nietzsche had a keen vision and he said religious people were condemning sex, renouncing sex, but since the very bases of life is sex, it is so deeply rooted in biology, it constitutes his whole body, he is born out of sex, he cannot get rid of it except by suicide; the religions failed, the men failed, sex remained, but as poisoned sex. The same situation exists about other things, e.g., life of comfort, life of luxury, the religions have denounced these things, they condemned riches, wealth, comfort life since the "blessed are the poor for there's the kingdom", but then who becomes a terrorist, a wealthy man, no, the terrorist are persons who have nothing to eat, no financial resources. Rajneesh says that, "The terrorism is not in the bombs, in your hands, the terrorism is in your unconscious". . . . . . . The blind people, the conscious people are having bombs and are throwing them to kill mankind.

Rajneesh says, "The religions have done immense incalculable loss to all human values, to human life, to human understanding, to human evolution. And it is time that they should be exported, because that will prepare the ground for the birth of my rebel, for the birth of great rebellion against these ugly institutions. It will bring the whole humanity into a loving relationship, without nations, without religions, but with deep religionness, with a great respect for life, and great gratitude for existence". The remedy of terrorism lies in silence, in meditation, in the therapy which is contained in meditation. Terrorists require therapy of meditative silence. Communism is no remedy to terrorism, because it is psychologically, it is another tyranny of the proletariat, it is just another trap. Jesus said, the poor are the blessed for theirs is the kingdom of God, but a feeling of destitution remains simmering in the minds of the poor that if these have many things of control, they do it here. The Marxist contention that "the workers of the world unite, you have nothing to lose and you have the whole world to gain" you have to snatch away things from the other lot of persons, the rich ones and distribute them, take things from them, is another trap.

Another illustration of the politics of religions high handedness leading to terrorism has been explained by Rajneesh, i.e., the creation of Israel by England-America. Palestine was the place where the population was of only Muslims. As a part of strategy and conspiracy, Israel was created, then Palestine was under American and British troops. So, they forced the Jews on Muslims. It created constant trouble to the Jews living between Muslims from all sides. Hitler killed six million Jews, and the Jews in treble by the conspiracy of America. Everyday, some killing goes on. The question Rajneesh asks, who creates the terrorists?

Violence is not needed

Violence is not engrained in man. Violence is animals nature, it is the nature of the beasts. Animals kill, man murders. Animals kill their prey for food, man murders man for self-fulfilment, self-satisfaction. Animals have no alternative but to kill for food. Man has choice, he can live quite happily without murdering. They can live without killing. It is in their right choice whether to murder or not. Man can be violent or non violent as he wishes. It is man's freedom. It is not the freedom of animals, it is their helplessness.

Animals have no past nor future. Man has past and future. The beast is what it is, there is no question of possibility or actuality with beasts. Violence is acquired. Non-violence is the nature of man. Animals have only present, no history. Man has a future. He has history, he has the responsibility for future. There is potential in man, to become a vilest criminal or to be a saint in future. Animal has no possibility. Man can take a decision to be non-violent, animal is helpless. It has no choice. If any man says that violence is my nature, he is mistaken. Violence is not man's nature, it is acquired, and what is acquired can also be left out. Beast can be pardoned for violence, but man cannot be pardoned, since man has a freedom to choose. He can take a decision, decision to be either violent or non-violent. Man has got plans to implement. Animals have no plans. Man becomes violent by planning, and if one becomes violent by planning, then it is furrier and more brutal than animals. The Chengez Khan, or Taimur or Nadir or Hitler are examples, only a few examples. We cannot find out a history of beast parallel to these. If you ask any animal of such of his memory, it will reply no, I have no memory. Memory is for man, not for animal. So, we have the freedom to choose between violence and non-violence, between terrorism and love for humanity. Man is the only animal who kills other man. Can it not be changed? It is possible to have total transformation. Man should engage in prayer, to pray rather than "prey". Pray brings love to all creatures, reverence to life and the very existence, 'prey' is snatching life, it is hatred-based, selflessness-based, avarice-based Satan-based, devilishness-based, animally-based, and man has the power and potential to be God-like, to lighten the torch of divine light within himself.

The *Jehad* – Real/Unreal

Osho Rajneesh cites the story of a killer bandit Angulimal whose daily routine was to kill persons and prepare garland of finger to keep in the neck. The very word 'Angulimal'. *Anguli* means finger, *mala* means garland. People had forewarned Buddha not to pass by the path where Angulimal lived, but Buddha said, had I not been knowing, I would not have gone on that way, but when I have known about him, I shall pass by that road and see what he does. Buddha passed by that road, the bandit and this *sannyasi* and was moved, he said, go away soon, otherwise I shall kill, you don't know me. I am Angulimal, and I kill man everyday. Buddha insisted him to kill, but he was hesitant and trembling. He was surprised at his own trembling, as if someone has done some magic. Buddha asked him to finish his job soon, but he was not finding himself able to kill. Buddha said, you kill physically, I kill psychologically. Buddha asked, can you cut a branch of a tree and then again join it with the tree, you cannot. Real thing is growing not cutting. Destruction is easy, but creation is the real thing. The killer was moved, he said, "You have already killed me before I could kill you. You are right—destruction can be done by everybody. Now, teach me how to be creative".

The real *jehad* is purity, creativity, and compassion. It is moral *jehad* to kill the evil in man. The Sufis called this *jehad* of morality, freedom *Jihadun-Nafs*, it is real *jihad*, to purify one's soul from all evil influence, it is a cleansing process. It is bringing an inner transformation of one's being. This type of *jihad* is not *jihad* of war, to kill who does not accept our religion or other which *jihad* is an unending process, but the real *jihad* is the *jihad* of reason, conscience and pure consciousness which can bring a total change of heart, a change of being. This *jihad* is deathless, unending. It is a reply to *jihad* of tyranny, *jihad* of terrorism.

12

The Gandhian Concept of Welfare

Bijayananda Kar

Gandhi is undisputedly one of the topmost thinkers of modern India. He represents the typical Indian point of view in various important public affairs of socio-economic as well as socio-political importance. His deep concern for the flow of morality in different faces of human life has been considered as deeply illustrious. Even those who do not fully share with his viewpoints cannot afford to bypass his unique philosophy of life. That is why, to some of the great thinkers of the present century including Albert Einstein. Gandhi appears to be somewhat wonderful and is difficult for a normal ordinary estimation.

The peculiarity is: Gandhi, despite his original thinking in diverse fields, never is an advocate of any distinct theory. In fact he clearly gives his dissent to leave any 'ism' after him. In his manifold speeches and writings, he has, doubtlessly, left number of flashes which later scholars and writers have viewed differently and consequently attempts have been made to bring those ideas together to form some sort of unitary pattern. Thus, Gandhi is viewed differently by advocates and critics as well.

Gandhi's concern for human welfare need not be underestimated. All through his life, he advocates for human dignity and prestige. It is not for his more self-satisfaction and personal honour that he has launched a movement of protest all alone at Johannesburg in South Africa. It is precisely the germination of that big non-cooperative movement which at later time has become the point of considerable human significance in India. There are innumerable instances in his life which show how sincerely he moves for the cause of his fellowmen. Wherever humanity suffers either in temple or in war field or in civil life, everywhere Gandhi advances unhesitatingly to render his valuable service. It is this feeling of humanity which forces him to differ from the established sociological theorists. While such thinkers, more or less, emphasize the role of society more than that of individual, Gandhi, on the other hand, has a firm conviction that the individual "is superior to the system he propounded".[1] Individual to him, is not merely a 'cog in the machine'. The freedom of the individual cannot be surrendered for any cause of mechanization.

However, this does not imply that he echoes the Protagorean maxim : man is the measure of everything. He pleads rather for individuality and not for individualism. His appeal is not to break all social ties, but only to resist the imposition of certain rigid social rules and regulations which upgrade one group of social members (even if that constitutes majority) and degrade the other. It matters least whether the group belongs to majority or minority. Society, if its basic aim is to bring the welfare of individuals comprising it cannot be said to have done its duty by only supporting the cause of a section of individuals. Gandhi's message for *sarvodaya*, in this context, is of striking importance.

The ideal of *sarvodaya* stands for the welfare of all and not of some. Gandhi's point of view is not anti-democratic. Of course, he, in one sense, transcends the naive or popular sense of democracy that only emphasizes on the decision held by the majority as the rule of the law. The concept of majority if it is extended to such an extent, say, 51 per cent then it is evident that in what measure it is fulfilling the cause of social justice. But, it is worth-noting that from the Gandhian point of view, even if the concept of majority is extended upto, say, 99 per cent, it need not crush the view of minority. Because, if minority's stand is not abnormally ill balanced, but is placed on the sound track of judicious temper, then its angle of vision ought not to be evaded. It is from this point of view, a specimen of sound democratic order, instead of suppressing the voice of minority by means of upholding the voice of majority by some sort of ruthless coercive procedure, prefers rather to persuade and convince the minority not by force (since that is never practically feasible), but by appealing to its finer sense of rational justification. The majority that overlooks and neglects the minor section's needs and aspirations (which are of course just and legitimate) is never approved in the Gandhian framework. So, instead of force and brutality, Gandhi advocates for peaceful co-existence and welfare of all the members of the society in a balanced proportional measure. Hence, his view-point is not incompatible with the spirit of democracy, if it is held in the wider and liberal sense as indicated before.

It is this sense of democracy that has possibly given rise to the concept of *sarvodaya*. Welfare of all is not to be construed as a visionary utopian ideal. It need not be taken as impractical and improbable if pursued in right earnest with the background of honesty and integrity, it is never difficult to be implemented. As a matter of fact, if one looks to the pages of history in an unprejudiced manner, one comes across several illustrations. (even if those are in small sectors and groups) where this type of socio-political relationship among the members of one community has remained quite firm and steady. Of course, it is to be marked here that the bond or unity among the different members remains strong as long as they continue to rely on the efficacy of balanced and steady rational procedure (*sthirabuddhi*). Gandhi seems to have emphasized on this point basing upon the great message found in his national cultural tradition.

The aim of Gandhi is not to uphold the numerous individual or personal peculiarities but to point out that there is a clear sense in which the harmony between social and personal interests is possible. Individual considerations need not be opposed to the social requirements. The primary aim of society is surely to get rid of conflicts and to bring reconciliation among its members. Gandhi does not deny the very reality of society as a system of relationship of individuals. But to him, society does not have a personality transcending and eclipsing the individuals. Of course the personal interests have got to be moulded and adjusted in accordance with the common interests. In this context Gandhi's saying "we must die that the family may live, the family must die that the country may live, the country must die that the world must live"[2] is quite significant.

Gandhi concedes to the point that the objective of attaining *sarvodaya* is difficult. This is, no doubt, an ideal. But, simply because, an ideal as such cannot be made actual, there is no justifiable ground as to why it cannot be pursued. Rather, if something is accepted as an ideal, it seems quite reasonable in following that at the practical setting. To think of well-being of all members in a community or group sound encouraging. There are, however, many obstructions and hindrances in accomplishing that objective. At the practical front, there is considerable amount of gap between individuals within a social group. Not that all are equally meritorious or equally sound both mentally and physically, there is even remarkable amount of economic disparity. Even naturally also, all are not of the same status. But, all these need not necessarily stand in the way when one sincerely proposes for upliftment of all. Proportionate development, taking into account the factor of quality as well as ability may be regarded as a sound step in this direction. When there is large breach between the rich and the poor, the social welfare cannot be thought as drastically changing the social scenario by forcibly reducing one group to the other. Everybody cannot be turned overnight either as rich or as poor. Even if that is made possible through certain radical measure, that will not be contributive of social justice or social welfare. Effective change or reform must be slow and steady, backed by the spirit of moral justice. The exploiters need not be crunched but, on the contrary, he is to be reasonably persuaded; and only when he is convinced, it becomes perfectly smooth in commenting the cleft between him and the exploited. The move, in other words, must be non-coercive, and non-violent and this is basically what the Gandhian approach stands for. His concept of non-violence thus does not seem to have a negative flavour.

Social reform according to Gandhi, must be directed to reform the individual and not to smash him. Here the deep sense of humanity seems to have been lurking in his thinking throughout. In this sense, the move towards the implementation of social welfare is not to adopt any forcible violent procedure. Because violence, even if at times is found to be easier in practical front, it, in the long run, is also found to be breeding hatred, jealousy and unhealthy competition. All these are obviously detrimental to the establishment of social peace and solidarity. It is by means of adopting persuasive measure, the unsocial elements can be effectively reformed for the better.

Here, the point that is often raised as to how at all any such persuasive measure be taken as convincing. What guarantee is there that the sole emphasis on tender sentiment of human appeal would be productive in this regard? To meet such points raised from the side of the critics, sometimes a view is advanced that Gandhi finally takes resort to some sort of intuitive flash which he himself has termed as 'inner voice'. This point is explained in terms of the saying that the adoption of such moral principles like truth and non-violence in different walks of social life is backed by some mystical touch transcending reason. For, it is thought, reason has its own limitations and certain crucial problematic situations in human life cannot be satisfactorily accounted by any rational procedure. In this context, reason has to give way to mystical intuitive flash and Gandhi is pictured as an ideal figure advocating for moral-based socio-political life which is considered as supremely sacred and religious. For, he has identified truth with God.

But, it seems, the appeal for 'inner voice' is not necessarily suggestive of any form of mystical intuition. At the time of social conflict and clash between different communities the Gandhian point of view does not invoke some sort of escapism. Taking resort to silence or attending to, what he terms, 'inner voice' does not imply to leave the profane and to move into some form of transcendental ecstasy. Gandhi is a profound practical thinker. At the moment of social tension and communal conflict he never has remained idle but has moved to the troubled spot without caring for his safety and comfort. He has moved on to appease the situation by means of his impeccable practical wisdom and, in that way, he has been found acceptable to different groups who even sometimes do not hesitate to stand opposed to each other. So, by 'inner voice', he virtually refers to the sober temper wherein the matter is tested through sound reason with a view to re-establish confidence on human unity and solidarity. Gandhi emphasises on reason as the basic parameter for setting any controversy. He maintains that the opponent can be dealt with by way of appealing to his or her reason. On many occasion, his mission has been found immensely fruitful and where it has become somewhat ineffective, it is not due to any inherent weakness in his approach but because of certain external factors that are beyond his control. Even in such cases, his sincerity in pursuing the cause of human welfare can never be seriously questioned.

Moral based socio-political life, as proposed in the Gandhian framework, is neither impractical nor suprarational. It conforms to that rational standard which never sets down the concern for human welfare. That sense of humanity always remains at the background and a proper rational set-up is adopted throughout his active life. It seems that he has deliberately avoided the formation of any 'ism' because he does not want to profess bare theorization. The moral principles and the ethically prescribed code of conduct become otiose if those are not practically viable. If truth, honesty and integrity are accepted as ethical principles both at private and public sectors, then there is no point in keeping those as impractical visionary ideals. Those principles seem to have their vitality only in so far as those are worked, out in the living situations. Even if one cannot be fully truthful that does not reasonably suggest that one should remain content being untruthful. It matters most if one follows the principle as far as he is capable. It seems Gandhi's appeal for moral basis in each and every walk of life including politics and other public affairs is not rooted on any absolute and uncompromising standard but is quite flexible in view of the individual's potentialities as well as social needs and requirements.

It is this angle of vision which amply justifies the rational foundation of the Gandhian point of view. The objective of human welfare is never sought in an egoistic spirit of only protecting the cause of man at the cost of other animate and inanimate objects but with due regard for the protection as well as preservation of all that is conducive of peace and prosperity in the universal perspective. In this respect the Gandhian approach appears to be *deeply secular.*

But is not Gandhi, a strong advocate of religion.[3] He has covertly claimed truth as God. He follows sincerely a religious life by going for prayer everyday. Hence, it is widely held that Gandhi's adherence to morality is based on his religious conviction. And that is the reason, why in certain critical circles, his socio-political view are regarded to be extremely based on ethico-religious-ideologies, much away from actual concrete set-up where different social issues are operative. His religious and spiritual background, it is thought, cannot accommodate a secular temper as indicated before.

Thus, Gandhi personally adopts a religious view of life. So there is nothing wrong in presenting him as religious. Even his advocacy for human welfare may be viewed in the religious background. But the question, here, seems to be equally pertinent; as to how or in what sense Gandhi is religious? Though born as a Hindu, he transcends the communal framework in so far as he prefers for the unity of different religions. His religious dictum : Truth is God and God is truth is something unique and, in that way, his distinctive approach can be well seen. Most of the major classical religions of the world are basically theo-centric and all those present diverse speculations about other world basing on their respective mythological set-up. In spite of their recommending certain common humanistic as well as humanitarian measures those religions continue to have their individual distinctiveness and that is why the sense of communalism and some sort of divisionism seem to be inbuilt in such religious framework. But, on the other hand, Gandhi, as a religionist, never supports any form of communalism, fundamentalism and divisive tendency. His main emphasis is on social stability. So, in that set-up, any social form of theologism that aspires for trans-secular or trans-social sacred beatitude can find no legitimate place. In his framework, there seems to be no scope for *salvation/moksha/nirvāṇa* in the non-secular sacred sense. Rather, because of this observation, it is preferable to read his framework as trans-religious (in the sense having conspicuous difference from other classical theistic religions). True, he tries to bring harmony and unity among different religions, specially the Hindus and the Muslims. His prayer: *Ramdhun* is a move in this direction. But, it is also noteworthy that despite his leanings towards a theistic vision (based on *vaishnava* faith) at the personal level (That again, may be due to his specific family and social background), he remains evidently concerned (in the equal sense of the term) for the welfare and stability of believers as well as non-believers. He transcends, in this sense, the dichotomous setting of theism as well as atheism, His human concern and secular outlook can never afford to neglect the welfare of the non-religious and even the irreligious people. That clearly shows that his basic thrust is not on theo-centric but rather on ethico-centric world-picture. And, in that way, the dictum, Truth is God is profoundly non-theistic secular expression having, of course, strong moral background. Anybody who is disciplined, cultured and displays honesty and integrity in his thought and action both in personal and social sphere can be regarded as religious in the Gandhian framework irrespective of the point that he is a believer/disbeliever/non-believer. In other words, the Gandhian concept of human welfare seems to have been grounded on a sort of moral secularism and not religious secularism.

REFERENCES

1. *Harijan*, 20.03.1936, Ahmedabad, 1946.
2. *Young India*, 13.07.1921, Madras, 1935.
3. M.K. Gandhi, quoted by Bandyopadhyaya, *The Illustrated Weekly of India*, 10.10.1964.

13

Religious Integration : An Estimate

Bijayananda Kar

At present time, much emphasis has been laid upon the issue concerning the integration of all religions (*sarva dharma samanvaya*) particularly in the Indian context, where people belonging to diverse religious faiths, have settled down the ages. In the pre-Independence as well as post-Independence days, the Indian National Congress has almost given sole emphasis on the conception of religious integration for the social and political stability of the Indian national. In order to unite the Hindus and Muslims (the two great religious communities residing in India), Gandhiji has advocated the idea of identity so far as the Hindu concept of *Īśvara* and the *Islam* concept of *Allah* are concerned. It is primarily basing upon this idea of religious integration, the Indian concept of secularism has been developed. It is said that in a country like India where people of different religions remain, secularism is acceptable as the proper political ideal wherein no scope is left for religious communalism and fundamentalism. There shall not be any interference on personal religious faith or belief. Each must be allowed to thrive and grow within its own sphere. Maximum facility should be provided for mutual religious tolerance and the political decision must be free and neutral so far as religious affairs are concerned. In a word, politics must be free from religious fanaticism. This move, it is thought, is a definite boosting for social harmony.

Such attempt for religious integration is not new in India. In the medieval times, Akbar (the famous Mughal emperor) had made a religion called *Din-e-Illahi*. The attempt was not, however, successful because of certain grounds. The great saint, Kabir had made a sincere effort to unite the two communities in his most inspiring devotional lyrics. In the present century the great religious devotee, Ramakrishna Paramahansa has advocated for Hindu-Muslim unity also which has been well taken up by his able disciple, Swami Vivekananda who has moved one step further by emphasizing on the essential sameness among all religions and, by that way, he has visualized the ideal of *Viśva Dharma* (Universal Religion).

But, even though, there has been such numerous moves advanced by great socio-religious leaders towards inter-religious unity and integration, somehow or other, this sort of enterprise has not achieved considerable amount of success at least in the Indian context. Well, what is the cause of such failure? Is it because there are certain factual hindrances that are there in the Indian context for which the ideal of integration remains as unworkable and unrealistic? Or, is it because of certain essential differences among various religions, the issue of integration becomes futile? Right after the post-independent days, there has been great emphasis laid by the politicians, social workers, reformers and general intellectuals on the issue of religious integration. More or less there is found to be a basic agreement in all such approaches that all religious doctrines basically advocate faith in some form of divinity and spirituality. They all are almost unanimous in propagating an honest living based on moral discipline and also seek for the welfare of humanity at large. If that is the case, then it can be concluded that the divergences which are noticed among different religious faiths and practices are only peripheral and not central. Once there is the tendency to bypass such peripheral differences and to remain firm over the central points of similarity in thought as well as action, the issue of religious integration no more remains a mere theoretical ideal but can easily be concretised in the actual situation.

But, whatever may be the intensity of propagating this made by such thinkers and whatever may be their tone of sincerity and devotion in this regard, it is painfully noticed that during the period of almost half-century, since the time of independence, the issue of religious integration has not attained considerable amount of success in the actual front. Perpetual violence, mistrust and animosity continue to remain not only among different religious communities but even among their sub-groups, cults and orders. In certain cases the differences are so acute that it gives rise to terrible violence inclusive of brutal murder and assassination. Communal riots have almost become a normal affair and, at the face of all that, it obviously becomes an extremely difficult step to accommodate the sense of integration at the religious sector. Not only in the present time, it is also noticed that there had been the presence of religious intolerance and severe antagonism among different religious communities in different ages both in India and outside. The Crusade war of the Christians and the *Jehad* of the Mohammedans can be treated as some cruel instances in this respect.

However, it may be said here in defence that such strife and antagonism among people belonging to different religions were/are possible only because there has been some misunderstanding and confusion about the fundamentals of all religions. It is because of such misunderstanding and misapprehension, the Hindu is suspicious of a Muslim and *vice versa*. But if, on the other hand, there is the creation of congenial atmosphere to understand as well as appreciate the basic tenets of different religious faith and belief, then issue concerning dispute and difference becomes considerably weak. The manner of offering prayer and showing devotion, no doubt, varies from one faith to another. If one sincerely goes for a study of religious practices and rituals, one will, of course, observe number of vital points of dissimilarity and difference. But, though rituals, etc., figure most prominently in different religions, the fundamental aim and objective of all religions, it is thought, are remarkably of similar nature. There is the spark of divinity and spirituality more or less in all religious formulation. The belief in divine order and to attain the moral and spiritual excellence continues to be ideal in all classical religions. And, if at all, there is any deviation from that standard, as noticed in some cases like Marxism and Communism, it is said in reply that in all such cases there is the use of the term: religion purely in a different sense. To put differently, religion in its usual sense continues to be based on some fundamental sense of theistic divine order with the background of morality and spirituality. Religion, in its basic sense, also aims at the welfare of the entire mankind. And, in this regard, the sense of humanity is central to all religions.

Now, the point is : If what has been observed here is accepted, then there is no room for any doubt and apprehension. One may suspend all such queries concerning the issue of religious integration and may conclude that religious integration is very much feasible. It can meaningfully contribute towards social justice and harmony. But in spite of all such persuasive remarks, problems concerning religious integration seem to have still persisted. Even if one casts off the modern concept of religion like Communism, etc., and remains confined to such usual classical types like Hinduism and Mohammedanism, one notices that the so called points of similarity and unity are not only absent but, on the contrary, the points of difference continue all along to be the distinguishing features of different religious faith and belief.

Take, for instance, the case of a Śaiva and that of a Vaiṣṇava. It is true that both of them belong to the common Hindu order. Both the deities: Śiva and Viṣṇu are accepted within the Hindu framework. But, so long as one adheres to Śaivism or Vaiṣṇavism, can he consistently maintain that Śiva is Viṣṇu and Viṣṇu is Śiva? He has to hold the belief that the ultimate is only Śiva or only Viṣṇu and thus his prayer and devotion are addressed to Him and none else. In his framework one is supreme and the other is never on the same par but, at best, it has to be accepted as subordinate. This shows that from the doctrinal points of view, different religious cults are bound to stress upon their individual peculiarities and differences in order to preserve their distinctness and uniqueness. This implies that even within the general theistic framework, the different religious cults/groups, etc., can be properly identified by virtue of their distinctness and not on the footing of commonality.

In this context, the Muslim concept of *Allah* and the general Hindu concept of *Īśvara* can be fruitfully investigated. Though, at a popular front, there is great appeal for the identity of these two religious concepts and this move for identification has been found to be somewhat effective in establishing socio-political unity and harmony in certain circle, it is also to be noted that such moves are neither boosted up by doctrinal basis of respective religion nor are effective so far as religious practices are concerned. The concept : *Allah*, as a typical Islamic religious concept, has its specific significance. It does aim at a transcendent supernatural theistic. Being who is supposed to be absolutely formless. Any anthropomorphic form is simply inadmissible within this framework. But the concept of *Īśvara* is, on the other side, found to be noticeably different. Though it is rooted in the sense of divinity and spirituality, it nevertheless, accommodates a definite sense of anthropomorphism. That is the reason as to why there is no inconsistency and incompatibility within the Hindu religious framework to visualize *Īśvara* in human form. *Īśvara*, in this sense, is very much close to human person. There is, thus, the meaningful propagation of reincarnation in Hinduism which is remarkably absent in Islam. Thus, the concept of idol-worship which is so much compatible within the Hindu tradition is found to be not at all workable in the Islamic tradition. Further the Christian concept of God is said to have established a supernatural personal being who is supposed to be omnipotent, omniscient and omnipresent. But so far as the plural number of Hindu deities are concerned, their powers, intelligence, etc., are distinctly considered to be limited and finite in nature. Viṣṇu can only sustain and it is Śiva who can only destroy, but creation solely belongs to Brahmā.

Well, it may be pointed out here that the Hindu framework also subscribes to one monotheistic conception of *Īśvara* and, in that way, the attribution of omnipotent, etc., is not quite implausible in the Hindu religious framework. In this context the Vedic *mantra* "*Ekam sat viprā bahudā vadanti*" has been cited. But it can be noted here that such reference from the Vedic source seems to be more suggestive of certain metaphysical theory of impersonal absolutism than a religious doctrine of personal theism. Even if one concedes there some monotheistic implications in the modified sense of Henotheism, it seems to be too much to hold that the Vedic conception of *Brahman* and the Islamic concept of *Allah* are one and the same. Even within the Hindu set-up there is no unanimity to regard *Brahman* and *Īśvara* as identical. The Vedic/ Upaniṣadic formulation of *Parā Brahman* and *Aparā Brahman* clearly reveals the valuational point of difference between the two. Further the theistic conception of God as creator is found to be remarkably absent in many major religions like Buddhism, Jainism, Taoism and Confucianism. Buddha's sayings that are embodied in the well-known eight-fold path of virtue deal with a code of conduct for this world. Jaina conception of *dharma* is distinctly non-theistic rather than theistic. Both Taoism and Confucianism are remarkably naturalistic instead of accommodating any form of theism. In view of all this, is it not somewhat a forced conclusion which holds that religions are basically one and there is the acceptance of theistic spiritualism in each and every religion? Instead of supporting a theistic world-view Buddhism. Jainism and even a definite version of Vedic/Upaniṣadic *dharma* are revealed to be predominantly having moral foundation. And such conception of morality is not rooted in a trans-human supernatural theistic realm but is found to be highly significant in the earthly human planes of existence. Again, on the issue of morality, different religions never advance identical or even sometimes similar views. On certain occasion, their conception of morality is found to be radically different. The Jaina code of conduct is, while noticed to be so much puritanic, the Buddhist code of conduct is rather distinctly liberal and catholic. Moreover while in general, the concept of *ahiṁsā* is observed to be conspicuous in both Buddhism and Jainism, in some form of radical Hindu ritualism, the practice of sacrifice and immolation are clear instance of violence. It may be interesting to note that the tail of *ahiṁsā* is tied up with both Buddhism and Hinduism to a considerable extent. But, in spite of the fact that the expression "*jīve dayā*" is so well advocated in these religious set-up, the pernicious practices of offering animals like goats to the Goddess: *Kāli* or the Lord Buddha are found as something common and unobjectionable.

Not only in the practical form of operation there is the presence of so much sharp differences, there are also noticeable form of doctrinal divergences between different religions. Because of that it becomes almost entirely misleading to suppose that each and every religion essentially points to the same ideal. While the creation of the world is due to the sinful activity of Adam and Eve in the Christian religious set-up, the creation is due sport (*lilā*) of the Lord and further the entire human race is supposed to be the off spring of nectar *(amṛtasya putrāḥ)* in the Hindu *dharmic* set-up. While attainment of heaven and attaining supreme pleasure there are supposed to be the ideal in some major religious conceptual framework, attaining bliss or *mokṣa* here in this worldly set-up and thereby indirectly bypassing all such other-worldly mythical conceptions are also well noticed in some important religious standpoint.

If this is accepted, then perhaps the only legitimate conclusion to be adored is that the concept of religion is not primarily to integrate or to unite but rather to go for division and disintegration. For, different religions are logically forced to uphold their respective points of imagination concerning the supernatural phenomena, the nature of divinity, the conception of God, etc., and, in that way, the point of departure, instead of the point of assimilation, becomes obviously conspicuous. So, the critical remarks that religion is to grow divisive tendency, perhaps, is not entirely pointless. If this is acknowledged to be the goal to which sooner or later religious conceptual framework has to coverage, then what role can it play for social justice and stability? In the name of religion, there is the propagation of different orders and hierarchies irrespective of social needs and expectations. If some one is well-placed and another is ill-placed in the social level, then the so called explanation that the former is so placed because of good fate or performance of good *karma* in past life and the latter is so placed because of bad fate or performance of bad *karma* in past life is neither convincing from scientific angle nor is acceptable from unbiased, impartial rational point of view. Both fatalism and *karmic* hypothesis, from such point of view, can hardly be taken as satisfactory explanations.

Perhaps, it is not so much by religious background but by means of moral standard that is found to be appropriate and acceptable at the social front. A prescriptive move can be meaningfully advanced at this critical juncture. Religious spirit may be fruitfully grounded on pure moral foundation that is acceptable to social norms and requirements. Further it should keep itself away from all sorts of mystical fantasies, dogmatic prejudices, anti-social bias and superstitions. That needs radical change both in religious practices as well as in religious doctrines. The theological framework has to be replaced by an ethical framework that can purposefully maintain a balance between the individual as well as social needs and, perhaps, in this regard, the ideal of *sthitaprajñātā* (the state of rational compositeness) found in *Gīta* can be taken as a sound directive. In the Indian context, where there is the presence of multi-religious demands at the social sector. But this does not also mean that one is to succumb to such religious pressures that arrest social progress. It, on the other hand, has to boost up that sense of moral order which is a harmonious blending of the individual and social requirements in a balanced reasoned manner and, for that, any religious rigidity cannot be allowed to stand as a stumbling-block.

14

Trusteeship Theory: A Mean of Social Justice in Indian Society

Vinod Kumari

John Rawls in his Theory of Social Justice (while conceiving of the original position of human society) presumes two basic principles led by social justice:

1. Equal right for all members or basic liberty compatible with a similar liberty for others.
2. Arrangement of social and economic inequalities in such a manner that these are expected to be to every one's advantage.

He gives primacy to the first principle in recommending that the distribution of wealth and income and the hierarchies of authority to be consistent with both the liberties of equal citizenship and equality of opportunity.

The first principle has been at the basis of all constitutional states protecting individual liberties and providing conditions where maximum number of members of society may be able to avail equality of opportunity The social and economic policies take into consideration the second principle. Attempts are made to lessen the gap between different social groups in society. These differences may be based on economic social or political grounds. The purpose of lessening the gap is to provide that common level at which communication between two individuals of a society belonging to any two different sections is possible without the possibility of the other being used as a means. This requirement indicates to a deeper reflection into the very nature and functioning of society.

There is an external control and systematization of society which is controlled through state policies and social norms. The society is ultimately constituted of the relationships of individuals and each individual has unique nature, potentialities. capabilities and certain attitude of reaction to external circumstances. The inner nature of the society is the value structure, the moral sense, and the sensitivity of each member to the environment. It is this aspect of society that is to provide any society harmony and richness.

The idea of justice adopted in state policies for distribution of money, power and offices is keeping in view that liberty and equality of opportunity is provided to each member. Since it is merely the external arrangement of society that is controlled by state, the inner change requires a revolution in the very outlook of the individual members towards life and social institutions as such. The first step in this direction would be the development of sense of accountability in the hearts of those who are in a position to help one's getting less share in the distribution of economy. The money and property either self-earned or inherited have so much attraction for us that even if it is unused we like to hold it. The owner if he thinks of those who contributed in the earning of the wealth will come to the conclusion that all of them have share in the wealth Moreover the social reality of different cultures and countries in different periods have class inequalities quite different and unique. In every social system roles are divided and individuals live at different levels of economy. knowledge and beliefs. Any generalization about class differences has to be contextual to a social system. It is only then that a proper understanding of the real problems of a certain society may be obtained. Any borrowed ideology. not firmly grounded in the psyche of a social group is bound to be unsuccessful in long run.

Gandhiji realized this fact and he always tried to apprehend the Indian social reality in a unique manner. He suggested in his article in *Amrit Bazar Patrika* (3-8) that we should study our eastern institutions in that spirit of scientific inquiry which is characteristic to the western culture. Only then we can evolve a true socialism and a truer communism than the world has even dreamt of. The class division that existed in western industrialized countries was quite different from class inequalities present in India. Gandhi was very much inclined to the requirement of change in subjective attitude of the members of society as insisted upon in Ancient Indian culture. Jainism has always talked of *Aparigraha* as a moral virtue to be pursued. One ought not accumulate wealth more than is sufficient for his own livelihood and satisfaction of necessary desires. Gandhi was also appreciative of the functional division of society as it was initially accepted by ancient Indian society. Merely reversing the external condition provides no lasting solution for a happier and harmonious society until and unless there is a change in the attitude of the members of the society.

The trusteeship theory has been gradually formulated in Gandhi's thinking. It was an alternative to Marxian theory of class struggle and violent revolution. Gandhiji based his theory on the awareness, reflection and introspection on the side of those who are the privileged ones. Those who belonged to this class, i.e., the rich landowners, the industrialists and the wealthy ones had the responsibility to realize the fact that they were the owners of their fortune only as a trustee of those who had a share in their wealth through their contribution of labour in the attainment of their fortune. On the other hand the labour class had to be aware of the importance and dignity of its labour and might put its demands as a right. It was through these opposing aware classes that an equilibrium in the domain of class-division could be achieved. Gandhiji was not in favour of elimination of the wealthy class and the capitalists. What he wanted was only a change in outlook of this class towards the havenots of the society. In *India of My Dreams* he wrote what was needed was not the extinction of landlords and capitalists but a transformation of the existing relationship between them and the masses into something healthier and purer. Further, he wrote that those who talked about class war as being inevitable had not understood the implications of non-violence or had understood it only skin-deep:

> "Though Gandhiji doubted the inevitability of class conflict. He was always in favour of giving labour its due place. He was of the view that to inflame labour against wealthy is to perpetuate class hatred and all the evil consequences flowing from it. The strife is a vicious circle and he was of the view that it ought to be avoided at any cost. For him it was an admission of weakness—a sign of inferiority complex. Gandhiji was optimistic that the moment labour recognizes its own dignity, money will find its rightful place, i.e., it will be held in trust for labour. Speaking against *zamindari* evil, he wrote.
>
> . . . . In reality the toiler is the owner of what he produced. If the toilers intelligently combine, they will become an irresistible power. That is how I do not see the necessity of class-conflict".

Gandhi made frequent reference to the *power of work* in contrast to the *power of capital*. These are interdependent and either of them can be used either creatively or destructively. He wanted a harmony between the capital and labour so that, the immense positive possibilities of creativity could be explored. The main thing was that the labour became aware of its capacity. In 1937, he wrote in *Young India* that the moment the worker realized his strength, he was in a position to become a co-sharer with the capitalist instead of remaining the slave.

Ignorance is the greatest obstacle for the achievement of social transformation by lessening class inequalities as vigilant ever conscious masses are required for it. Gandhiji had a conviction that with a growing knowledge of the labour of its natural strength, the inequalities must disappear. His view was that if the revolution was brought about by violence, the position would be reversed but not altered for the better, He had great hope that by adopting non-violence, i.e., conversion of attitude, the new era of social relationships must be born.

Gandhiji realized the dichotomy of capital and labour, but he never favoured the solution of this conflict through state ownership of means of production, as for him, state represented violence in a concentrated form. It was the spiritual aspect of human iudividuals that distinguished them for soulless mechanical relationship of the state machinery which has never been free from violence. The inner urge, the moral responsibility and initiative is possible only when it is left to the decision of free responsible moral agents. State interference and violence was of little help in this regard. He was not in favour of producing a dead equality where even· person becomes, or is rendered incapable of using his ability to the utmost possible extent. Gandhiji always declared that such a society was ultimately to perish. He suggested:

> "I, therefore suggest that my advice that moneyed men earn their crores but so as to dedicate them to the service of all is perfectly sound तेन त्यक्तेन भुञ्जीथाः is a *mantra* based on uncommon knowledge". *Harijan*, 22-2-42

At another place he explained trusteeships theory that all wealth that one has does not belong to one. What belongs to one is the right to an honourable livelihood, no better than enjoyed by millions of others. The rest of one's wealth must be used for the welfare of community.

Gandhi's conviction was so strong that he would not bother whether the followers of his trusteeship theory were more or less. It is true that the ideal of trusteeship was too high an ideal, possible only in a society of autonomous moral agents. Gandhi too, was quite aware of the difficulties of pursuing such an ideal. But he had firm belief that if people reflected on trusteeship theory constantly and would act upto it the life on earth would have been governed far more by love than it was. Though absolute trusteeship is an abstraction like Euclid's definition of a point and is equally unattainable, but one could go further for realizing a state of equality on earth. This situation is not peculiar to trusteeship theory only. In moral domain the ideals do guide human action yet they always lie ahead of human achievements and are never attained entirely. But it does not imply that the efforts to achieve those ideals are futile or something is lacking with the ideal itself. Moreover, an ideal like trusteeship that is mainly concerned with individual relations in a society has its psychological dimension also. It is the greed, the consumerist culture and insatiability of human desires, which proves to be an obstacle in the realization reference to this part of human nature.

> ". . . . . . The mind is a restless bird. The more it gets the more it wants and still remains unsatisfied".

Gandhi's view was based on religious faith and selfless service to humanity having their metaphysical foundations: For him, true humility was most strenuous and constant endeavour entirely directed to the service of humanity, reason being the continuous action of God.

The above discussion leads us to the following presuppositions of trusteeship theory.

1. Each individual is free moral agent.
2. Each human being has an element of goodness however evil may be.
3. Individual dignity of human beings.
4. Social relationship ought to be based on mutual acceptance and sense of acceptability of its members.

The first and the third presuppositions remind us Kant's idea of morality and his insistence on being a member of the kingdom of ends. But for Kant it was an ideal not fact which is to be achieved and guide one while deciding of his moral action. Gandhiji somewhat blurred distinction of value and fact when he presumed it for advocating his theory Since a relationship of mutual acceptance of each other is possible only in a society in which majority of its members are not only aware but have sense of moral responsibility also. Awareness itself does not entail moral commitment of an individual. It has to be something emerging from the inner nature of mankind for which no external pressure of political system may be of great help. There is a dichotomy in human thinking and action that is at the root of this problem. Gandhiji wished to blur the distraction between thinking and action that is why he wanted the steps towards lessening the class gap to be taken by those who had the capacity and privilege of doing so.

As regards his forth presupposition, it is possible only in an ideal society since ideal is somewhat projected in future, the existing social structure and the privileged class in it can be appealed to act in direction. But this appeal may turn out to be merely a request for charity if the labour class or the have-nots do not realize their dignity which has been submitted through the social pressures and ignorance. Unless ignorance is eliminated this theory has remote possibility of practicability.

Since it remained Gandhi's mission to prove the primacy of mind over matter, he emphasized subjective transformation as a means for resolving class conflict. He fully realized the role of private ownership as a strong motive force and incentive for human action and creativity. For Gandhi, means were as important as the end. His demand for the purity of means would never accept any social change or effort to resolve social conflict that was imposed from outside as he strongly believed that the system that is consistent with human nature is more stable.

In contemporary world the growing demand for better productivity by providing better work environment and greater incentives is the recognition of the fact that appeal to the inner elements of human nature is essential, if any change in social domain is to be made for the betterment. Gandhi was a visionary, who had realised this aspect of change long ago.

15

Gandhi and Secularism

Manisha Barua

'Secularism' is a word that has become immensely popular in the present times. Almost every political party makes the utmost use of this concept and accuses other parties of being non-secular or communal. There have been different descriptions and definitions of this word. Secularism has been defined as a moral code of conduct based on the well-being of mankind irrespective of religion, creed or form of worship. A secular state has no particular religion of its own. In the west the word 'secularism' was used to mean the rejection of the papal authority in the management of the state.

'Secularism' though a much widely used word in modern times was alien to Indian culture in the ancient period. The Indian mind was always deeply rooted in spirituality but no necessity was felt to coin words like 'secular' to maintain the unity or integrity of the masses. To others spirituality may be one condition among so many other conditions but to the Indian it is one great sustaining force pertaining to all the aspects of their lives. This spirituality acted as a great tree which allowed shelter to all the schools of thought and allowed each individual to practice his or her religion with fearlessness and pride. The Indian spirituality which broadly may be interpreted as *Dharma* was thus secular in nature.

In India the word *dharma* is used to mean religion. But it should be noted that the word *dharma* in Hinduism has a much wider connotation than what we ordinarily mean by the word 'religion'. The word *dharma* comes from the root *dhri* which means to sustain *dharma* is thus the *greatest sustaining force or the binding force of the society*. The goal of *dharma,* is to create mental and spiritual fellowship among all men and to regulate its relation with all living entities. It thus tries to keep the world in perfect equilibrium. Thus, *dharma* which literally means holding together or binding together would mean a chain of duties essential for the sound organisation of the human society. A careful analysis of the concept of *dharma* on the basis of opinions put forward by different scholars proves that this word *dharma* may also be interpreted to mean what is approved by the society, though it may not be found in the *shastras* and may not be supported by any custom. It may also mean actions performed after due reflection and reason and also to mean what is conducive to the welfare of all beings. It is thus clear that the word *dharma* was not used in connection with any particular religion. Any religion, any custom, any creed could be brought within its fold and was thus out and out secular.

Mahatma Gandhi who was born and brought up in the Indian soil could not escape the influence of this *catholicity* and tolerance. India is called *Bharat* and the word *Bharat* has a special significance. In ancient times we have reference to *Bharat* as follows:

> *"Uttaram vat samudrasya*
> *Himadrakshaiva dakshinam*
> *Varsham tad Bharatam nama*
> *Bharati tatra santatih".*

The country that lies north of the sea- south of the Himalayas is 'Bharata' and there dwell the descendants of Bharata, that is, the 'Bharati'. Thus, it is clear that people who dwell in this land are all `Bharati' irrespective of caste, creed or religion. Gandhi's view of religion and society was similarly all comprehensive, wide enough to accommodate all human beings irrespective of any caste, creed. or community who lived a peaceful existence in the *Ramarajya* of his dreams.

A deep analysis of Gandhi's view of religion points out to its secular nature. Gandhi refers to 'God' as 'Truth' and this has very important bearings. The word 'Truth' has a much wider connotation than the term 'God'. There may be non-believers in God. But no one can deny 'Truth' for even the atheists must accept the power of 'Truth'. Every religion believes in the power of Truth and there is no religion in the world that can deny the mighty role played by this concept. 'Truth' for Gandhi was the highest religion. This acceptance of God as Truth gives a secular colour to his religion.

To Gandhi religion is that which underlies all particular religions. Religion is not equitable with particular religions: it transcends Hinduism, Christianity, Islam and all other religions. Yet it harmonises them and gives them reality. It is that which binds man indissolubly to Truth. The one, true and perfect Religion can never be equated with any particular religion because no particular religion can embody the whole of Truth. Yet particular religions, according to Gandhi, are necessary to convey the meaning of Religion in the same way as particular truths are necessary to convey the meaning of Truth. But as particular truths do not embody the fullness of Truth so particular religions do not embody the fullness of Religion.

Gandhi describes religions as human constructs or expressions and, therefore, to some extent may be imperfect or erroneous. All religions, according to Gandhi, are different roads to the same goal and that there will always be a variety of religion corresponding to different human temperaments and environments.[2] Gandhi says "Even as a single tree has a single trunk, but many branches and leaves, so there is one true and perfect Religion, but it becomes many, as it passes through the human medium. The one Religion is beyond all speech.[3] Therefore, Gandhi maintains that we should have an attitude of respect and reverence towards all religions since they all contain an element of truth. Gandhi rejects the outright claims made concerning the superior or inferior status of religion.

Mahatma Gandhi was a Sanatani Hindu. His love for Hinduism was great. He was proud of being a Hindu, but his love for Hinduism was not blind love. Gandhi spoke about the lofty ideals preached by Hinduism but he was also aware of the defects of Hinduism. His belief in the Hindu scriptures could not force him to accept every word of the scriptures as divinely inspired. Gandhi refused to accept anything that did not conform to reason and moral sense. To quote Gandhi, "My religion is Hinduism. . . . . . I can no more describe my feelings for Hinduism than for my wife . . . . . . Even so I feel about Hinduism with all its faults and limitations . . . . . . I know the vice that is going on today· in all the Hindu shrines. . . . . . My zeal never takes me to the rejection of any of the essential things in Hinduism".[4] Gandhi was aware of the liberal attitude in Hinduism. It did not have one central book for reference, no particular God of worship nor one particular way of God realisation whether he is a theist or an atheist, he is a Hindu. Whether he believes in one absolute or many gods, he is a Hindu. Whether he believes in the Vedas or not, he remains a Hindu. Gandhi was similarly liberal enough to accept anything which was in conformity with reason. Gandhi did not believe in idol worship, but he was liberal enough to take idol worship as a part of human nature. Similarly, he was ready to accept the concept of incarnation. Gandhi also accepted the Hindu ideal of *Varnashrama Dharma* with certain modifications. He describes *Varnashrama* as a healthy social division of work based on birth, but he regards the present idea of caste a perversion of the original. He did not support the restriction on inter-dining and inter-caste marriage Gandhi regards untouchability as the greatest plague of the Hindu society, which is the duty of even· true Hindu to combat. Gandhi was also against animal sacrifice, though prescribed in the Vedas as it went against his concept of non-violence. Gandhi did support the sacrifice of animality in us in the form of lust, anger, hatred, ill will, etc.

Gandhi in the course of his views referred to *Rama* and Kṛṣṇa, the two most popular gods of Hinduism. It should be remembered, however, that Gandhi had no anthropomorphic conception of God. Gandhi says, "My Rama is not the historical Rama. He is the eternal, the unborn, the one without a second. Him alone worship"[5]. Again he said, "My Kṛṣṇa has nothing to do with the historical person. I would refuse to bow my head to the Kṛṣṇa who would will because his pride is hurt, or the Kṛṣṇa whom the non-Hindus portray as a dissolute youth. I believe in Kṛṣṇa of my imagination as a perfect incarnation, spotless in every sense of the word, the inspirer of the *Gita* and the inspirer of the lives of millions of human beings. But if it is proved to me . . . . . . that the Kṛṣṇa of the *Mahabharata* actually did some of the acts attributed to him, even at the risk of being banished from the Hindu fold, I should not hesitate to reject that Kṛṣṇa as God incarnate". Though deeply religious by nature Gandhi did not believe in rituals, customs, traditions, dogmas and other formalities observed for the sake of religion. Like Swami Vivekananda and Rabindranath Tagore, Gandhi's religion was not confined to temples, churches, books, rituals and other outer forms. In the words of Swami Vivekananda, "Temples and Churches, books and dogmas are simply the Kindergarten of religions to make the spiritual child strong enough to take higher steps . . . . . Religion is not in doctrines, in dogmas nor in intellectual argumentation, it is being and becoming and it is realisation". So was Gandhi's view of religion.

Though theoretically Gandhi calls God 'Truth' or *Satyam* yet for practical purposes he says that God may be different to different people according to their needs. He may be a personal God to those who need his personal presence. He may be the law to those who concentrate their minds on the orderliness of the universe. He may be an embodied being to those who need his touch. The secular spirit in Gandhi made him believe that God may have a thousand names as *Iśvhwara, Śiva, Vishnu, Rāma, Kṛiṣhṇā, Jehovah, Christ,* and *Allah,* etc. according to the traditions in which a man is brought up. In the words of Gandhi, "Is there one God for the Mussalmans and another for the Hindus, Parsis and Christians"? "No, there is only one omnipresent God. He is named variously, and we remember Him by the name which is most familiar to us".

Equality of all religions was a manifestation of Gandhi's belief in secularism. Gandhi's religion was a federation of different religious treeds. Theological schools and sectarian faiths that have survived in India from ancient times. People belonging to different religions would go to him for his advice and blessings on different matters. All through his life Gandhi devoted much time and energy for the promotion of Hindu-Muslim unity and also fasted for this cause on many occasions. He had also supported the Muslims in the *khilafat* cause. In the wake of the partition of the country, hundreds and thousands of Hindus and Muslims were killed in Punjab, Bengal and Bihar. Gandhi threw himself into the struggle to heal the breach between the two communities. Gandhi wanted communal harmony and peace not only between the Hindus and the Muslims but between all sections of the people who believe India to be their home, no matter to what faith they may belong. Gandhi had the good fortune to have as his colleagues and followers people belonging to different religions. Two important examples are those of C.F. Andrews and Moulana Abul Kalam Azad. The *Ashram* prayers of Gandhi had passages from the holy books like the *Gita*, the *Bible* and the *Qur'an*. This tradition still continues in India in most of the public prayers and meeting. Gandhi also maintained that a reverential study of the different religious tradition is necessary. He felt that it is the duty of every cultured man and woman to read sympathetically the scriptures of the world. To respect other's religions, a study of their scriptures is a sacred duty, according to Gandhi. The study of the scriptures, however, should not be motivated with the aim of coversion. To understand the point of view of another faith requires tolerance, sympathy, broadmindedness, humility and willingness to recognise Truth wherever it is to be found. If we possess these qualities we can appreciate other faith, traditions, customs, culture and way of life. The prophets and seers of different religions have brought to mankind the consciousness of the unity underlying the whole universe and a deep sense of brotherhood of man.

But though Gandhi had a deep respect in the different religions, he was against proselytisation. He was against certain forms of missionary activities specially those relating to conversion. Gandhi finds no justification in the use of force in order to lead man to the love of God. The presupposition of superiority of a particular religion as is propagated by the missionaries was strongly disliked by Gandhi. Gandhi was not opposed to conversion if it was based on one's own will but he was against any use of force or propaganda in the matter of conversion. Gandhi expressed this view almost poetically when he said: "A rose does not need to preach. It simply spreads its fragrance. The fragrance is its own sermon . . . . . . The fragrance of religious and spiritual life is much finer and subtler than that of the rose". Gandhi never subscribed to the fanatic view that there will be only one religion on earth. Gandhi's Catholicism was clearly evident when he refused to allow a Christian to declare himself a Hindu by being influenced by the *Bhagavat*. Gandhi said, "What *Bhagavat* offers the *Bible* also offers. You have not made the attempt to find it out. Make the attempt and be a good Christian"[10].

Gandhi's religion acquired a true secular nature when he declared that religion should act as a guiding force behind all activities of man—political, social and economic. The view of Jesus: "Render to Caesar the thing that are Caesar's and to God the things that are God's"[11] did not find favour in Gandhi. Rather his view was not more in accordance with the writings of H.G. Wells according to whom "the doctrine of the kingdom of heaven as Jesus preached it, was no less than a bold and uncompromising demand for a complete change and cleansing of the life of our struggling race, an utter cleansing without and within".[12] Gandhi's religion was spiritual humanism because he declared that the service of the poor whom he called *Daridranarayana* is a true service of God. In other words Gandhi finds God amidst his creation. In the Ashrams founded by him, service of the poor was the greatest object they aimed at. Gandhi had great sympathy for anyone who was in trouble and he tried to console them with his advice and help. His vast correspondence contained a good proportion of letters from and to those who needed his help. In his *Ashram* it was his habit to go round every morning to visit the sick people. He was keen on making the life of every villager comfortable and clean—physically and mentally. He was deeply touched by the sufferings and humiliations of the so called untouchable whom he called *Harijans* and he fought hard to remove the long standing evil of untouchability. To improve the economic condition of the masses he advocated some economic measures to ensure economic progress and create employment.

Gandhi was a spiritual humanist. His humanism is strikingly different from some of the important supporters of humanism in the west. In the west, the fashion at one time was to champion the cause of man against a theological world view. To mention a few are humanists like Exams and Herder who were opposed to the claims of the *Bible* of and Ludwig Feurrbach and Karl Marx who were totally materialistic in their outlook. The Indian humanism advocated right from the days of Asoka in the third century B.C. to Sankaracharya in the seventh century, to Kabir and Tulsi Das in the medieval period to Vivekananda, B.G Tilak and Aurobindo in the modern period tried to bring about a complete revolution. They advocated a humanism by maintaining its spirituality and so did Gandhi. Thus, Gandhi's concept of secularism did not reject spirituality and religion. Rather it gave a new dimension to 'secularism' which preached equality, humanity, universal love and tolerance. It did not mean anti-religion but it meant equality of religions in the eyes of the state.

REFERENCES

1. All Men are Brothers, pp. 56, 59.
2. *Selections from Gandhi* by N.K. Bose, p. 256.
3. *Ibid.*, p. 254.
4. *Young India*, 6. 10.1921.
5. *Harijan*, 4.4.1946.
6. *Young India*, 1.10.1925.
7. N.B. Sen (edited) *Wit and Wisdom of Mahatma Gandhi*, p. 14.
8. *Facets of Gandhi* by B.K. Ahluwalia and Sashi Ahluwalia, p. 133.
9. *In Search of the Supreme*, Vol.III. p. 83.
10. Gandhi, M.K. *'Mahatma'* edt. by D.G. Tendulkar, Vol.IV, p. 121.
11. *Mark* 12.17.
12. H.G. Wells: *A Short History of the World*, p.154.

16

The Meaning of Secularism

Dipak Basu

In India, everyone is confused about the definition of secularism. They equate secularism with religious tolerance. Secularism is defined in the Webster's dictionary as: "A system of doctrines and practices that rejects any form of religious faith and worship" or "The belief that religion and ecclesiastical affairs should not enter into the function of the state especially into public education." The Oxford English Dictionary states that secularism is the doctrine that morality should be based solely on regard to the well-being of humankind in the present life to the exclusion of all considerations drawn from belief in God or in a future state.

George Holyoake and Charles Bradlaugh were two leading secularists and atheists of England in the nineteenth century, from whom we have obtained the word 'secularism'. According to Holyoake, secularism maintains the sufficiency of secular reason for guidance in human duties. Secularism implies complete elimination of religious elements from life. A secularist is someone who rejects every form of religious faith. Thus, Guru Nanak, Sri Chaitanya, Swami Vivekananda, Ramakrishna Paramahamsa, Sri Aurobindo, although highly tolerant and respectful of other religions, were not secularists. Similarly, Mahatma Gandhi, Rabindranath Tagore, Subhas Chandra Bose, Maulana Azad, and Khan Abdul Gaffar Khan were not secularists, as they were devoted to their respective religions. Hindu religion, which teaches us to respect other religion, cannot be a secular entity as it is a religion.

The definition of secularism implies acceptance of "secular reasoning", which is utilitarianism of the English philosophers Bentham and John Stuart Mill. Utilitarianism suggests that the pursuits of happiness should be the goal of all human actions. According to Bentham "what is good is pleasure or happiness, therefore one state of affairs is better than another, if it involves a greater balance of pleasure over pain" ("Theorie des peines et des recompenses, ouvrage extrait des manuscripts de M. Jeremie Bentham", in *The Collected Works of Jeremy Bentham*, Oxford University Press). John Stuart Mill said: "Pleasure is the only thing desired, therefore, pleasure is the only thing desirable" (*Principles of Political Economy*, Oxford University Press).

Sri Krishna has described 'Secularist' and 'Utilitarian' persons very clearly, "They say, "this world has no truth, no moral foundation, no God. There is no law of creation" (Ch. 16, verse 8, *Bhagavad Gita*). "Their highest goal is sensual enjoyment and they firmly think that is all" (Ch. 16, verse 11). "In their chain of selfishness and arrogance, of violence and anger and lust, these malignant men hate me" (Ch. 16, verse 18).

Hindu ideals are based on selfless work without expecting any rewards. "When work is done as sacred work, unselfishly, with a peaceful mind, without lust or hate, with no desire for reward, then the work is pure" (Ch. 18, verse 23, *Bhagavad Gita*). Sri Krishna also said, "when a man dwells on the pleasures of sense, the lust of possession arises, which leads to anger, ruin of reason and ultimate destruction" (Ch. 2, verse 62). Thus, Secularism embodied in Utilitarianism is against the Hindu ideals.

In India, secularism is translated as *Dharma Nirapeksha*. The intended meaning of *Dharma Nirapeksha* is equal treatment of all religions. However, Government of India does not treat all religions equally either. Equality before law (Article 14), prohibition of discrimination on the ground of religion (Article 15) and equality of opportunity in public employment or for holding any public office (Article 16) are there in theory in the Constitution of India, but a series of amendment to the Constitution make those inoperative.

Article 14 is not observed at all. Police cannot start

investigations or prosecute any member of the parliament or the politicians holding high offices or even civil servants above the rank of a joint secretary without proper permission, which may not be available at all. There are separate laws for members of different religions.

Article 15 is completely submerged under the layers of special privileges and different systems of laws for different religious communities. There are discriminations on the grounds of caste, religions, tribes, and languages approved by the state. Positive discriminations based on caste and tribe are discriminations against those who are unfortunate enough not be born in those specific cases and tribes. There are various types of discriminations on public employments based on language as well, particularly in Tamil Nadu. Thus, Article 16 is not observed at all.

Article 28(1) lays down that no religious instruction shall be provided in any educational institution wholly maintained out of the state funds. However, Article 28(3) permits a state-recognized or a state-aided school to give religious instruction or to hold religious worship provided no student is compelled to attend the religious instruction or the worship. In India, states fund religious schools where religious instructions are compulsory. Religious schools receive generous grants. Purely religious educations in *Madarsa* for the Muslims are considered equivalent to the standard secular education.

Articles 29 and 30 that went beyond equal protection by giving special economic, legal, and political privileges to Christianity and Islam in the name of 'minority protection' and 'Secularism'. Even religious pilgrimage of the Muslims can be subsidized by the state. The 1981 Act on the Aligarh Muslim University describing it as an institution to promote the Muslims and established by and for the Muslims is fundamentally against every premises of secularism. Both Muslims and Christians can insult Hindus or Buddhists openly, and expel Hindus from their homes unless they accept conversions. Some Tamil politicians since the days of the language riots of 1960s regularly insult Hindu religion. Christian priests openly describe Sri Krishna and Gautam Buddha as devils.

Hindus were expelled from Kashmir by the Muslims and from Mizoram, parts of Tripura and Nagaland by the tribal Christians. Buddhists were expelled from both Nagaland and parts of Arunachal Pradesh by the tribal Christians. Efforts are going on in Andhra Pradesh and Kerala to have positive discriminations for the Muslims as well. Indira Gandhi started the practice of giving Iftar parties for the Muslims during *Ramadan*. Now political leaders compete against each other to throw lavish parties at national and state capitals. Former Muslim President of India, Zakir Hussain has established a mosque inside the presidential palace. Similarly, there is a mosque inside the Calcutta airport. Government of India cannot take any actions against the illegal Muslim immigrants from Pakistan and Bangladesh due to the fear of antagonizing the Muslims politicians. Religious groups like Muslim League and Akali Dal, and various Maulanas and Muftis are elected to high positions in the government. Muslim League is a part of the former 'secular' government of Man Mohan Singh. Thus, in no sense India has religious neutrality in the affairs of the government.

There is hardly any secular states anywhere in the world. A few countries like USA, France, Turkey are officially declared secular, but a closer examination may reveal that these countries are not that religious neutral either.

Secularism in USA

In the Constitution of United States explicitly calls for the separation of church and state. However, the overwhelmingly Christian population allows for some lapses in this policy: for example, money bears the words "In God we trust", and the Pledge of Allegiance includes the phrase "under God".

In USA, the First Amendment, confirms the religious neutrality in the Constitution in 1791 : "Congress shall make no law respecting an establishment of religion or prohibiting the free exercise thereof; or abridging the freedom of speech or of the press; or the right of the people peaceably to assemble, and to petition to government for a redressal of their grievances.".

However, there are traces of non-secular legal systems in the states of the U.S. In the Constitution of South Carolina, Protestantism is specifically noted as their state religion, and even election of clergy as part of a state election process. The Constitution of Pennsylvania advocates religious work for building human virtues.

Secularism in UK

In England, there is a close alliance between the Church and the State. The Church of England became independent of the Pope in the Sixteenth Century and is the official Church of England. The Monarch of England is the head of the Church. Though there is religious freedom in England, the Church of England has a special status inasmuch as the monarch of England must join in communion with the Church of England. A Catholic or any one who marries a Catholic cannot be the monarch of England. It is probable that a Catholic may not even be Lord Chancellor. The Established Church in Scotland is the Presbyterian Church and the General Assembly of that Church is the supreme legislative and judicial body. Higher levels of Priests (Bishops and Arch-Bishops) are automatically members of the upper house (House of Lords) of the British Parliament and thus, take part in the legislative process.

Secularism in the USSR and Russia

Although, USSR theoretically was a socialist atheist state, in reality religions were never banned or banished. The government used to employ priests from the three approved religions, Christianity, Islam, and Buddhism and to pay their salaries and pensions along with all other facilities. It has publicly funded religious training institutions for the priests, and used to maintain the religious places of worship along with the monasteries. Thus, the Soviet Union was not secular in the true sense of the term either.

In Russia today, these three religions are officially patronized as well, but Orthodox Christianity has the supreme position. Just like the USSR, Russia pays for salaries of the priests, maintains the places of worships, and builds new churches. In addition, just like in Britain, there are reserved positions in the state and central parliaments in Russia for the priests of these three religions. Priests from the Orthodox Church preside over the inaugurations of the parliament and the new government after any election.

Secularism in Germany

In Germany the state collects taxes for two Christian groups, while other religious or atheist groups have to collect their membership fees without the help of the state. Furthermore, there are religion lessons at school given by the state, but only for those two Christian religions. Communists are not allowed to be a teacher in a school or an academic in the university. A large number of teachers and professors of the former East Germany were fired after the unification of Germany in 1989. Thus, there is neither secularism, nor non-discriminations.

Secularism and Japan

Since sixth century until 1934, Buddhism was the state religion of Japan. In 1934, after a military coup in which the elected Prime Minister of Japan was killed, Buddhism was banned and Shinto, the original Japanese religion became the state religion. After 1945, in the new Constitution of Japan, religion and the affairs of the state were separated out. However, Shinto priests still preside over all inaugurations of public ceremonies, even the inaugurations of an industrial plants or a new machinery. Buddhists have their own political party, New Komeito, which collaborates with the ruling Jiminto party for decades. Thus, Japanese state system is not secular or religious neutral.

Secularism in Turkey

Turkey is supposed to be the only secular Muslim country, but it is a specific kind of secularism, which excludes all non-Muslims.

During 1915 to 1925, the Ottoman Empire and particularly Kamal Attaturk have committed genocides against the non-Muslim Armenians and Greeks, in which about 2.5 millions Armenians and Greeks were killed and rest had escaped to the Soviet Union. As a result, there are hardly any non-Muslims today in Turkey.

In the so-called secular Turkey, all religious affairs are carried out by a central government organization affiliated to the Prime Ministry, namely the Department of Religious Affairs, established in 1924. The function of this organization is to carry out tasks related to the beliefs, divine services and moral principles of Islam, and to enlighten citizens on religious matters. One cannot bring *Bhagavad Gita* into Turkey. This is hardly a great example of secularism.

Muslims and Secularism

Muslims in India are the most vocal supporters of secularism. Even members of religious groups like Babri Masjid Action Committee, Syed Shahabudeen, and Prof. Irfan Habib claim to be secular and Marxist. However, secularism has no support in Islam.

According to Islam, what Mohammed spoke is the law that controls everything in the Universe. "God can guide you to the Truth. Who is more worthy to be followed: He that can guide to the Truth, or he that cannot and is himself in need of guidance? What has come over you that you so judge?" ('The *Qur'an* 10:35) The Rule of *Allah* (*Shariah*) is compulsory and has basic laws and regulations that cannot be changed.

Secularism makes adultery lawful if the male and the female are consenting adults. *Riba* or interest on borrowed money is the basis of all financial transactions in secular economies. On the contrary, The *Qur'an* forbids these. As for alcohol, all secular systems allow the consumption of alcohol and make selling it a lawful business.

Secularism is based on separating religion from all the affairs of this life and hence, it rules by law and regulations other than

Allah's laws. Hence, secularism rejects *Allah*'s rules with no exception and prefers regulations other than *Allah* and His Messenger's. For Muslim societies, the acceptance of secularism means abandonment of *Shariah*, a denial of the divine guidance and a rejection of *Allah*'s injunctions

Ancient India and Secularism

In ancient India, the functions of the priest and king were separated. The priestly function belonged to the Brahmins while the political and administrative functions were vested with the Kshatriyas. The king was expected to encourage piety and virtue and aid religious institutions. Government was not based on a theocracy and considerable impartiality was practiced in the treatment accorded to various sects irrespective of the sect to which a king belonged. The ancient India was tolerant towards all religions, was equidistant from all religions, and generally gave equal promotion to all religions.

Thus, the foundations of religious tolerance are indigenous to India. Max Weber puts it: "It is an undoubted fact that in India, religions and philosophical thinkers were able to enjoy perfect, nearly absolute freedom for a long period. The freedom of thought in ancient India was so considerable as to find no parallel in the west before the most recent age". (*The Religion of India: The Sociology of Hinduism and Buddhism*, Free Press Publishers, Glencoe, Illinois, U.S.A.)

Analysis

India is not secular if we accept the true meaning of the term. India is not religious neutral or *Dharma Nirapeksha* either. Existence of differential legal system for different communities and reservation systems based on caste make India discriminatory towards religions. India particularly discriminates against the Hindu religion and Hindu ideals in the name of secularism.

Absence of religious learning in the schools in India in the name of secularism has the effect of creating a new generations who are hedonistic and without any moral values, as they see the politicians and the business community are prospering because they have no moral values at all. Along with the 'Economic Reforms' introduced in 1991, the doors of India are now open to all kinds of sexually stimulating materials encouraged by a very relaxed censorship. Sexual attacks on women and children are very frequent today in India. This is the result of lack of any moral and religious teaching in the schools and lack of proper censorship of the popular media, films, and television. In India, after independence there was an opportunity to maintain the idealism of the freedom movement. However, that opportunity was wasted; as a result, we now have a highly immoral society in India.

In *Bhagavad Gita* Sri Krishna said very clearly, "Even those who in faith worship other gods, because of their love they worship me, although not in the right way" (Ch 9, verse 23). That is the reason Swami Vivekananda has declared that Hinduism is the only religion that respects other religions. To ensure that there would not be any religious persecutions or differentiations, there should be very strict laws against discriminations. That would automatically demand a number of significant changes in the legal and political system.

(A) Just like in UK, USA, Germany, and France and indeed in other developed countries, the legal system in India should have uniform criminal and civil laws for all religions, tribes, castes, and races. When millions of Muslims in USA, UK, France, Russia, and Germany can live under unified legal systems, Muslims in India cannot raise any objection. If they want to live under the *Shariah*, they have the choice to leave India for their new homeland Pakistan (and Bangladesh) created in 1947. Christians cannot object either, as their position would not be affected adversely in any way.

(B) All system of positive discriminations or reservations based on caste, languages, tribes, must be removed. Positive discriminations for the disadvantageous groups should be based on poverty and physical disability only, irrespective of religion, caste, tribe, or language.

(C) All citizens must be allowed to take up employments or to live anywhere in India. Special status of Jammu & Kashmir, Nagaland, Mizoram, Meghalaya, and Arunachal Pradesh and employment restriction on non-Tamils in Tamil Nadu must be removed as well so that every citizen can move freely within the domain of India.

(D) Communal political parties, like Muslim League, with past crimes against humanity and parties with direct links with the anti-Indian terrorists, like Hurriat, Mufti Mahmoods' political organization, violent tribal organizations in Tripura, Mizoram, Nagaland and Assam, all must be banned, no matter what would be their reactions. Continuous recognition of their existence itself is discriminatory against their victims.

In Indian political system, secularism is a hypocritical word to demonstrate gross bias in favour of Muslims and tribal Christians, who are not secular in their thoughts and actions. It also has the effects of making the evil caste system of the Hindu society, which should be abolished completely, a permanent feature because of the caste based positive discrimination system.

Secularism itself is not superior to any alternative systems that exist in various countries of the world. There is hardly any country, which is secular. It would be absurd for India to claim to be morally superior just because it is so-called secular, where all kinds of discriminations and social evils exist in India at the same time. Time has arrived to get rid of this false secularism, and make Indian society and the political system devoid of any discrimination of any kind.

17

Was the Buddha : A Misogynist ?

Angraj Choudhary

As the doctrine of the Buddha is basically monastic in character, so his attitude towards women is determined by it. It is typical of monastic sentiment not to have any sympathy with woman, because she is a great snare. She is the most attractive but at the same time most insidious and dangerous. When Ānanda asks, "Master, how shall we behave before women," the Buddha says, "You should shun their gaze and if you happen to see her, you should not speak to her and if you should speak to her, you must watch over yourself."[1]

As far as monastic view is concerned, there "can be no falling in love, because it is a kind of *moha,* infatuation." As Anand K. Coomarswamy says, "To compare *nibbāna* as the *Bṛhadāraṇyaka Upaniṣad* compares the bliss of *ātman* intuition to the self-forgetting happiness of earthly lovers locked in each other's arms, would be for Buddhist thought a mockery."[2] He further says, "no less remote from Buddhist Sentiment is the view of western chivalry which sees in woman a guiding star or that Vaiṣṇavas or Platonic idealism which finds in the adoration of the individual an education to the love of all."[3]

In answer to a question, put by Ānanda, the Buddha once said, "Women are soon angered, Ānanda; women are full of passion, Ānanda; women are envious, Ānanda; women are stupid, Ānanda etc."[4] But he never disdained to accept the hospitality and the gifts of devout laywomen like Khemā, Uppalavaṇṇā, and Paṭācārā etc. He not only accepted offerings from the respected women, but also from the sinners. He accepted Ambapāli's invitation and refused the alternative invitation for the Licchavī Princes.

In this chapter I shall try to bring out the Buddha's overall view of women.

There are at least a few passages in the *Tipiṭaka* where the Buddha has directly or indirectly expressed his opinion about women.[5] There are some passages among them on whose basis one can prove his misogynic outlook. One such passage occurs in the *Cūlavagga* where the Buddha says to Ānanda, "If, Ānanda, women had not received permission to go out from the household life and enter the homeless state under the doctrine and discipline proclaimed by the Tathāgata, then would the pure religion, Ānanda, have lasted long, the good law would have stood fast for a thousand years. But since, Ānanda, women have now received that permission, the pure religion, Ānanda, will not last so long; the good law will now stand fast for only five hundred years."[6]

The tone here is confessedly apprehensive of the dangers that the order would be exposed to and the repetition of the name of Ānanda, as pointed out by I.B. Horner, for as many as four times more than confirms the Buddha's acknowledgement of his colossal mistake in permitting women into the Order. What he seems to imply by 'one thousand years' and 'five hundred years' is that the religion he took so much pain to propagate will not last long. Hence, he seems here like a tired man who has staked something very dear to him by giving permission to women to enter the Order. He seems to rue the fact that women have been given permission to enter the Order. On the face of it, it is quite clear that the Buddha in the heart of his heart, perhaps, did not approve of the idea of women entering the Order. But he yielded to the request made by Ānanda on behalf of women, because he loved Ānanda so much that he could not think of disappointing him. It was Ānanda who had pleaded the case of women headed by Mahāprajāpati Gotamī. To Mahāprajāpati Gotamī who brought him up after the death of his mother, he could say 'a flat no' "Enough, O Gotamī, let it not please thee that women should be allowed to do so,"[7] but to Ānanda's request he acceded, although he was full of misgiving, remorse and apprehension that were to follow as a necessary consequence. On the basis of this passage one can glibly say that the Buddha did not hold women in high esteem, thought them incapable of leading a religious life and so looked down on them.

There are other passages in the *Saṁyutta Nikāya* and *Aṅguttara Nikāya* where the evils of women as a race are brought out at length. "Women-folk are uncontrolled, Ānanda; women-folk are envious, Ānanda; women-folk are greedy, Ānanda; women-folk are weak in wisdom, Ānanda. That is the reason, that is the cause why women-folk do not sit in a court of justice, do not embark on business, do not reach the essence of the deed."[8]

"Monks, women-folk end their life unsated and unreplete with two things. What two?

> *Sexual intercourse and childbirth."*[9]
> *" 'Tis women that doth stain the higher life."*[10]

The very fact that a woman is said to possess the above mentioned evils proves beyond doubt her inferiority to man.

There is another passage in the *Majjhima Nikāya* where very authoritatively and forcefully the Buddha proves the inferiority of women. "It is impossible, it cannot come to pass that a woman who is a perfected one could be a Fully Self-Awakened one. . . . . . but the situation occurs when a man who is a perfected one could be a Fully Self-Awakened One—this situation occurs. . . . . . It is impossible, it cannot come to pass that a woman should be a wheel-turning king. . . . . . could be a Sakka . . . . . . a Māra . . . . . . a Brahmā... but this situation occurs when a man might be a Sakka . . . . . . a Māra, a Brahmā . . . . . . this situation occurs."[11]

It is clear from this passage that a woman can gain Arhantship and may become perfect, but she cannot rise to the status of a Sakka, a Māra, a Brahmā, let alone to the status of a Buddha. On the strength of this passage one would naturally arrive at the conclusion that the Buddha saw some inherent weakness in women on account of which they cannot achieve the perfections of a Fully Self-Awakened one. This passage, therefore, most seriously stresses the inferiority of women and it is this passage once again which more than anyone else reveals the Buddha's misogynic outlook. Perhaps passages like this were later responsible for the development of the view that *purishindriya* is superior to *itthindriya* and also that the former is acquired by observing higher morality (*mahantena kusalakammena*),[12] and the latter by observing lesser morality (*mandena kusalakammena*).[13] It has been said in the *Buddhavaṁsa*[14] that one has to have eight attainments (*sampatti*) before one can become a Buddha. One of the attainments obviously is to be born a man.

Buddhaghosha explains it in the *Suttanipāta Aṭṭhakathā* that *paṇidhi* (aspiration, resolve) can be fulfilled only by man, not by woman. *Liṅga sampattīti purishabhāvo, mātug manapuṁsa-kaubhatovyanjakāṇaṁ hi manussajātiyaṁ ṭhitānaṁ pi paṇidhi na samijjhati.*[15]

> *Manussattaṁ liṅgaṁ sampatti, hetu satthāradassanam/*
> *Pabbajjā guṇasampatti, adhikāro ca chandatā/*
> *Aṭṭhadhammasamodhānā, abhinīhāro samijjhatī ti//*

In the *Aṭṭhasālinī* also it has been explained at length that the faculty of male sex is caused by strong *kusalakammas.*

Tasmā purisalingaṁ balavaṁkusalena antaradhāyati, itthilingaṁ dubbala-kusalena patiṭṭhātta. Itthilingaṁ pana antaradhāyantaṁ dubbala akusalena antaradhāyati, purisalingaṁ balvakusalena patiṭṭhāti. Evaṁ ubhayaṁ pi akusalena antaradhāyati, kusalena patiṭṭhāti ti veditabbaṁ.[16]

On an analysis of these three passages one finds that all of them, in a way, point to the inferiority of woman as a race. The second passage concerns itself primarily with making a psychological analysis of her character but the first and the third which are chiefly concerned with her capacity or otherwise to adopt a religious or ascetic life and achieve Buddhahood prove that women are inferior to men as a race.

Before we make a thorough critical analysis of these passages and bring out their real import, it will be better to refer to some more passages from the *Tipiṭaka* which prove that the Buddha was not a misogynist. On the other hand, he was full of compassion for women. He poignantly felt their five woes[17] deeply cared for their hopes and aspirations and even looked beyond his age as has been pointed out by I.B. Horner, "to secure for them a status", social as well as spiritual which most of the social philosophers and ascetics of his time could not even conceive of. It was the Buddha and Mahavira who had the courage of conviction to rise above the prejudiced public opinion. They actually took good care to see that women got their just and right place.

For quite a long time, women were looked down upon, were regarded as no better than chattels and were subjugated by men. A time came when daughters were regarded as unwelcome. Dowry may have been one of its reasons. The second and perhaps the most important reason was the belief that a son by performing rites could secure for father (parents?) a place in heaven, but a daughter could not do so. As a result, daughters gradually lost their prestige, which they had during the Vedic period and even during the Upaniṣadic period. We hear of women such as Maitreyī and Gārgī who were great seers, perhaps as great, if not greater, as *ṛṣis* like Yājñavalkya. But, by the time of the Buddha women came to have a very low place. One instance among many will make this amply clear. When a messenger told King Pasendi that Queen Mallikā had given birth to a daughter, he became very sad.[18] The Buddha's outlook, which is evident from what he said to King Pasendi on the occasion, is quite different from the general public opinion, which prevailed at that time. His appreciations of the qualities of women are couched in excellent language.

A woman-child, O lord of man, may prove
Even a better offspring than a male.[19]

He does not have any doubt in his mind that women do have virtues and qualities and at times they can be better than men.

If we take into account the time when the Buddha pronounced this view of women, his revolutionary idea about them will be obvious. I am not using the term 'revolutionary' in the modern sense which implies some kind of demolition, but I am using it in the sense in which one can be revolutionary without resorting to violence and demolition and by just holding a view which is unheard of in one's time. The Buddha was very much advanced for his age and he saw clearly that women did deserve a higher status than they had been given and also they deserved immense sympathy and compassion. He took a liberal view in an age the atmosphere of which was not congenial for it. From this point of view, the Buddha can be said to be the holder of new view concerning women, the view which centuries later came to be known as the Emancipation of Women – a movement which epitomised their hopes and aspirations. It may legitimately be said that the Buddha fully espoused the cause of women and in his own way fought hard to secure for them a status which they had lost for quite some time.

Now, let us see what he thought of them from the religious or spiritual point of view. Did he consider them inferior to men as far as religious aspirations and ascetic practices are concerned? It will be clear from what he said to Ānanda that women are not incapable of ascetic practices and are not inferior to men as far as living a spiritual or religious life is concerned. When Ānanda asked him if he thought women incapable of practicing religion and making spiritual progress, he gave a categorical reply in the affirmative.

"Bhabbo nu kho, Bhante, mātugāmo Tathāgatappavedite dhammavinaye agārasmā anagāriyaṁ pabbajitvā sotāpattiphalaṁ vā sakadāgāmi phalaṁ vā anāgāmi phalaṁ vā arahatta phalaṁ vā sacchikātuṁ ti?"

"Bhabbo, Ānanda, mātugāmo. . . . . . sacchikātuṁti."[20]

He has absolutely no prejudice against women and unlike

others[21] very frankly admits that the door of salvation is not closed for women nor are they unfit by their nature to attain *nirvāṇa.*

"And be it woman, be it man for whom such chariot doth wait, by that same car into *Nirvāṇa's* presence, shall they come."[22]

In the *Aṅguttara Nikāya*[23] also he says that both mother and son can overcome the three terrors by following the Noble Eightfold Path.

From all this, it is clear that the Buddha did not say anywhere that women cannot lead a religious life nor are they incapable of attaining *nibbāna* (*nirvāṇa*). He never presumed that the nature of women stands in the way of realizing *nibbāna.* Somā replies boldly to Māra that being a woman does not mean that *nibbāna* is impossible for her.

Itthibhāvo no kiṁkayirā, cittamhi susamāhite/
Ṇaṇamhi vattamānamhi, sammādhammaṁ vipassato//[24]

What shall we say about the Buddha who emerges out of these passages? Can we justifiably call him a misogynist. The Buddha, who is so full of sympathy for women, who almost took up arms against those who wanted to keep them subjugated and did not allow them to have their social status, who thought women as capable as men of tasting the *dhammarasa,* who unequivocally declared that women are capable of gaining Arhantship cannot be labelled as a women-hater. In fact, he is a real revolutionary who is trying to get for them the status, social as well as spiritual, that they once enjoyed and lost during the centuries that intervened between the glorious Vedic period and the rise of Buddhism.

It is unthinkable that the Buddha who declared in emphatic terms that people attain superiority and greatness not by birth but by their actions[25] and did not attach any importance to caste, should have thought women inferior to men and relegated them to a lower position. Had it been so, he would not have so readily accepted the invitation extended to him by Ambapālī—the courtesan. The verses of the *therīs* amply bear it out that he espoused the cause of women and when occasion demanded, he gave them sermons to lead a religious life so that they could work out their own salvation and release themselves from the shackles of sufferings as also from the rounds of births and deaths.

Now, while interpreting the passages mentioned in the beginning we must remember this aspect of the Buddha. We should not interpret them in isolation. If we do so we will miss their real import. It is only when one reads them in isolation and out of context that one is inclined to call him a misogynist.

Let us take the third passage first where the Buddha says that it is impossible for a woman to become a *cakkavatti,* a Sakka, a Māra, a Brahmā or a Buddha. As a matter of fact, he is not giving vent to his prejudice against women nor is he looking down on them, when he says so, for any inherent weakness in them, but he is making a statement of fact here just as he does when he says that there is suffering in the world. It is possible for a woman to gain Arhantship, it is also possible for her to put an end to her suffering and better her lot, but it is impossible for her to become a Sakka or a Māra or a Buddha.

We know that for becoming the Perfectly Enlightened One, one has to work very hard. One has to fulfil all the *pāramitās*[26] (perfection), *upapāramitās* and *paramatthapāramitās* in order to attain Buddhahood. Besides, one has also to have what is called *paṇidhāna* (resolve) and *abhinīhāra* (aspiration). To fulfil all these one is required to be born several times and make immense efforts. Women in general are tender by nature and not capable of hard labour. Their physical build is such as does not enable them to make sustained efforts and keep hard vows. If we also take into account what the Buddha said in the second passage where he has made an objective psychological analysis of women's nature, it will be clear that both physically and psychologically, they are not strong enough to fulfil the conditions necessary for becoming a Buddha.

Had the Buddha said that they are incapable of gaining Arhantship and attaining salvation, his observation would have smacked of prejudice against them. But what he said about them is based on psychology which could have been ignored only at the cost of being unrealistic. A realist as he was, he knew that women in comparison to men are physically weak and psychologically weak-minded. But, this second passage should not be interpreted to mean that he regarded women inferior to men from social and spiritual points of view.

The first passage, too, should not be taken to mean, as pointed out by Horner, any kind of discourtesy to women. The Buddha hesitated to admit them into the Order because he thought the time was still unripe for this revolutionary step. Almost all the contemporary philosophers and ascetics were against women pursuing religious and spiritual life and none of them except Mahāvīra had established any Order for them (*Bhikkhuni Sangha*). "The dead weight of public opinion" according to I.B. Horner was too heavy to shake off. He was not a narrow-minded and conservative Hindu, but a broadminded and liberal one. I do not agree with I.B. Horner who says that "a man is bound by the chains of the past and these go clanging in his ears too insistently to be ignored." This may be true of an ordinary man, but this cannot be said to be true of the Buddha. He was not prejudiced as others were against women. But he hesitated to admit them into the Order because of "a whole host of reasons in their complicated relationship in the India of that time." Public opinion was one of them. He did not want to stir hornet's nest about his ears.

So, when Mahāpajāpati Gotamī accompanied by a large number of women strongly desirous of renouncing the world and tasting the elixir of the *dhamma* approached him and requested for being allowed to do so three times, they were given the same reply, "Enough O Gotami, let it not please thee that women should be allowed to do so". They were indeed very much sad by this refusal, but they did not lose heart. After some time they again went to him. This time they first met Ānanda who made out a case for them. Finally, the Buddha did agree to admit them into the order, but he did so hesitatingly because he thought that some unnecessary complications would arise if women were admitted into the Order and there would be obstacles in spreading the *dhamma*, as a consequence.

It is quite likely that the Buddha would not have invited women of his own accord to join the Order, but knowing their keenness, sincerity and strong desire, he could not have ultimately denied their entry into it.

We have made a detailed study of the Buddha's view of women and in the light of what has been said it does not appear reasonable to call him a misogynist. He was too full of the milk of human kindness and in no case he would have allowed public prejudices against women to get the better of him. "That he hesitated to admit them into the Order and he prescribed rules such as a nun even one hundred years old must stand in reverence before a newly ordained monk, can be surely ascribed to monk-editors of the texts", as has been observed by I.B. Horner, "who possibly could not rise above their prejudices against women."

REFERENCES

1. D2. 106.
2. *Buddha and the Gospel of Buddhism*, p.160.
3. *Ibid.*, pp. 160-61.
4. See below f.n. 7.
5. To get through to the Buddha's view of women it is appropriate to concentrate on the earlier layers of the *Tipitaka* and not on its later layers such as the *Jātakas* which do not faithfully represent the Buddha's view of women. The respect and deference paid to women can be inferred from the two Aniyata rules. (see *The Book of the Discipline*, Vol. 1, p. xxiii, Tr. by I.B. Horner).
6. Sace, Ānanda, nālabhissa mātugāmo Tathāgatappavedite dhammavinaye agārasmā anagāriyam pabbajjā, ciraṭṭhitikaṁ, Ānanda, brahmacariyaṁ abhavissa, vassasahassaṁ saddhammo tiṭṭheyya. Yato ca kho, Ānanda, mātugāmo... pabbajjito, na dāni, brahmacariyam? ciraṭṭhitikaṁ, Ānanda, bhavissati. Pañceva dāni, Ānanḍa vassasatani saddhammo, ṭhassati. Cv. (Nalanda Edition), p. 377.
7. Alaṁ Gotamī, mā te rucci mātugāmassa Tathāgatappavedite dhammavinaye agārasmā anagāriyaṁ pabbajjā ti. C.v. (Nalanda Edition), p. 373.

8. Kodhano, Ānanda, mātugāmo; issuki, Ānanda, mātugamo; maccharī, ānanda, mātugāmo, dupaṇṇo, Ānanda, mātugāmo-ayaṁ kho, Ānanda, hetu ayaṁ paccayo, yena mātugāmo, neva sabhāyam nisīdati na kammantaṁ payojeti, na kammojaṁ gacchatī ti. A 2.87 (Nalanda Edition).
9. Dvinnaṁ dhammānaṁ, Bhikkhave, atitto appativāno mātugāmo kālam? karoti. Katamesaṁ dvinnaṁ Methunasamāpattiyā ca vijāyanassa ca. A. 1.72 (Nalanda Edition)
10. Itthīmalaṁ brahmacaryassa, etthāyaṁ sajjate pajā. S. 1.36 (Nalanda Edition).
11. *The Middle Length Sayings*, tr. I.B. Horner (PTS) III, p. 109. 'Aṭṭhānametaṁ anavakāso yaṁ itthi arahaṁ assa sammāsambuddho, netaṁ ṭhānaṁ vijjati' ti pajānati, 'ṭhānaṁ ca kho etaṁ vijjati yaṁ puriso arahaṁ assa sammāsambuddho, ṭhānametaṁ vijjatī pajānāti. . . M 3.128-129 (Nalanda Edition).
12. See *Aṭṭha*, ed. P.V. Bapat, p. 259.
13. *Ibid*. p. 259.
14. *Bu* (Nalanda Edition), p. 309.
15. *Sn* A. p. 60, ed. Angraj Chaudhary.
16. *Aṭṭha*, ed. P.V. Bapat, p. 259.
17. *S 4*. 212-1. *ā213* (Nalanda Edition)
    See *Āvenikadukkha suttaṁ*
    ... a woman, at a tender age goes to her husband's family; ... is subject to menses... is subject to pregnancy,... has to bring forth... has to wait upon a man. *The Book of the Kindred Sayings*, IV, tr. F.L. Woodword (PTS), pp. 162-163
18. S 1.85 (Nalanda Edition).
19. *Ibid*., p.85.
    Itthī pi hi ekacciyā, seyyā posa janādhipa/
    Medhāvinī silavatī, sassudevā patibbatā//
    Tassā yo jāyati poso, sûro hoti disampati/
    Tādisā subhagiyā putto, rajjaṁ pi anusāsatī ti//
20. Cv. p. 374. (Nalanda Edition).
21. The *Digambara* Sect of the Jains holds that women are incapable of salvation.
22. S 1.31 (Nalanda Edition).
    "Yassa etādisam yānaṁ, itthiyā purisassa vā/
    Sa ve etena yānena, nibbānasseva santike//
23. Ayaṁ kho, Bhikkhave, maggo ayaṁ paṭipadā imesaṁ ca tiṇṇaṁ

samātāputtikānaṁ bhayānaṁ imesaṁ ca tiṇṇaṁ amātāputtikānaṁ bhayānaṁ pahāṇāya samatikkamāya saṁvattatī ti A.1.167 (Nalanda Edition).

24. How should the woman's nature hinder us.
    Whose hearts are firmly see *Psalms of the Sisters*, p.45.
25. Na Jaccā vasalo hoti, na jaccā hoti brāhmaṇo/
    Kammunā vasalo hoti, kammunā hoti brāhmaṇo. Sn 142.
26. Ten pāramitas are : Dāna pāramitā, Sīla pāramitā, Nekkhamma pāramitā, Paṇṇa pāramitā, Viriya pāramitā, Khanti pāramitā, Sacca pāramitā, Adhiṭṭhāna pāramitā, Mettā pāramitā and Upekkhā pāramitā.

18

Religious Pluralism and National Integration

Avinash Kumar Srivastava

By 'integration' we mean human unity and solidarity in diversity. In fact, the term 'integration' means the harmonization of loyalties and diverse interests. This unity is not an organic unity but an emotional attachment, which binds one another, whether it is group, region, religion, society or individual, by a general feeling of oneness in them.

National integration may be understood as cohesive attitude among different groups and individuals at the national as well as local level. It implies a feeling of common fraternity and oneness among the nationals of a country.

Here a question arises, "what is the ground or basis of this unity or cohesion? There must be cause for that. In fact, this common cause of unity or emotional attachment is nation itself. Nation is the pivot around which the common feeling of the different groups or individuals revolves. It also implies a loyalty to nation, which is above petty considerations. Thus we find, broadly, three elements in national integration :

1. It is an attitude of mind that regards loyalty to the nation being above group and sectional loyalties.
2. It is an attitude of keeping the interest of groups or sections subordinate to the wider interest of the nation.

3. It is an urge to think of the interest of every citizen of the country irrespective caste, creed and religion.

Now, it can be said that by 'national integration' we mean a harmonization of loyalties that the citizen of any country feel for different groups in the context of the nation as a whole.

Another term is 'religious pluralism'. This term is conjugation of two words—'religious' and 'pluralism'. Normally, religious pluralism means coexistence of different religious faiths and beliefs as we have in India. Before, we examine the concept and implication of religious pluralism, it would be proper on our part to examine what do we mean by religion.

Galloway opines that, "Religion is a man's faith in a power beyond himself whereby he seeks to satisfy emotional need and gains stability of life and which he expresses in acts of worship and service." Marxism, Leninism consider religion a historically transient phenomenon of social consciousness and shows that main factors that determines its existence at different stages of society's development.[5] When we analyze religion in a scientific way, we find that it is a complex social phenomena, a system of specific ideas, feelings and rituals. In the Indian context religion is translated as *dharma*. Etymologically, the word *dharma* has its origin from the root '*dhri*' which means 'to maintain', 'to continue' and 'to possess'. In that sense religion is a unifying force in a social structure.

We need to accept as well that as men became conscious of their existence, which consisted in the chain of BIRTH and DEATH, they realized how helpless they were in nature's set-up. This instilled a sense of 'wonder' and greater than that 'Fear'. To emotionally stabilize themselves, they worked out esoteric methods that in due course was systematized. Thus, a system to repose faith in something beyond control took the form of religion.

'Pluralism' as a concept is opposed to monism and which means that all that exist consists of a multiplicity of equivalent, isolated substance, irreducible to a single principle. In the field of social sciences pluralism serves as the basis for denying the existence of a singly determining principle of society. For understanding history as a current of accidental events and in context of religion it means different community of society believing in different divine powers, using different sets of rites for their religious purposes. In fact, religious pluralism, as we have already suggested above, is a state of different religion coexisting simultaneously and with a sense of adjustment on social plane.

To understand the term religious pluralism it seems proper to trace the stages of development of religion. In early stage of human civilization there was, probably, no religion. If at all, there was any, it was the religion of food, drink and shelter. But this stage could not continue for a longer period. With the evolution of mankind habit and tendency of men living into groups increased. This was primarily due to security of life and property. The economic theory of the origin of the state accepts that state came into existence for the fulfilment of human necessities. Aristotle points out that state come into existence for the sake of good life. Persons of sound body and sound mind emerged as leaders who made a study of the environment and situations around them and established a code of values that were necessary for the regulation and growth of their society. In this very sense the word *dharma* is defined in *Mahabharata* as the factor, which sustains the society.

In fact, their social values, in the long run, were transformed into different sets of religious commandments. And thus, in course of historical evolution different religions emerged on the different parts of the world.

When we give a glance over the present situation we find that there is a plurality of religion such as *Hinduism, Buddhism, Jainism, Islam, Christianity, Zoroastrianism, Sikhism,* etc. Every religion is divided into so many internal sects, *viz,* in Christianity there is a division of Catholic and Protestant, Islam is divided into *Shiya* and *Sunni, Daudi* and *Vohara* etc., *Buddhism* is divided into *Hinayana* and *Mahayana.* In Hinduism also there are several inner religious sects such as *Shaiva, Shakta, Vaishnava,* etc. In *Sikhism* there are two sects *Akali* and *Nirankari*, etc. Thus, the entire human population is divided into several religious camps.

As we have tried above to explain in brief the connotations of the two phrases 'religious pluralism' and 'national integration', we have come to understand that the conjunction or the two means persons of different religions or religious sects living in a country with a common allegiance and intention to defend the country.

A question may arise, is national integration possible behind the plurality of religion? Can religions generate a feeling of oneness among the nationals of a country? If we look back and take into account the history of mankind, we will find that religion had been one of the potent factors responsible for disintegration at many points. Disunity of mankind is, in great part, due to the prevalence of many religions in the land. It is evident from the history that in past, religions have played active role in disintegrating a nation and injuring the solidarity of mankind. There have been instances of religious strives, such as *Jihads*, Hindu–Muslim and Hindu–Sikhs riots, etc. Several religious warfare were staged and nations were divided on the basis of religions. India has been the victim of religious fanaticism. Even after fifty years of independence, the divisive forces of religion are at work and are threatening the national integrity. An enquiry into the working of Christian missionary in Bihar and Madhya Pradesh reveals that Christian missionary had been primemover for the proposal of a separate *Jharkhand* state for tribal people. The conversion of large number of *Harijans* to *Buddhism* under the leadership of late Dr. Ambedkar was due to communal bias. Our country has already been divided on the basis of religion, followers of Islam forming a new state, The Islamic Republic of Pakistan after independence. Even today the national integrity in India is at stake due to religion's sponsored terrorism. The demand for separate *Khalistan* was primarily a religious issue.

How religion tends to be a factor of disintegration? How religion functions in antagonizing the people of different religions? In order to find out the answer of these questions we will have to take into account the present purpose of religion in the society, and how the leaders of different religions have exploited it.

When there is more than one religion in a nation, religion becomes the cause of disunity due to the following reasons :

1. Different pattern of behaviour of the people of different religions;
2. When expectations of some members of some particular religious community is frustrated;
3. Religious chauvinism;
4. Religious intolerance;
5. Role of politicians and religious leaders;
6. The problem of minority; and
7. Conversion of religion.

1. When there is more than one religion in a society, there will be different patterns of behaviour among them. This is mainly due to different places of origin of different religions. For instance, in India, Christianity, Zoroastrianism and Islam came from outside the country. They have always tried to preserve their separate entity and distinctive features. They did so partly due to self-defence. Since they came from different climate and culture, their behaviour was different from the followers of the Indian religions. Often some of their activities were opposed to others that touch the sentiments of the religious followers of India, *viz.*, cow slaughtering, which is common in Islam and Christian. These practices have touched the religious sentiments of the Hindus, Jainis, Buddhists and Sikhs. In the same way, pork is a taboo among the Muslims and if unfortunately pork is found near a mosque or a house of a member of the Muslim community, tension is bound to stir. In the same way, different behaviours of the people of different community create enmity in them, which result in human unrest and disintegration of the nation.

Not only that, there has been difference of existence and approaches of behaviour of other religions and the religions of the Indian soil. But even the religions born and nursed in India are found at logger's head. This variation of behaviour of the people of different religions creates trouble, unrest and ultimately injures the solidarity of mankind in a country.

2. The members of every religion expect favour, and special privileges from the Government as well as from the followers of other religious community. They also expect that the followers of other religions pay regard and reverence to their religious deities in the same spirit they pay to them. The failure of the same, causes injury to their communal feeling. These expectations are confined not only to social level; they are extended to political favour such as favour in government service and also in political berths. When any of these expectations is frustrated it makes them violent, intolerant, which is deterrent to the national integration. Really speaking, the man is obsessed with two qualities.
   (i) Sense of belongingness, and
   (ii) Sense of self-identification.

Religion has inherited these qualities. Due to the sense of belongingness, the followers of every religion expect that there should be some institutions to foster, encourage and expand their religion. This sense of belonging generates in them a sense of separateness and exclusiveness. If it is ignited, it creates a problem for a nation. The demands of separate *Tamil* state in *Sri Lanka, Islamic Chechnya*, Palestine State, etc., are due to these elements of religion.

The sense of self-identification also creates a sense of separateness. The followers of every religion want a separate recognition and identification. They do not want to mingle into the main stream and lose their identity. That's why reservation in service and berth in cabinet and other political posts is often demanded by different religious leaders. When these elements grow they became violent and separation of the nation is demanded.

3. *Religious Chauvinism*—Religious chauvinism and fanaticism to great extent, are responsible for the tragic situation of disunity among mankind. In fact, these give rise to religious communalism. The followers of every religion consider their own religion superior to others. They consider their God mightier than the God of other religions. They plead that their religious rites and norms are better than those of the others. They also keep it in their mind that their religion alone has the capacity to enlighten the mankind and redeem its suffering. This false notion compels them to think that only their religion has the right to survive. In this hypnosis they raise their voice against the other religions that culminate in riot, arson, *jihad.* They treat these battles as *dharmayuddha.* Here lies the germ of terrorism. In fact, it is a false notion. No religion prescribes conquering others through brute force or might.
4. *Religious Intolerance* – The false notions regarding religion generate a sense of intolerance. If any procession is taken out before any temple, Hindus become angry. If any drum is beaten near any mosque the riot begins. Religion has become so weak that its sanctity is broken by the sound of drums, music and procession of other religions. This religious fanaticism and dogmatic outlook has generated a sense of greater loyalty to one's own religion than to the nation. It is, in fact, threatening to the national integration. When sense of intolerance attains maturity it becomes dangerous and violent. They treat them outcast and do not want to tolerate them. This cult of terrorism has received strength and is creating threat to the harmony of the nation and cohesiveness.
5. *Role of Politicians*—The so-called religious and political leaders exploit the situation. In order to maintain their leadership they seldom miss a chance to condemn other religions and its followers and declare them the cause of all the evils. They exploit the religious instincts of the people in the way they like. The dissatisfied people get

ignited into action. The suppressed tension is released in the shape of riots and showdowns. It creates emotional imbalance that results in crisis, troubles and disunity in nation.

In fact, these leaders for their political gain utilize religion and exploit religious sentiments for their own ends. They twist anything in their own interest. Britain was quick to perceive this inherent weakness and took advantage of it for strengthening her political hold. They roused the communal feelings as a matter of official policy. The rationale behind her policy is that Indian integration and unity was against their political interest. The Anglo-Mohammedan nexus achieved its positive result—Pakistan.

Really speaking, religion is simply a shield. The main reason of arson, riot and human unrest is personal gain and lust for power. The demands of percentage in the Government clearly indicate that liberal tolerant Indian society is now burning into flames of communalism, separatism and terrorism. Selfish elements are making their hay at the cost of innocent life of mankind. Mahatma Gandhi rightly perceived that it was the greatest deterrent to the national unity. His major task was to finish this religious communalism. He became martyr in his mission. Our late Prime Minister Smt. Indira Gandhi and Saint Harchand Singh Longowal met the same fate that was on the path of Bapu.

6. *The problem of minority* – In India Muslim, Christian, Parsi, Buddhist, Jain and Sikhs are in minority. Some of them look at the national integration from the point of view of adjustment. They are much concerned with their security and freedom in their religious affairs. On the other hand, Hindus are more concerned at the threat to communal aspects of integration. In this respect their way of thinking is very close to that of the minorities, i.e., Muslims, Sikhs, and Christians. "Due to mutual suspicion, prejudice, preconceived notions and false ideas much avoidable friction is caused."[6]

In fact, the majority Hindus are suffering from minority complex. There are two reasons for that—

(a) They had been under other's rule for centuries;

(b) They themselves are divided into so many castes, sub-castes and groups. The psychology of smaller group persists in them. That's why the concept of *Hindu Rashtra* appeals to them so much.[7] If we equate India with *Hindu*-India, we degrade *Hinduism* and destroy its catholicity.[8]

7. *Conversion of religion* – In fact, much of misunderstanding prevails regarding conversion of religion in our country. Often it results in strong difference of opinion. It creates unnecessary feeling of insecurity and fear in the mind of religious minorities and on the other hand it arouses an undue sense of power under stress of emotion which causes serious damage to life and property. The smooth relation becomes impossible and it creates an atmosphere of mutual suspicion. It also creates a sort of tension that often results in riot, arson, etc.
8. When religion fails to explain the oppressive factor of the hierarchical division of the society, the oppressed class being frustrated became antagonist to the majority, which often creates a chaotic situation.

On the basis of above analysis, it becomes clear that religious pluralism with its consequent, culture and social divisive tendencies put up a great obstacle in the way of solidarity in a nation because it functions in isolating the human populations in different groups and camps. Religious fanaticism, narrowness, intolerance, dogmatism give rise to violent separatist tendencies and man becomes the enemy of man. That is why religion has been called opium of society. Religious following is considered to be the symbol of backwardness.

Often it is said that the function of religion is to unite and integrate and not to disintegrate. Even if it is true, it binds together only the followers of one religion but in the process of binding them, it separates the followers of other religions, which shows that religious pluralism and national integration cannot go together.

When we peep into the meaning, use and the function of different religions of the nation we cannot agree with this hastily arrived conclusion regarding religious pluralism in the context of national integration. It will be the darkest day for the nation when its unity will be achieved by suppressing all religions. If the price of national integration is to sacrifice all religions, religious beliefs and practices, it will be a heavy price indeed. Religion cannot be got rid of. However, we should decide the ways and means to achieve national integration despite plurality of religions. Broadly, there seems to be two ways through which our goal could be reached. They are negative and positive ways.

Negative ways : Negatively it is abstaining from such work, which may injure the harmony of the country by causing harm to its uniting forces. They are as follows :

1. There should not be any objection with regard to the external behaviour of the followers of other religion, if it does not do any positive harm to person, society or nation as the external behaviour and different modes of worship do not form the essence of religion. The difference among them is due to their different birthplaces. Every mode of worship, rites, bears an impact of culture, geography and climate of the place. We should not attach much importance to them. The different prayers and different names of God are nothing but the different expressions of religion. In *Veda* it has been rightly said, *"Ekam sad viprah bahudha vadanti"*. It should be borne in the mind that various religions of the world are various paths to achieve the common goal of religion, like various rivers which travelling through straight or crooked routes reach the same ocean. Religions try to understand their view point with open mind. If we live together, accepting the right of everybody to follow his own conviction, we should be able

to form the family hood of all religions through love, sympathy, service and self-secrifice.[9]

In fact, Hinduism and Islam, Buddhism and Jainism, Christianity and Sikhism all have a uniform goal of human welfare, a common programme of social regeneration and a common aim of solidarity of mankind. Their characteristics are common and aims are identical. *Every religion has R—Righteousness, E—Enlightenment, L—Leniency, I—Impartiality, G—God fearing, I—Inspiring, O—Objectiveness,* and *N—Nobility.*

If this basic fact is understood and accepted, conflict between religions and different sect of religion will cease and national outlook will emerge. We can have national integration despite religious pluralism.

2. No class, community or religious group, whether minority or majority should bolster up narrow and exclusive group interests as absolute. Then interest should be subordinated to the larger interest of the nation. Religious groups should not stress on rights and privileges at the cost of duties and obligations. No religion advises to have undue expectations in this regard because these are not religious in true spirit.

Secondly, people of any religion who have settled down in any country for a considerable period and have contributed to the cultural stream are expected to accept the secular way of life consistent with the geography and the history of the country. Particular religious beliefs cannot be imposed on others and one should not expect in this way. The Muslims cannot be expected to look at gods and goddesses of Hindu mythology exactly with the same eye as the Hindu do, and *vice versa.*

3. To consider one's own religion better than others and on that ground to think that only his religion has the right to

survive is a wrong notion and unhealthy sign. In fact, different are the roads leading to the same goal. They differ with other due to the difference in three aspects i.e. *philosophy, mythology* and *rituals*. Different religion emphasize the different qualities of religion, such as Islam lays emphasis on universal brotherhood, Hinduism on spirituality, Christianity on self purification for entering into the kingdom of God. It does not mean that one is superior and other is inferior, one is real and true and the other is wrong and false. Buddhism decries this tendency. In twelfth *Ashokan* inscription it is written that one should not decry other's religion while praising one's own. If he does so he causes harm to his own religion.

In this connection Jain religion provides a nice solution. According to *Anekantavada* various religions should not quarrel with one another because everyone of them has some amount of truth, which the other side may be wanting. Our concepts of truth are often partial. One should, therefore, be ready to express respect for other stabilizing and destabilizing factors to our development. And it is they who have created the problem of national integration.

4. The religious tolerance should be developed instead of intolerance. No religion advises to be intolerant rather it preaches love to the creatures of the world. In fact, religious faith is the matter of personal conviction. One should not interfere in that. Worship should defend pure and sincere faith. We should not compel anyone to accept a particular religion. No religion preaches to be intolerant. In the *Sura Kafirun* of the *Holy Qur'an* it has been clearly said, "Say, O ye, that reject Faith, I worship not that, which ye worship, nor will ye worship that which I worship. And I will not worship, That which ye have been went to worship, Nor will ye worship That which I worship, To you be your way, and to me mine."[10]

Jain religion believing in *Anekantavada* does not ask anyone to give up his or her religion and embrace Jainism. Hindu religion has the concept of tolerance, which is based on the validity of all religions, and the same with Sikhism. In Christianity we find that Christ himself is the symbol of tolerance. He crucified himself for the sake of others. Thus, we find that every religion preaches to be tolerant. It does not ask anyone to be intolerant for religions sake. If we follow this message of religion honestly and sincerely the problem of disintegration will never arise.

5. If religion is not polluted by politics, there will be no problem of disunity, nor there will be any conflict among the followers of different religions. Religious pluralism cannot create any problem to the national integration provided it functions in the true religious spirit without being polluted by politics. It is politician who twists the religious preaching in a communal sense and utilizes it for his personal gain. It is evident from the history that when Islam entered in India as a religion, in hundred AD Hindus welcomed it, accepted it and liked it. The kings were benevolent to provide land and resources to the Muslim Mullahs for constructing their mosques. But when Islam again entered India under the patronage of Mohammad Bin Kasim, Mohammad Gazani, which was more a political force than a spiritual light, both stabilizing and destabilizing factors to our development vehemently opposed it. And it is they who have created the problem of national integration.

It is imperative on the part of majority people to take them into confidence by extending them a sense of positive security and generate in them a sense of 'we feeling'. Jaya Prakash Narayan is of opinion, "They have to be tuned out of the smaller circle into the large circle of nationhood as they still persist in their minority psychosis. On the other hand, they should also establish rapport with the people of majority religion in order to become part and parcel of Indian culture and loyal to the soil, while remaining free to follow their own religion and worship their God in their own way. Last year I saw a nice caption "Muslim with the religion part of the nation". It is the real spirit of nationality which should generate in each and every man of this nation.

The Positive Approach

Positively by following the sanctions of one's religion, national integration can be maintained. It has already been mentioned earlier that etymologically the import of *dharma* is integration. It is uniting factor. In Indian context, it has different sheds and meanings. *Dharma* means duty. If we all do our duty honestly we can keep our country integrated and we can maintain harmony and peace. In the *Bhagavad Gita*, different types of duty have been assigned to the different people of different castes and it has been further said that by doing one's own duty one can get liberated. Today, the first and foremost duty of every citizen is to serve the nation and save it from the internal danger and external aggression. Thus, the followers of different religion can remain honest to their nation by holding on their respective duties and thus can remain faithful to their own religion also.

Concept of National Integration in Different Religions

When we peep into the internal references of scriptures of different religions and their ways of worship, we find that every religion has given stress on national integration, directly or indirectly. Here a brief account of the elements of national integration as found in different religions is needed. Hinduism is full of feelings for national integration in most of the worships or *yajna* the different Indian nationals. Due to iconoclastic zeal of Mohammad Gazani, Hindus became hostile to Islam. It is a fact that Mohammad Gazani caused a great harm to Hindu religion but indirectly it was no less a harm to Islam which he wanted to perpetuate. These two religions did not meet for a longer period at the higher level of intellectual discussions or philosophical understanding. It was the *Bhakti* movement (religious movement) that softens the ills and agonies of the followers of both the religions (*Hindu* and *Muslims*).[11] Kabir preached that Allah and Rama are the different names of the same God. Hindu and Turks were the poet of same day. During the time of Akbar, Hindu venerated Muslim saints and the Muslims respected the Hindu saints. (Both Hindus and Muslims worshipped *Satya, Pir*).

In the same way, the Sikh religion emerged in India and became the main stream of Indian culture. Every Indian has regard and reverence for *Guru Granth Sahib, Guru Nanak, Guru Govind Singh* and other saints of *Sikh* religion. Most of the Hindus go to *Gurudwara* to offer their prayers. Even now the matrimonial relation between Hindus and Sikhs is very common. But when the political leaders get their access in *Gurudwaras*, they motivated people for terrorism developed in Sikh religion. Innocent people were slain at the altar of religion for the political gain. It antagonized all the true Indian nationals; a rift took place in the relation of these two communities. Many Hindus stopped going to *Gurudwaras* in Punjab, not out of hatred but because of fear. Really speaking, it is an indirect loss to Sikh religion. To my mind if the religion is purged of politics it will be an ideal situation and again the harmony will be established.

6. *Problem of Minority :* In Indian, *Christian, Muslim, Parsi, Buddhist, Jainis* and *Sikhs* are in minority from the point of view of religion. They are very much Indian in food-habits, appearance and ways of living. They are very much components of our nation and contribute to our heritage. They add to our diversities and lend colour to our varieties. Perhaps, because of them, we claim to be secular and composite in our colour. It is because of them, we have survived the vicissitudes of history. Interestingly enough, they by themselves are rivers of India are offered prayers and participate in it. The Hindus do pilgrimage and offer their prayers to the different gods in different temples

situated in the different parts of the country. A Hindu devotee starts his pilgrimage and reaches each and every part of the country right from *Kashmir* to *Kanyakumari*. Thus, they meet the people of different region, language, class and culture and feel affinity with them. It generates in them a sense of oneness with the people of the nation and unites them through the threads of religion. Keeping in view the Indian integration *Adi Guru Sankaracharya* established four *Mathas* on the four corners of India.

Buddhism – Buddha travelled on foot every nook and corner of this country, met the people of different places, cultures languages and religion and also asked his disciples to do *charika* everyday for the welfare of the people.

Buddhists have also constructed their temples all over India which unites the people of whole country with one thread.

Jainism – Jain solution to the problem may also be taken into consideration. According to it if everyone believes in the metaphysical theory of *Anekantavada* and epistemological theory of *Syadvada*, the religious pluralism will not create any threat to national integration, as every religion will be considered as the expression of the same truth. This will lead men to respect other religions also. A believer of *Anekantavada* never asks anyone to give up his or her religion and embrace Jainism. He can very well say purify yourself, even without giving up your religion you can become a true *Jain*. It is the main spirit of the universal religion of Vivekananda.

Sikhism – Sikhism emerged in reaction to the disintegrating forces of India. It has always fought against those element and forces that tried to disunite or create a disharmony in this country right from *Mughal* period to British reign their contributions are laudable. Their role in Indian National Movement is praiseworthy. *Sikhism* always thought of maintaining and preserving the *Hind ki chadder*.

It is evident from the history that the great *Guru Nanak* spent his twenty-two precious years of his life in *padayatra* to every part of the country in order to knit together the entire population of India. *Guru Amar Das* opened the gate of *Gurudwara* for the people of all class and community. There everyone could lunch and dine together in a common kitchen irrespective of caste, creed, class and community. This generated in them a feeling of equality, which was helpful in promoting an atmosphere of communal harmony.

Islam—The historical references of Islam reveal the fact that even there the concept of religious pluralism and national integration is available. In the year of 622 Prophet Mohammad entered into a contract with the Jews of Madina that the people of both the religious communities will fight against the Arabs and save their town and in the same time one will be at liberty to follow one's own religious life. This is a beautiful example of religious pluralism and national integration.

Every religion permits the peaceful coexistence of the followers of different religion. Today one speaks of this but unfortunately our national consciousness has become meaningless in the present atmosphere.

A question arises what is the cause of this deterioration and these are two fold : (1)The Dual culture, (2) Lack of proper knowledge of religion.

(1) *Dual culture* – Today our national character has become dual in nature. Any Indian whether he is Hindu, Mohammedan, Sikh, and Christian whatever he may be is living under the layer of two cultures :

   (a) A culture inside the house; and

   (b) A culture outside the house.

(a) *A culture inside the house* – Any Indian who looks to be liberal, catholic or secular is not at all an Indian inside the house. He is a dogmatic *Hindu, Muslim, Sikh, Christian* and nothing more than that. In fact the culture used in our house is of a dogmatic religion rather than Indian. That is why a man sitting inside the house does not remain an

Indian. He is a Hindu, a Muslim, Sikh or a Christian. Thus, our houses do not produce a patriot Indian national rather they produce a Hindu, Muslim, Sikh or Christian patriot.

(b) The culture outside the house—The *Hindu, Muslim, Sikh* or *Christian*, who is a dogmatic disciple of his religion pretends to be a secular and patriot Indian national, the moment he comes out of his house. But this drama is not the part of his personal belief rather it is a condition for living in a secular state. It is a mask, which is thrown out in a corner of the house once he steps into the door. Next morning when he comes out he wears it again so that he may be designated as a secular or a nationalist.

This is the inner conflict the majority at the Indian nationals is living. Today a man is identified not as an Indian, but as *Hindu, Muslim*; forward, backward, *Brahman, Kshatriya, Vaishya, Shudra*, etc. In this secular state the leader of Muslim must be a Muslim, only Hindu can lead the Hindu people, only Sikh can be leader of the Sikh community and so on.

(2) *Lack of Proper Knowledge of Religion*—In fact, the people of different religions do not understand their religion properly nor have they the firm faith in it with the scientific development and rise of modern mechanical civilization of seventeenth century there came a radical and revolutionary turn, in their behaviour, culture and moral values of the modern man. The old religious beliefs received a strong threat and shock with continuous changing of moral values, culture, belief of modern society. Science has cut the rational behind the religion, which resulted in loss of religious values. The hold of basic principles of religion is continuously disappearing from the heart of the people. Today a man inherits his religion. He does not become a Hindu or Christian rather he inherits it. He does not believe honestly in values of the religion

on a national plane rather he holds the religion dogmatically. That is why this secular state which was meant to preserve human values, which was declared in the Constitution, "There will be equality before law and equal protection of law", has failed in its mission.

REFERENCES

1. *Marxism and Question of Nationality*, p. 6.
2. *Nationalism*— A report by a group of members of the Royal Institute of International Affairs, Oxford University Press, 1939, p. XVI.
3. *Political Ideals*. p. 78.
4. Galloway.
5. *Dictionary of Philosophy*, Ifroloy, p. 357.
6. *Report of the Committee on Religious and Moral Instruction* (New Delhi, Ministry of Education, 1960).
7. Narain, Jaya Parakash, *Challenge of Nation Building*, p.108.
8. *Ibid*.
9. Kaka Kalelkar, *The Orient*, Part Two, p.11.
10. *The Holy Quran*, S. CIX I – 6.
11. Narayana, Jaya Parakash: *Challenges of Nation Building* (New Delhi, Orient Book, 1974), p.108.

19

Civil Liberties and the Armed Forces (Special Powers) Act

Mahi Pal Singh

The economic policies based on the principles of globalization and privatization have, in their wake, brought to this country, imported consumer goods from developed countries for which India has provided a market with a vast potential, even if at the cost of the closure of a very large number of local manufacturing units resulting in the unemployment of a still larger workforce. This has done tremendous harm to the conditions of physical survival of those for whom keeping together their body and soul was never an easy task. At the same time the increased inclination of the youth belonging to the middle class, (in any case, the elite sections have always shown a tendency to be consumerist going to the extent of a blatant and vulgar display of their wealth earned, nay, amassed through the exploitation of the working classes, corrupt means or speculation in the share-markets—those legally sanctioned, unproductive gambling houses of the rich meant to deprive the unsuspecting people belonging to the lower middle class of their hard-earned and frugally saved money, if our experience of the last 13 years is any evidence), has taken away all his sense of honour, human dignity and the commitment to protect his civil liberties and human rights. His commitment towards his fellow human beings and their welfare has also received a serious jolt as a result of the mad pursuit of his self-centred motives.

To cater to the needs of the elite sections of our society, including the neo-rich, who have reaped the fruits of the new economic order, and also the not-so-rich, who emulate the other two classes because people from these classes spending a lot of money on luxuries, (and also the trigger-happy film hero killing people with impunity), attract them to the extent of becoming their role models, are coming up the costly shopping malls and multiplexes in all metropolitan cities as a result of which the new culture of consumerism has drowned the culture of human rights discourse in the country.

How else should one interpret the trend as reflected by the print as well as the electronic media where indecent photographs —so much so that, thanks to the efforts of the journalistic fraternity, some sections of the papers have come to be known as 'porn pages' —and stories from the film and fashion world and descriptions of marriages and parties of the rich invariably fill a large portion of the front pages of most of our national dailies and they also get a place of prominence on the news channels, and people's struggles, protests and movements even for their basic rights and tales of their sufferings and deaths due to hunger, malnutrition and at the hands of various agencies of the state hardly find a mention even in an obscure corner of the newspapers? Otherwise, how does one explain the complete obliteration of everything related to the imposition of emergency in the country on 26th June, 1975, the greatest danger to democracy, civil liberties and human rights this country has faced ever since attaining independence in 1947, from the newspapers and the electronic media even on the anniversary of that black day, and of any reports of meetings held on that day to observe anti-emergency day to keep alive a continuous struggle for the protection of our civil and political rights from the next day's newspapers, as if an emergency had never been imposed in this country, or perhaps to remember such events is considered a useless exercise to be undertaken only by some intellectuals in their seminar rooms as a ritual having nothing to do with the present day life.

It would be a happy turn of events if we were no more required to recall such events, if they really became a matter of the past, never to recur again. But as things stand today the danger to our civil and political rights has not diminished a bit even after the 44th Constitutional Amendment to Article 359 disabling the President from suspending Articles 20 and 21 of the Constitution of India, thereby denying him the power to forfeit the fundamental right to life and liberty of any person even during a period of promulgation of Emergency in the country. Although promulgation of Emergency has been made more difficult, than it was in 1975, because 44th Amendment has introduced 'armed rebellion' in place of 'internal disturbance' as the condition for such a promulgation, and such a promulgation has also to be endorsed by a special majority in Parliament, yet there have been lesser laws which have been depriving people of the country of their basic civil and political rights with impunity, and what is worse, they do not require any such sanction of 'special majority' in Parliament for their imposition.

Why to Remember the Emergency?

For those who suffered the excesses of the Emergency, it will always remain a nightmarish experience never to be forgotten. But the young generation can hardly understand the importance of keeping its memories alive; we must not forget that those events took place twenty nine years ago. How can the youth of today know that "the darkest chapter in the history of independent India was written on the midnight of 25-26 June, 1975?" and that "With the imposition of Emergency on that day, thousands of people including opposition leaders were arrested and put in jail, and all the important fundamental rights were suspended. There were violations of all standards of morality, justice, and freedom; acts of barbarism and violence were committed. With the promulgation of Emergency, all rights and justice, civil liberties, law and order were trodden under feet. The Emergency waged war upon democracy. Excesses that were committed were not accidental, but the logical and deliberate acts of an authoritarian political philosophy. The object of this philosophy was the destruction of all freedoms, and triumph of the strong." (Remembering the Emergency—Dr. R.M. Pal, *PUCL Bulletin*, June, 1997).

We have to remember that the Emergency was imposed in the country because on a petition filed by Late Sh. Raj Narayan who had been defeated in a parliamentary election by Mrs. Indira Gandhi, the then Prime Minister, from Rai Bareilly, in its judgement delivered on June 12, 1975, the Allahabad High Court had held Mrs. Gandhi guilty of corrupt practices in her election, and declared her election as null and void, and that in a meeting on June 25, all opposition leaders had declared that if she did not quit as the Prime Minister of the country, they would start a civil disobedience movement from June 29. Defying the court judgement and making a mockery of the rule of law, Mrs. Gandhi declared a state of Emergency in the country, usurping all authority into her own hands, suspending fundamental rights including the right to life and liberty only to perpetuate her illegal, immoral and authoritarian rule by ruthlessly silencing all opposition by putting all opposition leaders behind the bars, without warrants or charge-sheets and for periods nobody knew how long, and also gagging all the national press, first by ordering their electric supply to be cut and then through the introduction of very stringent censorship laws which did not allow anything to be published against the Prime Minister or her decisions, or any of the excesses perpetrated by her or her son Sanjay Gandhi, who enjoyed the status of an extra-constitutional authority and whose orders, as a member of the Nehru family wrote later, "sometimes verging on criminality were obeyed without question". Under his leadership the Youth Congress, the youth wing of the Congress (Indira), had acquired the notoriety as a band of goons and its leaders as the unelected executives of the areas under their command, and government officers including police SHOs thought it to be their most solemn duty to obey their word of mouth as if it had come from the Prime Minister herself. Such was the atmosphere during the Emergency regime of Mrs. Gandhi and her infamous son Sanjay Gandhi that one could not move freely, talk freely or breathe freely in this very democratic country of ours. What is even more disturbing is that "the fundamental lack of commitment to values of freedom and democracy, tolerance of dissent, and the capacity to look beyond one's immediate interests which had made the intellectuals, with a few honourable exceptions, accept the Emergency and abide by its soul destroying demands." (Remembering the Emergency).

If democracy as a form of government, by and of the people, and the cardinal values like civil liberties and political rights, the freedom of the press, the right to profess any faith and the right to elect any government are to be preserved and protected, then the people themselves have to exercise an eternal vigilance to ensure that those in power do not succeed in subverting the democratic system to satisfy their greed to stick to power through unconstitutional, corrupt or divisive means because all shades of politicians and political parties have adopted these means to come to power, and once in power, to stick to it. If Mrs. Gandhi's Emergency regime was an example of the first kind, Narsimha Rao's government was an example of the second and Narendra Modi's government in Gujarat was an example of the third kind. Atal Behari Vajpayee's NDA (National Democratic Alliance) government also came to power riding the chariot of Hindutva, moving on the wheels of the divisive agenda of building the Ram temple at the site where Babri Masjid stood earlier at Ayodhya, to consolidate the majority Hindu vote and garner its support for achieving its narrow political end of capturing power, and his government also made a frantic effort of keeping to stick to power by adopting the corrupt means of spending something like Rs. Seven hundred and fifty crores from the public exchequer to boost his own image, and his party's, through the 'Feel-good' and 'India Shining' campaigns. It is a different matter that these slogans invented by the think-tanks of the BJP could not befool the uneducated and poor people of this country who thwarted their attempts to regain power at the Centre. To quote once again Dr. Pal from the article cited above, "We must take note of increasing corruption, manipulative politics, and other evils in the system which have been systematically eroding the values of democracy and destroying it".

Anti-democratic Draconian Laws in the Garb of Public Order Laws

In the name of bringing under control various terrorist and disruptive activities, the state of India has brought about various legislations and Acts ever since the country got independence in 1947. While it is true that various groups in different parts of the country took to arms or indulged in unconstitutional methods to press their demands, the methods adopted by the state to bring them into the mainstream have also been dubious. While nobody having a faith in the rule of law can and should support the use of arms to press any demands, however legitimate they might be, it is also equally true that a serious attempt has never been made to understand their problems, or to find out the compelling reasons which might have made them take to arms against the state. Poor, deprived people who had hoped to get a better deal at the hands of local rulers after attaining independence from foreign rulers, felt neglected and cheated when nothing was done to improve their conditions and they continued to suffer from starvation and disease. Their appeals of SOS continued to go unheeded and unheard and when they tried to organize themselves into a movement to force the powers that be to listen to their voices they got bullets in reply. When out of desperation they took to arms, they got Maintenance of Internal Security Act (MISA), Terrorist and Disruptive Activities (Prevention) Act (TADA), National Security Act (NSA), Armed Forces (Special Powers) Act (AFSPA) and Prevention of Terrorist Act (POTA). While it is true that all these special Acts came into being with the purported intention of bringing under control only those few who were thought to be uncontrollable otherwise, and that too for a limited time and purpose, the fact remains that all such people could well have been brought under control under the ordinary criminal law, under Sections 121 to 130, 153A, 294 and 295 of IPC. Another fact that cannot be contradicted is that all of them have invariably been used for a much longer period than they were originally planned to exist for. And the most dangerous common factor amongst them is that all of them have been used against the most innocent people to deprive them of their life and liberty, when these hapless people have tried to voice their grievances, and that too for excruciatingly long periods. All of them have been misused, by those in power, to subvert democracy they were purported to protect. All of them have been used ruthlessly against the people they were supposed to protect, to silence the voice of dissent, to crush the right to demonstrate against injustice and to decimate political opposition.

For example, TADA, which came into existence a decade after the imposition of Emergency in June 1975, following the assassination of Prime Minister Indira Gandhi which in turn was followed by a ruthless collective massacre of the members of the Sikh community, is still considered by the Sikh community as an Act which was brought into force as a measure of continuing vengeance against Punjab. It was later extended to Kashmir, Andhra Pradesh, Assam, LTTE Tamils in Tamil Nadu and against Muslims after the demolition of Babri Masjid. This Act has been perhaps the most criticized law ever since independence. It was also one of the most 'lawless' laws along with the Armed Forces (Special Powers) Act and N.S.A. It gave wide powers to the police to arrest and to detain people without trial under its custody for periods which could run up to one year and confessions made before a senior police officer were admissible as evidence before the court of law. The Act thus made a mockery of civil liberties and the fundamental rights of the people as laid down in the Constitution of India, and in fact, of democracy itself.

The following statistics prove beyond any doubt how this law was misused against the so-called 'terrorists': "This law was abused in almost every state for silencing activists and political opponents. According to the "NHRC 165 men above the age of 75 years, 160 women, and 43 children below the age of 15 years were detained under this Act until the end of 1994, and the oldest detainee was an 83 years old woman in Gujarat," ("Open Letter to the Prime Minister for the Repeal of TADA" by K.G. Kannabiran – *PUCL Bulletin*, May, 1995.)

Within a short period of its passage by the Parliament, POTA has also achieved the same notoriety which was earlier enjoyed by TADA, and the list of those arrested under it in a short period in Chhatisgarh alone reads like the list given above. Its misuse to silence the opposition is exemplified by the detention of Vaiko, a prominent opposition leader in Tamil Nadu, by J. Jaylalitha's government, and his release by the POTA court under the directions of the Supreme Court, as the charges framed against him were not found tenable under POTA. The very fact that of the 76,166 persons arrested under TADA till 1995, when the Act was allowed to lapse, only 843 (that is only 1.11 per cent) were convicted, as per Union Home Ministry's own statistics, is enough to show how widely and wildly the Act was misused to deprive people of their right to life and liberty by various governments.

Armed Forces (Special Powers) Act, 1958, a Tool to Subvert Democracy in the North-Eastern States

The Armed Forces (Special Powers) Act [AFPSA] which has been in force for forty six years since 1958 is in clear violation of the letter and spirit of the Constitution and has led to an undeclared Emergency and Martial law in the North-Eastern States of the country. The AFSPA has been responsible for the untold misery, death, rape and torture and the denial of civil and political rights to the people of Nagaland, Manipur and Assam. Extra-legal killings have become the order of the day there and people are denied their civil and political rights because the armed forces there enjoy unfettered powers over areas declared as 'disturbed area' prohibiting the assembly of five or more people. The citizen is wholly dependent upon the whimsical and subjective satisfaction of a warrant officer or a non-commissioned officer who becomes the ultimate officer to define "order" and determines the steps to be taken to maintain "order". Under Section 4(a) of the Act if the concerned officer is of the opinion that it is necessary to maintain public order, after giving such due warning as he may consider necessary "fire upon, or use such force, even to the causing of death," and under sub-section (c) arrest any person without warrant who has, or is likely to commit a cognizable offence; and under sub-section (d) enter, and search without warrant any premises to make such arrest." And the worst part of it all is that to take such action the officer needs no permission from a superior and is not answerable to anyone. Under Section 197 of the Code of Criminal Procedure (Cr.P.C.) no court can take cognizance of an offence alleged to have been committed by a public servant or member of the Armed Forces while acting or purporting to act in the discharge of his official duty except with the previous sanction of the Central or State government whereas the permission of the Central government has to be obtained to prosecute a military officer under Section 7 of the Armed Forces (Special Powers) Act, which practically means that people have no right to approach the court and launch prosecution for atrocities committed by any such officer. Even various commissions of enquiry appointed by the government have found security forces guilty of gross human rights violations but in most of the cases the guilty officials have not been prosecuted for the offences committed by them.

In Manipur, where AFSPA was extended 27 years ago in the name of fighting militancy, successive governments have retained it and there have been complaints of military excesses from the people. Only recently a 30 years old woman, Manorama Devi, was allegedly raped and killed by Assam Rifles personnel. Students supported by many NGOs and human rights organizations there have been agitating for action against the guilty as well as for the repeal of AFSPA which has become a tool in the hands of rifle wielding criminals to perpetrate such crimes.

Can the Courts Provide any Relief?

The Constitution of India has laid down the responsibility of protecting the fundamental rights of the people, as guaranteed under the Constitution, on the shoulders of the Supreme Court of India and the various High Courts. In individual cases these courts have given some historical judgements thereby extending the scope of some of the fundamental rights. The Right to free and compulsory Education as a fundamental right emanated from the judgement of the Supreme Court in 1993 in Unni Krishanan's case (AIR 1993 SC 2178) wherein the Court observed that the 'Right to Education' is also a right to life, which is implicit as it flows from the right to life guaranteed by Article 21, though it had been present in the Constitution of India as a Directive Principle of the State Policy under Article 45 ever since the adoption of the Constitution in 1949 without being considered a fundamental right by any government before that. Right to know and information have also emanated from the interpretations of Articles 19 and 21 of the Constitution by the apex Court.

However, in the matter of such draconian laws as the TADA, the POTA and the Armed Forces (Special Powers) Act, the courts have somehow failed to fulfil their responsibility as the protectors of the Fundamental Rights of the people as assigned to them by the Constitution and as recognized by themselves as such, when, in the Keshvanand Bharti case, otherwise known as Fundamental Rights case (AIR 1973 SC 1461) the apex Court observed that the democratic form of government and the fundamental rights are some of the basic structures and framework of our Constitution and they cannot be abrogated or whittled down even by the Parliament in exercise of its plenary powers of amending the Constitution. Yet the Court has gone against its self-assigned, and constitutionally mandated, duty again and again. On the allegations of "administrative liquidation" of two men by personnel of the Manipur police, the Supreme Court had ordered a district and sessions judge to conduct an investigation on a public interest petition filed by the People's Union for Civil Liberties (PUCL) in 1992. The Court, however, gave orders only for monetary compensation, in its judgement on February 6, 1997, to the relatives of the victims. It did not exercise its authority to refer the matter to the trial court for the criminal prosecution of the perpetrators of the crime.

When the necessity to examine the Armed Forces (Special Powers) Act arose as a result of a letter-petition addressed to the Court in 1982, it was converted into a petition under Article 32 of the Constitution. The judgement came after 14 long years and the Court ruled that *none of the provisions of the Act can be characterized as arbitrary*. Though utterly bizarre such judgements might seem, they are in perfect consonance with the *status quo* and its character of the establishment, be it the legislature, the executive or the judiciary. Otherwise how does one view the judgement of the apex court, during the Emergency in 1976, wherein the Habeas Corpus Case, which came to be known as ADM (Jabalpur) Case, (AIR 1976 SC 597) the majority of the four Judges headed by Chief Justice A.N. Ray (Justice Khanna alone differing and paying the price for it) ruled that "Article 21 is the sole repository of the right to life and liberty and that since that right was suspended, Habeas Corpus petitions were not even maintainable," which practically meant that the Government had a right to kill a person without the authority of law and, in fact, contrary to the rule of law.

The National Human Rights Commission is even prevented by Clause 19 of the Protection of Human Rights Act from investigating directly complaints of human rights violations against the armed forces.

How Can an Atmosphere Conducive to Human Rights be Secured?

The National Democratic Alliance (NDA) government led by Shri Atal Behari Vajpayee could not find time to pass the Women's Reservation Bill to empower women during its six years rule because, as it claimed, it wanted to bring about a consensus on the issue. The same government passed the POTA within no time by calling a joint session of Parliament when it realized that it would not be able to get the bill through in the Rajya Sabha where it did not enjoy a majority. The same Congress party, which was opposing the move then, and later declared that it would abolish the Act as soon as it came to power, has still not found ways to do so, although, if Justice Rajinder Sachar, a retired Chief Justice of the Delhi High Court and expert in legal matters, is to be believed, the Act can be abolished overnight by an ordinance issued by the President. Not

20

Questions Arising from the Mumbai Terrorist Attack

Mahi Pal Singh

The terrorist attack of 26/11 on Mumbai by Pakistani terrorists, trained, abetted and supported by terrorist outfits based in Pakistan as well as by the Inter Services Intelligence (ISI) of Pakistan army, and connived at, if not directly supported by, even the civilian government of that country, has opened a Pandora's box of questions, answers to which must be found if we wish to avoid recurrence of a like event in future. The first and foremost question is whether our political class is really serious about ending terrorist attacks of all kinds and also whether it wishes to go about the job in a transparent manner and whether it really has the will to go a step or two forward in the right direction for ending this menace which takes a toll of innocent lives every time it occurs.

There has been a war cry from many quarters in India, some people talking of surgical strikes against the training camps of terrorists based across the border in Pakistan. Even our political masters have been saying that no option is closed—meaning thereby that the option of waging a war is very much open, though the Indian Foreign Minister has at times himself admitted that it is not possible for India to pursue terrorists and their supporters across the border. That, in any case, is absolutely true also. If America, with all its force, has not been able to pursue Osama-bin-Laden, the leader of Al-Quaida and the perpetrator of the 9/11 attack on the World Trade towers in the US in spite of the heavy presence of its forces in Afghanistan and its precision attacks across the border in Pakistan, how can India hope to pursue the perpetrators of the Mumbai attacks successfully by exercising the military option? It can only result in the larger numbers of innocent people losing their lives on both sides of the border, besides causing an irreparable loss to the Indo-Pak relations, which in any case are at its lowest ebb now. The supporters of the nuclear weapons should also realize, now at least, that these weapons have not given an edge to our position over Pakistan unless we decide to use these weapons, and if used, they can only cause untold suffering and devastation on both sides, leaving neither of the two sides in a position to claim an edge over the other. War mongering and ever increasing weaponization are no solutions to any problem. They have only taken a heavy toll of the financial resources that could otherwise have been available for development and providing education and healthcare to the people, and generating opportunities for employment thereby reducing discontent and alienation among the masses.

Although in the long run India has been able to garner the support of many countries and succeeded in building a pressure on Pakistan to act against the perpetrators of the Mumbai attacks, its handling of the matter has not been appropriate. First, our Foreign Minister continued to claim from the beginning that they had provided the proofs of the involvement of Pakistani elements in the attack to Pakistan whereas Pakistan continuously denied having received any such proofs. But when after about a month of the attack on Mumbai the chief of the Interpol, Mr. Nobel, declared at a press conference in Pakistan that India had not given any such evidence to the Government of Pakistan, or to Interpol, regarding the involvement of Pakistani citizens in the attack, the news was absolutely embarrassing and shocking. What had been given was a list of about 40 suspected terrorists and their supporters stationed in Pakistan and their extradition to India for trial had been demanded. It is only after about 45 days of the incident that a dossier has now been given to Pakistan, along with other countries;

containing whatever evidence India wishes to share with Pakistan. But what was even more shocking is the fact that no representative of the media, which had been so active in exploiting the terrorist attack for hyping the war theme, ever questioned Mr. Pranab Mukherjee, the former External Affairs Minister, even after the revelation by Mr. Nobel, about the evidence he had been claiming to have given to Pakistan, or asked to clarify the position on what Mr. Nobel had said in Pakistan. Not that Pakistan would have done much had the evidence been provided to it, but what is equally worrying is that we do not question our own politicians about the claims that they make, and blindly accept as gospel truth whatever they tell us. Pakistan stands exposed in the eyes of the world for being insincere in taking action against the terrorist outfits like the Jamat-ud-Dawa and Lashkar-e-Toiba. But at the same time we must also learn to question if we wish to be sincere in our search for truth, if we have to effectively tackle such issues as terrorism.

It is because of our habit of not questioning that we easily accepted the argument by some sections of our politicians that an stringent law like the POTA is a must for effectively tackling the menace of terrorism and our Parliament passed a law like the Unlawful Activities Prevention Act (Amendment) 2008, unanimously and without much debate, which was even in its earlier *avatars* nothing but a replica of POTA, which was scrapped by the UPA Government immediately after coming to power as part of a public promise, in the wake of strong protests against the history of its misuse against the minorities, other marginalized sections of society, people struggling against social and political injustices, working for human rights, and against the known opponents of those in power. In the amended act only the provision of legal admissibility of a "confession" made in police custody is left out. But, a most bizarre and anti-legal provision to treat an accused as guilty till proved otherwise and not to be granted bail unless the court finds the accused *prima facie* innocent, has been added to it. This evidently runs counter to the recent Supreme Court directive that during a trial, granting of bail should be the norm, and rejection an exception. The basic presumption in law everywhere in the world is innocence of a person until proved guilty whereas this Act presumes a person guilty of such grave crimes as terrorism until he proves himself innocent if the police books him for such a crime, thereby shifting the onus of proving him guilty from the police to the victim of proving himself innocent.

We do not question our politicians and legislators why they thrust such dreadful laws upon us which almost always result in depriving the marginalized sections of our own society of their civil liberties and human rights and provide unlimited powers to the police to book even innocent people under stringent laws and keep them behind the bars for long periods of time, only to be released later by the courts for want of evidence which never existed, with stigmas attached to them which deprive them of their normal position in society ever after, and such stringent laws almost never succeed in tackling terrorists against whom they are supposed to be used. Why do we not ask our lawmakers and administrators about the statistics and the history of success or failure of such laws in the past before they proceed to enact one more of such anti-people laws? Of course, the law implementing agencies will always demand such laws to cover up their failure to investigate, arrest and prosecute the perpetrators of terrorist activities, and fascist politicians willingly succumb to such demands which empower them with additional legal authority to throttle the voices of dissent and dissatisfaction among the people. This results in the arrest and detention for long periods of innocent people like Dr. Binayak Sen, the Vice President of National PUCL and General Secretary of the State Branch of Chhattisgarh, who has been in jail for 18 months without bail, on concocted charges. The governments, in their arrogance of power, do not even heed the protesting voices of Nobel laureates, human rights activists and those in whose selfless service the Doctor has spent more than twenty-five long years working as a doctor.

Such laws are counterproductive in the long run and lead to greater dissatisfaction among the people, denial of democratic rights to the people, and impede scientific inquiry and economic growth of the country, thereby leading to obscurantism and religious fundamentalism and intolerance. Justice Markandey Katju, a Judge of the Supreme Court of India, writing in *The Hindu*, dated January 2009 under the title 'Importance of liberty and democracy in India' observed: "To my mind, harsh and draconian laws will curb liberty. That will not only violate the right to liberty granted by Article 21 of the Constitution. It will also lead to great evils such as an increase in corruption in the police and other law enforcing agencies, which will have much more opportunity to extort money from the citizens, apart from impeding scientific and economic growth".

Then there was a news report that perhaps the perpetrators of the crime in Mumbai had secured their safe landing through the sea route by bribing the coast guards and other law enforcing agencies who had taken them to be ordinary smugglers, which only proves that it is a standard practice to allow smugglers into the country after taking hush money from them, not caring for the fact that these smugglers, most of them narcotics smugglers, cause a great damage to the country's economy and health of the youth, besides providing huge amounts of money to the D-company, which in turn pumps back this money for funding terrorist activities in the country. While it was an appreciable gesture of thankfulness to appreciate the Mumbai police for its brave handling of the Mumbai terrorists, it is surprising that nobody questioned the role of the same police in letting them in for money. The people of the country are with the administration for honouring those who made the supreme sacrifice while fighting the terrorists, they equally have the right to demand punishment to those who have been making money out of the whole bargain regardless of the danger they cause to the country. However, the media, which is supposed to be ever vigilant for the defence of democratic freedoms in its role as an important column of the democratic structure of our country, failed to question the administration and the police on behalf of the people.

Governments need to be reminded that voices of dissent and protests, whether non-violent or violent, arising from within the country can only be effectively controlled by addressing the problems of people through dialogue and not through use of brutal